DEPARTMENT OF TRADE AND INDUSTRY

The impact of foreign direct investment on the United Kingdom

by M D Steuer, Peter Abell, John Gennard, Morris Perlman, Raymond Rees, Barry Scott and Ken Wallis

STATIONERY OFFICE

SBN 11 511055 0

Preface

This study of the effects of inward direct investment on the economy of the United Kingdom was undertaken as an outside research project sponsored by the Economic Services Division of the Board of Trade, now the Department of Trade and Industry. The brief given us was a very wide one. We were not asked to explain why the multi-national firm is growing at such a rapid rate, but rather to study the consequences for this country of the direct investment which has been arriving here. In particular, we were asked to place emphasis on the implications of direct investment for the balance of payments, for the state of British technology, and for development regions, such as in Scotland, where it has a tendency to concentrate. Beyond these matters we were free to take up whatever subjects we took to be of significance. It was suggested that we concentrate on manufacturing industry and leave aside oil and services. On the whole these seemed to be appropriate limitations on a very broad area of investigation. To the three topics mentioned we added seven others; consideration of the policy options open, industrial relations of foreign-owned firms, questions of monopoly and concentration, the type of control exercised by parent companies over subsidiaries, foreign investment and national sovereignty, current United Kingdom regulation of inward investment, and a review of the relevant statistics. It was understood that a postal survey of all foreign owned firms would play a large part in our work.

The approach we adopted had three main features. We wished to avoid the more obvious and familiar aspects of direct investment. We wanted to be particularly alert to potential disadvantages to the United Kingdom as a host country. And we did not want to restrict ourselves to the purely economic aspects of this phenomenon. It is probably fair to say that the experience of undertaking this work made us more favourably disposed to direct investment than we were when we began it. This conclusion should not be generalized to other countries, particularly less developed countries, and it refers to current investment levels, not future and possibly substantially higher levels. Direct investment calls for closer monitoring by governments than has been the practice in the United Kingdom up to now.

Seven authors were involved in various parts of this study, and on the whole there was considerable interaction between them. They were Peter Abell of the University of Essex, now at Imperial College; John Gennard, Morris Perlman, Ken Wallis and Max Steuer all of the London School of Economics, the last now at the University of Ghana; Raymond Rees of Queen Mary College; Barry Scott of the Economics and Statistics Division 5 of the Department of Trade and Industry. We received help from economists and others in various Ministries and from many academic economists. There was often a high level of co-operation from foreign owned firms themselves. It would not be unreasonable for the Government to consider the possibility of compensating firms in the future for costs undertaken in providing data. Apart from the element of fairness, this might make officials more courageous and insistent if they were paying for information, as well as being more disciplined in their requests.

The Steering Committee organized by the Economic Services Division was helpful in reviewing our working papers. We would particularly like to thank Miss Margaret Groves and Miss Eileen Cope of the Division for able research assistance. Much help was given by John Heath, the Director of the Division and now at the London Graduate School of Business Studies.

The project was ably and helpfully administered by Denys Gribbin in the Division. It was a genuine pleasure working under the direction of the Board of Trade (now the Department of Trade and Industry). Final responsibility for the analysis and judgements expressed rests with the author in charge.

M D Steuer
and
Peter Abell
John Gennard
Morris Perlman
Raymond Rees
Barry Scott
Ken Wallis

September 1971

Contents

1. Characteristics of inward investment and policy options for the host country

Introduction

1.1 The central problem in analysis of inward direct investment is determining precisely what *are* the issues created by foreign ownership and control of subsidiaries operating here. Simple nationalistic sentiments and fear of large organizations generally are enough to induce a presumption that the growth of multi-national enterprise poses some kind of threat. But these vague feelings, however strongly held, are not specific enough either to establish that in fact a danger exists, or to indicate appropriate responses on the part of host country governments. To do that, careful investigation is required. In recent years considerable progress has been made along these lines. (Representative books are by Brash: 1966, which raises many issues of evaluation and economic analysis; Safarian: 1966, gives detailed results of a survey; Kindleberger: 1969, concentrates on important problem areas.) The present study, which emphasizes the United Kingdom, is one among a number of studies undertaken in various countries in an attempt to narrow down the direct investment phenomenon to a set of clear and significant questions.

1.2 We may distinguish three broad problem areas. The first has to do with the possibility that when a parent company undertakes production abroad through establishing subsidiaries in various countries, national governments can no longer exercise the degree of control over its activities or hold it accountable for its actions both to the extent that they can with respect to purely national companies and to the extent that is in the general interest. Bigness as such is a factor. But beyond bigness, the international operations of companies are held to place these organizations to some extent above the law and outside the control of law makers.

1.3 Where the first area has to do with governments generally *versus* the multi-nationals, the second area has to do with political losses for capital receiving countries. For this type of consideration, far from the multi-national being regarded as outside of governmental control, it is viewed as being an agent of the parent company country. The alleged losses resulting for the host country may be measured against the situation that would obtain if the foreign subsidiaries were owned by host country nationals, a clearly unrealistic and irrelevant comparison. Or they may be measured against the situation resulting if the proposed incoming investment had been excluded.

1.4 The third area is the more narrowly economic, in which the concern is with the effect of foreign investment on the domestic income of the capital receiving country. This topic may be broken down into a number of sub-questions such as the effects on host country technology, balance of payments, income distribution, and the like. It is important for analysis to recognize that the answers to many of these sub-questions have no welfare implications in themselves, and are of interest only in terms of their implications for the national income of the capital receiving country.

1.5 These three concerns, that multi-national companies may be eroding the power of the nation state, that source countries for direct investment capital may impinge on host countries, and the economic consequences for capital receiving countries, are all important. We give some attention to the first two in this study, but our emphasis is on the third. This does not imply that the first two are less significant. They are, however, more problematical, and responses to them are more dependent on subjective political preferences.

1.6 In the United States, the largest source of direct investment international capital, government-sponsored studies have naturally been mainly concerned with the economic effects of an outward flow. This, in turn, leads to a concentration on the balance of payments implications of capital exporting. The most comprehensive study, which also contains an excellent summary of the literature, is by Hufbauer and Adler: 1968. The outward flow, and again the balance of payments aspect for the source country, has also received extensive study in the United Kingdom, the second largest capital exporter, (Reddaway, 1968). Looking at the other side of the direct investment relationship, there are many examples of official interest in the phenomena on the part of host country governments. These countries in which foreign investment is a large proportion of total investment have understandably been more active in investigating the effects and publishing their findings, a notable example is the 'Watkins Report', *Foreign Ownership and the Structure of Canadian Industry:* 1968. Apart from published indications of interest, changes in official policy in the direction of a more or less welcoming stance can be seen, the biggest swings often occurring in France. At present Japan is in the process of reviewing a traditional policy of excluding foreign direct investment.

1.7 The British position has been consistently favourable to the incoming foreign investor. No cases of ultimate refusal have come to our attention. Conditions are often attached to permission to invest, but not of an extreme kind. This study is in the fortunate position of examining a topic at a time when it is not such an intense issue as to inhibit relatively relaxed and open consideration. However, in the United Kingdom, as in other developed industrial countries, foreign investment, and more particularly the growth of the multi-national firm, is regarded as being of interest, something to be watched, and a possible area for policy action. Evidence for this assertion can be found in a wide variety of places. These range from frequent questions in Parliament to television programmes devoted to the topic. Inward investment, especially in the form of take-over, gets considerable coverage in the press. The TUC, for example, is paying more and more attention to the foreign owned subsidiary, and in recent years bodies like PEP, the Fabian Society, the Trade Policy Research Centre, and others have produced pamphlets on direct investment. (Dunning: 1969, Turner: 1969, and Steuer: 1969.) The main embodiment of European popular concern with American international firms is Servan-Schreiber's *Le Défi Americain*, which focused on the effects on the Common Market countries, but enjoyed large sales and considerable attention in this country. Similarly emotionally charged books about American direct capital flows to this country have been written here in recent years. (Williams: 1962, MacMillan and Harris: 1968.) Britain clearly shares the general concern with and interest in inward direct investment. The purpose of this study is to at least partially satisfy that interest, and to provide a background for further consideration of the phenomena.

1.8 The far Left and the far Right have almost always found international economic interests to be objectionable. A not necessarily flatly opposed, but certainly a questioning attitude, is now more characteristic of more moderate political positions. Direct investment, in contrast to international portfolio investment, involves foreign control of subsidiaries and branches engaged in production and sale of goods and services in this country. In principle that need not imply the existence of a foreign parent company. It may simply be the case that controlling equity interest is held abroad. In practice in the significant cases of inward investment, whether they are cases of take-over of existing British firms or were set up as new establishments or as joint ventures, there is a foreign parent company. Any observer is bound to note four outstanding features; the sheer growth of direct investment at roughly twice the speed of growth of international trade, the dominant position of American capital being roughly eighty-five per cent of the inward flow in the United Kingdom, the move towards internationalization with subsidiaries in many countries and world-wide integration of economic activities, and the concentration of direct investment in science based industries. These four factors help to explain the concern which exists, though they do not give this concern much precision.

1.9 The growth of direct investment, the large United States role in it, and the multi-national firm operating as a coherent unit, together suggest a problem of national interest, or loss of national autonomy, along with potential economic problems, for important host countries. The United Kingdom remains, after Canada, the most important destination for United States direct investment, in spite of some recent tendency for this capital to gravitate to the Continent. And the three factors taken together are important for the vague fears. If the volume was small and the trends less steeply upward, or if many countries were equally involved, or if the subsidiaries were self-contained like domestic firms, in spite of being foreign owned, it is doubtful if the direct investment phenomena would be of interest to the extent that it is. And if we add two additional generalizations, the importance of giant and therefore potentially monopolistic firms in direct investment and their concentration in science based industries, the instinctive and unargued case for concern is probably complete.

1.10 It is natural to distrust the foreigner, to exclude or penalise him, but it may not be right to. In the case of foreign firms, a second's thought suggests such possibilities as current economic gain for us, in the sense of higher real income per capita, to be set against broadly social or political loss, or longer term economic loss. Where to look, how to set up the problem, what are the relevant theories and facts? These are the key questions. We have taken the primary purpose of this study to be to attempt to clarify issues and where possible to present evidence, rather than to engage in extrapolation into the future or in policy recommendation. But where they seemed natural we have hinted at both, and it is hoped that the study will be useful to both. At the same time, we have not stuck exclusively to scientifically manageable economic questions and have tried to see inward direct investment in the round, indulging in impression and speculation where necessary.

Method and scope

1.11 Much of the direction of our study was provided by the Steering Committee of the Board of Trade, now the Department of Trade and Industry. Two primary topics were suggested, the effect of inward direct investment on the balance of payments, and the effect on British technology.

Chapters Two and Three take up these areas. The balance of payments question has been most amenable to formal economic analysis, and the technology issue the least so, at least in our hands. Chapter Four is on the industrial relations and labour utilization of foreign owned firms, and contrasts these with domestic firms. It rapidly became clear that appraisal of the gains and losses of foreign investment depends to a great extent on issues of competition. And apart from appraisal, a characterization of the multi-national firm requires considering questions of size and monopoly power. This is emphasized in Chapter Five. The next three chapters lead increasingly in the direction of non-economic effects, or not exclusively economic effects.

1.12 A significant amount of direct investment is located outside of the main industrial conurbations, in depressed regions in Scotland and Wales. Chapter Six takes up some of the regional aspects. It affords a convenient focus for considering some of the less tangible effects. Part of the inward investment effect comes about through a change in the quantity of capital in this country. Another part depends on qualitative differences in behaviour between the foreign owned subsidiary and the domestic firm. A possible approach to illuminating these differences is through the areas and ways the foreign parent organization exercises control over its subsidiary here. This is the subject matter of Chapter Seven. Some attempt is made in Chapter Eight to tackle the wider issue of national autonomy. There we are asking the question, in what way does foreign decision taking with respect to some economic activity here affect this country beyond the confines of the specific subsidiaries involved?

1.13 Chapters Nine and Ten are relatively straightforward. The former summarizes current United Kingdom regulation of foreign direct investment in this country. The latter chapter marshals and comments on the statistics of inward investment. It draws on published and unpublished sources. In the next section of this chapter some general observations are made. These are followed by brief discussions of the major results of the chapters mentioned above. A concluding section points to some of the policy options.

1.14 The preparation of this study rests on eight elements. The first is the substantial literature of international direct investment. Bibliographies prepared at Harvard and Columbia contain about six thousand items, books and articles. Only a sample could be read. We concentrated on literature directed to host country implications, excluding that part concerned with direct investment in less developed countries, which is a separate issue. Second, we had many useful talks with Government agencies. A substantial number of these were with the Treasury and the Ministry of Technology. In the course of our work many academic specialists in the subject talked to us informally about their work. These were mainly, though not exclusively, economists from Canada, the United States, and this country. The fourth element was pilot interviews with foreign subsidiaries which were intended to help us with our postal survey. Our enquiry form is shown as an inset after page 10. This was sent to all the foreign owned firms we could locate by combining various official and unofficial lists. A ten per cent response, just under six hundred usable replies, was disappointing. The sixth element was a series of in depth interviews with a number of firms selected because of special interest. These interviews followed the general form of the postal survey, but were intended to supplement the more qualitative questions, and to some extent provide a check on the postal survey. It is unusual in economic research to engage in field trips. However, this seemed worthwhile in connection with the regional implications. Two members of the team went to Greenock in Scotland. The final element on which our study is based was unpublished information provided from the 1963 census. It is easier to list the inputs than to show exactly how they bear on the output. Often the output is simply judgemental, an impression, a feel for a problem area or a conclusion. In some ways the study is more like what we would have liked to have had when we started than like what we hoped to produce when we finished.

Approaches to direct investment

1.15 There is an easy road to an apparently statesmanlike position through finding a precedent for everything, dismissing interest as 'fashion' and concern as 'hysteria'. Traditional pure theory of international capital movements would, unwittingly, lend some support to this position. In a static, competitive, full information, general equilibrium setting, free trade and free capital movements maximise world output. From the point of view of a single country, some interference, either taxing or subsidizing current account trade or capital movements or both, can squeeze out a bit of an advantage over the free trade and capital movements position, this gain for one being at the expense of the rest of the world. (Jones, R W: 1967.) Apart even from the issues of possible retaliation by other countries, a potentially important consideration for a large capital exporter like the United Kingdom, and inhibitions due to international agreements through GATT and other agencies, the interactions are too complex to allow the analysis to guide a country empirically to an optimum interference policy. This leads to a single conclusion. Staying within the assumptions of the competitive model, free trade and free capital movements give a good approximation to the best position we can achieve.

1.16 This well known formal model is not concerned with uncertainty, research and changes in technology, managerial skills, externalities, and advertising and monopoly power. A growing school of thought in international economics sees these elements, in various combinations, as the potential source of a new paradigm better suited to explaining direct investment than arm's length market interactions. To the economist a particularly troublesome feature of direct investment among developed industrial economies is the observed simultaneous in and out flows. If capital migrates to take advantage of higher returns elsewhere, and there are certain disadvantages in operating a subsidiary in a foreign country, competition would insure that a country was either a capital exporter or a capital importer, but not both.

1.17 Investigators differ in where they place the emphasis. (Johnson: 1968.) A key difference is between those who emphasize monopoly elements, and those who emphasize uncertainty and frictions, including tariff and currency problems. There are, after all, many alternatives to direct investment. These include exporting, portfolio investment, and allowing foreign firms to produce under licence. Direct investment, especially in the cross-freighting case, implies a special advantage held by a particular interest. That this is realised through direct investment rather than an alternative usually implies a monopoly element.

1.18 The large firm with a large market can spread research costs over a large base. Product or cost saving innovations resulting from research may then preserve or extend the market share of a single producer. (Vernon: 1966.) This could help to account for the growth of the multi-national firm. It is getting returns to scale in research and possibly marketing and management. Three post-war developments have greatly expanded the possibility for relatively detailed and integrated control of an international business complex: improved management techniques, the computer, and jet travel. The scale of the multi-national firm may represent genuine economies of production and marketing. And it is this changed role of the subsidiary as part of an integrated world complex which stands out. In this way it is unlike an isolated, profit maximizing unit, whose equity happens to be held abroad, and who goes on about its business like a domestic firm.

1.19 If, in the capitalist world, the bulk of economic activity were to be undertaken by a few hundred multi-national firms, with a handful of oligopolistic producers in each industry, that would be something different from the past. If these firms had only an historical national origin, with no geographically fixed headquarter parent, with their equity capital held all over the world, that also would be something different from the past. Neither of these things has yet taken place. But signs pointing in those directions do exist. Yet even at present the direct investment phenomenon differs from the past, and our ways of looking at it are undergoing change. The purpose of this section is to summarize these changes.

The balance of payments

1.20 It is not always appreciated that what matters is not how direct inward investment effects the balance of payments as such, but what happens to domestic income per capita, with and without direct investment, and assuming appropriate policies to achieve balance of payments equilibrium in both cases. In one we exclude, by fiat, a certain proposed foreign investment from coming in. The government pursues policies of internal and external balance, and so generates a certain stream of income per capita over time. In the second case, we allow the inward investment. This generates a whole complex of in and out flows. Initially, our reserves rise by the amount of the investment. Then, as a result, there are exports and imports to third countries and to the foreign parent company country. There are repatriated profits, payments for research and development, and so on. Again, the government pursues appropriate policies for internal and external balance, and again a stream of domestic income per capita over time results. The important question is whether this second stream is higher or lower than the first.

1.21 The question of whether income rises or not is not the same as the question of whether repatriated profits exceed or fall short of the initial investment. Suppose that the subsidiary here did no exporting or importing, and simply repatriated its normal profits. Also assume that physical capital here rose by the amount of the investment, so there was no observed balance of payments gain. Output will be higher because, essentially, our labour has more capital to work with. But some of that output belongs to the foreigner, not all of the extra output. So in perpetuity a higher domestic income can result, even though the balance of payments effect, looked at naively and in isolation is adverse.

1.22 Nevertheless, in a world of imperfections, disequilibria, fixed exchange rates, constant policy problems and second best solutions, it is still important to examine the balance of payments effects of direct investment. The proper *ceteris paribus* conditions for such an exercise are unusually difficult to formulate. The same inward investment has different implications, in terms of rise or fall in reserves, when the receiving economy is in different conditions of over or under full employment. And what is to be assumed about the response of the authorities in changing the total pressure of demand and the supply of money? While every situation of the economy and every particular inward investment may reasonably be deemed to have unique properties, the topic calls for some sensible generalisation. In the following paragraphs we discuss briefly the approaches other economists have taken, the nature of the model we have developed, and the tentative results it generates for the United Kingdom.

1.23 A pioneering study is that of Philip Bell, who addressed himself to the question how long will it take for an American capital export, with its initial drain on United States reserves, to bring back in repatriated profits and other flows such balance of payments gain as to cancel out the initial drain, (Bell: 1962). His method assumes that all the flows, in both directions, are different but constant proportions in each year of the American direct investment capital stock abroad in the previous year. The proportions are calculated by averaging observed flows between parents and subsidiaries for a number of years. This method is rather mechanical and leaves little room for economic behaviour on the part of firms or the economy at large. It has been extended and elaborated, (Hufbauer and Adler: 1968), and yields answers to the question posed on the order of five to seven years, but covering a much greater range in some formulations, according to the assumptions specified. Staying within the terms of the analysis, one cannot say that the United Kingdom balance of payments experience is equal and opposite in sign, because investment here results in exports to, and imports from, third countries. But there are many other objections. Inward investment may be a substitute for imports of the same goods; no account is taken of the productivity of this investment here and the implications of a changed domestic income on macro behaviour of the system; and it concentrates on parent-subsidiary flows rather than all the flows between the source and host countries. An alternative high theory approach is that of Pearce and Rowan: 1966. A full general equilibrium model is specified by the authors and the system is allowed to fully adjust to the capital movement. Equilibrium positions are compared and the model indicates the terms of trade adjustment necessary for a zero external balance with a given international capital movement. While recognising the theoretical validity of the framework, we have been unable to make use of it for empirical estimation.

1.24 The essence of our model is the bringing together of micro and macro aspects of direct investment. For manageability this calls for making simplifying assumptions and then carrying through their implications fully. Scope is allowed for the direct investor in the case of take-over to change productivity and export proportions. The United Kingdom tax on corporations enters into the calculation, and a modified absorption approach allows the import substitution effect to be deduced, thereby removing the necessity of direct observation of something we cannot, as yet, observe. The changed income streams, both domestic and foreign owned, are fed into a simple Keynesian macro framework. Price and monetary effects are not taken into account. We believe this to be an allowable simplification given the current scale of inward investment. The time dimension of the model, with its use of comparative static multipliers, is a drawback. But this, too, does not appear to be a totally damning simplification. The model is convenient for sensitivity analysis, exploring how the implied balance of payments effect responds to changes in the assumptions.

1.25 The model leads to four effects on the balance of payments; export effect, import substitution, import effect, and repatriation effect. The final equation involves six fairly readily observable variables, and one that can be tried at various levels. The answer emerges in terms of a proportion of foreign output here which is the overall balance of payments effect. Depending on the policy response of the Government, this effect is generally favourable, on the order of ten per cent of the 'foreign' output. The model appears to be fairly robust over the range of plausible changes in such magnitudes as proportion of output exported by foreign firms and their extra efficiency.

Technology

1.26 It is difficult to discuss the effect of inward investment on United Kingdom technology without going into a thorough investigation of the economics of technology generally. This is an area which is dominated by impressions and catch phrases. Improved technology, in the sense of better methods of production, including managerial and organisational aspects as well as machines, skills and processes, and improved technology in the sense of better products, is held to be critical to the development and well being of the British economy. While not wishing to disagree with this view, we note that there are many ways of improving the performance of the economy, they all entail current costs and future benefits, and intelligent optimizing calls for a sensible mix of inputs, including inputs in improved technology.[1] And broadly, how do the gains from better technology arise? Do they accrue to the producers of new knowledge, to the appliers of this knowledge, or to consumers? No doubt comparative advantage, given the diversity of the knowledge producing industry, calls for some production of new knowledge here, and some should be brought in from abroad. The part which is brought in can come through a wide range of channels: it can be embodied in final goods and producer goods; skilled individuals can be hired here for short or longer periods; research contracts can be let abroad; processes may be used and products produced under licence; inward investment is a means of acquiring improved technology. It is this last possibility with which we are concerned. Here a number of specific issues arise. It is difficult to be authoritative about them without going into the wider context of the technology problem, and that is beyond our scope. Yet some clear points can be made.

1.27 In the technology chapter we examine some of the arguments that have been put forward, for and against, as to the effects of direct investment on technology. Most of our attention is directed to some popular theories, which we generally do *not* find convincing. The allegedly favourable considerations may be summarized as follows:

- (i) Subsidiaries may draw on the research efforts of the parent organisation, often at low or zero explicit cost.
- (ii) New products are made available at lower cost and are promoted more effectively.

[1] Is one not entitled to be sceptical of the seriousness of intent behind the national drive for better technology? The fundamental input here is better trained people, especially in the range of higher education. How is one to take current discussion of plans to double the number of university students without any increase in the teaching or other resources for higher education?

(iii) Spill-over effects diffuse better techniques through mobility of personnel, contacts with suppliers, and a stimulus to imitation through proximity.

The allegedly adverse considerations may also be summarized:

(i) Through take-over foreign interests acquire property rights in the research achievements of British firms, and so gain the benefits of exploiting certain ideas.

(ii) New establishments may fail to undertake research here, or may disband research organisations in cases of take-over.

(iii) The United Kingdom economy may in a general sense become technologically dependent on foreign economies.

1.28 Both the favourable and the unfavourable possibilities appear less persuasive on closer examination. For example, drawing on other sources, we characterize the United Kingdom economy as being especially heavily committed in science based industry. At the same time, the ratio of scientists to other workers is lower here than elsewhere, and there is excess demand for them. Why, then, do we want foreign owned subsidiaries to engage in research here? They employ almost exclusively British personnel, with effects comparable to the brain drain, which is a 'bad' thing. The various arguments can be looked at in this way from the point of consistency and plausibility, with a general result of down grading the importance of these particular technology considerations.

1.29 Autonomy and national independence is a particularly awkward policy to follow with respect to the production of new knowledge. Nationalistic research, with an emphasis on large, distinct and prestigious projects is to be contrasted, in our view unfavourably, with work which mingles freely with foreign efforts, pursues special advantages rather than completeness and is orientated toward economic gain. Nor does there appear to be a great deal, if any, scope for stimulating indigenous technology through excluding the foreign owned firm. At the same time, the very great benefits which some observers expect to follow, on technology grounds, through encouraging inward investment seem to exaggerate the spill-over effects, pay insufficient attention to the question as to who benefits from improved technology, and give little weight to alternative ways of promoting technological growth.

Industrial relations

1.30 The behaviour of the foreign owned firm in the British labour market is of special importance on two accounts. The first is that the parent company may operate in a country with different industrial relations practices, and it is interesting to examine the extent and ways in which it either imports its practices or adjusts to the British norm. And changes, when they occur, could either be useful innovations which spread to domestic firms, or they could be quite disturbing. We find, contrary to expectations, that the foreign subsidiary is less strike prone than its domestic counterpart.

1.31 It is quite widely believed that in so far as the foreign firm achieves superior performance, this is largely due to more careful use of more able labour. This, and related, propositions are examined in the text, taking the electrical engineering industry as a case study. We find that physical capital inputs tend to be larger for the foreign owned firm, and that inputs of knowledge need not be embedded in better educated workers employed directly by the subsidiary. One of the advantages of a multi-national firm is that it draws on knowledge in the entire organization which is not necessarily physically present in the United Kingdom.

Monopoly and competitive structure

1.32 One half of the giant United States firms, and one quarter of the non-American foreign giants, have subsidiaries in this country. These subsidiaries make up a large proportion of total inward direct investment in this country, and are often large firms compared to domestic companies. Ten per cent of the largest companies in this country are foreign owned, and their parent companies are giants among other firms in the source countries. Direct investment is very much an activity of oligopolistic firms.

1.33 In this country direct investment tends to go into industries which are more concentrated than average. The typical situation is that if there is any foreign ownership in an industry, there are several foreign subsidiaries, not just one. Oligopoly, rather than perfect competition, is the appropriate characterization of the direct investment phenomenon. From this it does not follow that inward investment reduces the degree of competitiveness within the economy. Competition is not perfect in the absence of the incoming firm. Indeed, in industries where scale is critical and entry very difficult, entry from abroad actual or potential, may be the strongest deterrent against domestic firms engaging in serious exploitation of a monopolist position. Of course, imports can do the same thing. But in industries where proximity affords a real advantage, or where tariff protection is significant, inward investment may well increase the degree of competition in spite of its own oligopolistic nature.

1.34 For direct investment to benefit the host country, real income must somehow escape from the subsidiary to the country in the form of either taxes on profits, higher wages or other factor payments, or lower product prices. Competition should serve this function. And it is sometimes argued that where competition is less than perfect, the host country does not gain. Our view is that this is too stringent a requirement, that gains come to the host country in the oligopolistic setting.

1.35 As is discussed above, a capitalist world where a few international manufacturing giants undertake the bulk of the production is something we may be headed towards, is difficult to speculate about, and suggests critically altered power relations in society. This is not the present situation. Domestic firms undertake at least half, and usually much more, of total production in all United Kingdom industries. (There is a problem of course, of defining industrial categories.) The direct investment which is here cannot usually be accurately described as perfectly competitive, but in our judgement, it does not worsen the competitive situation compared to what would be the case if the direct investment was not here.

Regional impact

1.36 There is some natural tendency for new establishments owned abroad to locate in depressed regions, and official policy reinforces this tendency.

Board of Trade Economic Inquiry into Foreign Direct Investment in the United Kingdom

1. Name of firm ....

Note: *In filling out the form, answer all questions from the point of view of the United Kingdom subsidiary* **and** *its sub-subsidiaries located in the United Kingdom. Exclude the contributions from your sub-subsidiaries located overseas.*

2. Name of parent(s) company and country in which it is incorporated.

(Name) .... (Country) ....

....

3. Indicate the percentage of your equity capital owned by the firm(s) named in question 2.

.... %

.... %

Note: *If none of your equity capital is owned by a foreign firm, you need not complete this form.* ***However, would*** *you please return it to the Board of Trade with a comment on question seven.*

4. Was this subsidiary established through a take-over, a joint venture, or was it a new establishment?

Take-over ☐ Joint Venture ☐ New establishment ☐

5. Date of establishment as a foreign owned firm in the United Kingdom

....

6. Indicate the dates and nature of subsequent principal changes in the composition of ownership.

....

....

....

Note: *Indicate "none", if appropriate.*

7. Indicate extra information, if any, which you feel is relevant to the question of ownership.

....

....

....

....

8. List companies, if any, where your United Kingdom firm exercises a controlling interest, as shareholder, in subsidiaries operating in the United Kingdom.

Company	Per Cent of Equity Ownership
....	....
....	....
....	....

Note: *Please indicate "none", if appropriate. Use additional space if necessary.*

9. List companies, if any, where your United Kingdom firm exercises a controlling interest, as shareholder, outside the United Kingdom.

Company	Country Located	Per Cent of Equity Ownership
....	....	....
....	....	....
....	....	....

10. What, briefly, are your principal classes of product (or activities, if more appropriate), and what is your approximate share in the United Kingdom market of these products ? (List in order of importance).

Principal Products	UK market share
1	%
2	%
3	%
4	%

Note: *Fill in less than four items, if appropriate. Give more only if necessary. Please list the products even if market shares are not known to you.*

11. In filling out the following table, please exclude, if possible, the contributions of your **overseas** subsidiaries, if any. Whe from these sources. Also indicate if contributions of your United Kingdom subsidiaries are or are not included. If your da that basis anyhow (by the nearest approximation), and state below the accounting period to which the data actually refer.

....

Note: All money figures in thousands of pounds *(*see definitions)*

			1955	1956	1957	1958	1959	1960
a*	Value of net assets							
b	Capital expenditure							
c*	Long-term indebtedness to United Kingdom interests at year end							
d*	Profits retained in the United Kingdom	(i) Undistributed						
		ii) Distributed in the United Kingdom						
f*	Repatriated profits							
g	Interest payments abroad							
h*	Payments to parent company for charges for services							
i	Sales in the United Kingdom excluding re-sales							
j*	Re-sales in the United Kingdom							
k*	Current expenditure on Research and Development							
l	Exports							
m*	Operative employees (Number)							
n	Non-operative employees (Number)							

12. Indicate in total for each of the past two years your annual payments to the parent company and/or a subsidiary of it abroad, and to any other firms or organisations abroad, for technical knowhow, payments for research work, royalties and fees, production under licencing etc.(but excluding payments for market research). Please give figures in thousands of pounds.

	1966	1967
Parent or subsidiary abroad		
Other company or organisation abroad		

Comment ....

13. Could you give some indication of the numbers of qualified scientific personnel and engineers employed in your Research and Development Department, and in management.

	R. & D.	Management
Those with post-graduate degrees		
Those with first degrees		
Those with qualifications equivalent to a degree		

14. Describe briefly the **nature** of the research work done by you (mainly pure, mainly development, etc.), and outline the **policy** concerning the allocation of research and development between your parent company and yourself. (For example, does it undertake research at your request?).

....

....

....

s not possible, can you indicate below roughly the share coming
t available on a calender year basis, please fill out the table on

....

1962	1963	1964	1965	1966	1967

DEFINITIONS FOR THE TABLE OF DATA OVER TIME

(a) Fixed assets after accumulated depreciation, plus total current assets, less total current liabilities.

(c) Include all long-term loans, debentures, bank loans, etc.

(d) Total profits after depreciation provisions but before tax and including income from trade investments.

(e) After U.K. tax.

(f) After U.K. tax.

(h) Include affiliates share of head office expenses, research and development expenditure, royalties, copyrights, patents, trade marks, technical assistance, know-how and the like.

(j) Items produced by the parent and sold by you with no, or minimal, additional processing.

(k) Expenditure by you in the United Kingdom, including any payments made to other United Kingdom firms and organisations for research and development, but not expenditure undertaken by the parent in the parent country.

(m) If you do not have a breakdown of operative and non-operative employees, give total employees in the 'operative' row and indicate this has been done.

P.T.O.

15. Roughly what proportion of your executive and technical staff, broadly defined, are nationals of the country of the parent company? .... %

16. Do you receive a grant from your Industrial Training Board; if so, what was the amount last year?

Total levy £ .... **Total grant £** ....

17. What share, approximately, of your total sales are to your parent company, or to a subsidiary of it? .... %

18. Has the establishment of your firm as a foreign owned subsidiary had any effect on exports to the United Kingdom from the parent company?

....

....

19. If this subsidiary was formed by take-over, did the take-over affect the proportion of the output exported?

....

....

20. In what way does the parent company influence your exporting behaviour, other than in its capacity as a buyer?

....

....

....

21. What is the maximum capital expenditure which can be undertaken without reference to your parent company?

£ ....

Comment ....

What changes have there been in this figure over the past fifteen years?

....

....

22. Describe briefly the procedure and policy with respect to the determination of your product prices, indicating the role of the parent company.

....

....

....

23. Does the parent company set targets for you (for example with respect to rate of return on capital, sales, etc.), and if so, please indicate their general nature.

....

....

....

24. Name of person responsible for the completion of the questionnaire.

(BLOCK letters please) ....

Tel. No. .... Ext. .... Signature ....

STD CODE (if outside London) ....

The potential gain is quite great. Instead of simply increasing the productivity of British workers, by raising the amount of capital per man, it may put people to work who otherwise would be unemployed. Our chapter on this topic concentrates on possible unintended and undesirable side effects of the presence of foreign owned companies in relatively isolated regions. In dense industrial conurbations, with a high level of employment and alternative employment opportunities in most skill specialisms, the employee is likely to have effective choice as to whether or not to work for a foreign firm. This may not be the case in an isolated region.

1.37 The distinction between working for a domestic and a foreign firm can, though need not in all cases, be a meaningful one, as the incoming firm may be an effective importer of a way of life. If we think of the British life style as involving choice, the expanded choice offered by the presence of foreign firms here is consistent with this life style. If we think of the British life style as having a definite, specific content, then the foreign firm is a potential disruption. However, even in a relatively isolated labour market area it is unlikely that a large proportion of the work force will be employed by a single foreign employer. This conclusion follows from a number of generalisations.

(i) The direct investing firm is typically in a 'new' science based industry, employing a set of skills that does not traditionally predominate in the area.

(ii) It employs people from the area, bringing in only small numbers from the outside.

(iii) With wages often above average, the emphasis is on high quality labour.

(iv) Hiring is done largely from other firms rather than from the pool of unemployed.

(v) Careful labour utilization, an emphasis on supervision, and the breaking down of operations means that surprisingly little training is undertaken.

This programme can only succeed if the incoming firm is employing a small proportion of the work force available in the area.

1.38 With certain possible exceptions, we were in general unable to uncover serious special problems arising from the presence of foreign owned firms in relatively isolated regions. There are indications, however, that they can make things more difficult for existing traditional industry in the area. Competition for better labour is an obvious example. The traditional industry may be perfectly economically viable, and nevertheless suffer if special advantages are given to new firms in the area. This cautionary note with respect to new firms coming to an area applies to domestic firms as well as to the foreigner.

Control of foreign owned subsidiaries

1.39 We have identified five decision making areas, and attempted to learn something about the degree and kinds of control which parent organizations exercise over subsidiaries in each of them. The areas are: financial decisions, including capital expansion; production planning, including changes in products and methods; pricing policy; personnel policy; exporting policy. Two-thirds of the firms in our sample indicated that they were given no explicit targets, such as rate of return on investment, by the parents. In the areas of capital expenditure and the related questions of products to be produced and methods of production, our tentative results confirm the view that multi-national organisations are becoming increasingly integrated, with less autonomy for individual units. Again, about two-thirds of the firms indicated that they set prices independently of the parent. About a third of the firms indicated that the parent did not interfere in their exporting policy. Geographic limitations were not uncommon, being reported in about a fifth of the replies. The most interesting result of our work on control is the tighter control exercised by 'network' companies with subsidiaries in many countries.

Inward investment and national autonomy

1.40 While a loss of national autonomy is not the same thing as the control exercised by parent organisations over subsidiaries located here, the two are related. Our findings suggest that those firms whose exporting policy is subject to foreign control, but not the other decision making areas, are less amenable to United Kingdom Governmental directive. However, these also tend to be the firms which are part of a multi-national network, rather than a part of a simple parent-subsidiary relationship. And it could be the network aspect, rather than control over exporting, which matters. This is consistent with our finding that links in multi-national organizations are less amenable to Government directive than bi-national firms and joint ventures, and have a greater awareness of responsibilities outside the United Kingdom.

1.41 In general, our search for concrete cases of loss of national autonomy through inward investment produced very little. Only the most minor indications were found here and there. It is also the case that in many ways the flow of inward investment increases the host country options. One important way is through raising domestic income. And the fact that the foreign firm is foreign, is here on sufferance, and the possibility of exchange control, tend, under present conditions at least, to make it more publicly accountable than domestic firms.

1.42 Future nationalization of industries with important foreign subsidiaries is clearly a difficult undertaking. A large part of the value of the subsidiary comes from its international links. Often it may be engaged in the United Kingdom in only one phase of a many nation production process. So this may make it impractical, or very difficult, to nationalize an industry. Of course, if the foreign investment is excluded, then it cannot be nationalised either, though the industry it was headed for may more readily be.

1.43 There is a growing feeling that proper control of the multi-national firm by nation states calls for international co-operation at the Government to Government level. But this co-operation itself can entail some loss of national autonomy. Current British regulation of foreign investment and the statistics of foreign investment conclude this study.

Conclusions and policy options

1.44 The force of our investigation, in a paragraph, is that concerns over the multi-national firm and inward investment on the grounds of monopoly power, technology, and the balance of payments are not well founded. At the same time, some drawbacks have been indicated, as well as a substantial amount of uncertainty with respect to our findings. We have tried to direct attention to effects on domestic national income, rather than to considerations bearing on this indirectly. While the foreign subsidiary means that some decision taking relevant to our economy goes on outside this country, there is not a great deal of interference and we have been unable to find substantial adverse effects due to it. Links in multi-national organizations exert their influence on the organization as well as being influenced, and excluding the foreign firm does not give us control over many decisions which still effect us. Nor is it realistic to regard the nation state as a single interest entity, with the foreign influence as an obvious disturbance.

1.45 When all is said and done, some may still wish to limit inward investment or to exclude it altogether. This may be because of political considerations analogous to trade embargoes on Rhodesia, or Cuba, for example. It may be due to a desire to move away from essentially capitalist forms of economic organization. Less dramatically, undesirable side effects may emerge from an increased amount or changed nature of inward investment. Alternatively, other investigators may uncover significant adverse effects in the current situation which have escaped our attention. If such action is contemplated, a very relevant consideration is what is the cost in terms of real domestic income of excluding direct inward investment? Put another way, what is the contribution to domestic income of the current stock of foreign investment here? As usual, the so called 'dynamic' effects, stimulation to innovation, improved competition and so on, are harder to measure than the 'static' quantitative effects of having more capital in this country. We argue elsewhere that the dynamic effects cut both ways and are usually exaggerated. On very extreme assumptions, using the increasingly discredited aggregate production function, and taking account of the United Kingdom tax take on foreign profits generated here, it is possible to get an insight, better than nothing, into the contribution to our real income from inward investment. This works out at around two per cent, as an order of magnitude. For a discussion of this type of estimate, undertaken for the Canadian economy, see Penner: 1966. By 'an order of magnitude' we mean here that the increase in real domestic income is not a figure like one half of one per cent, or less, a typical figure for the gains from joining the Common Market, for example, nor, on the other hand, is it a figure like twelve per cent, for example, a typical proportion of gross national product going to net investment. The figure two per cent gives the general areas, say, something like the annual growth rate. (How this two per cent contributes to our growth depends on what we do with the extra income.) The estimate tallies reasonably well with an estimate of about three and a half per cent for Canada, where inward investment is proportionately more important than for this country, (Penner: 1966).

1.46 One approach to the inward investment problem is to reason that there are firms that would be good for us that want to come here and also firms that would be bad for us who also want to come here, and a selective policy should be adopted. We have had in mind the aim of contributing to a sensible selective approach. One might envisage a handbook listing characteristics of firms to be avoided and characteristics of firms to be encouraged. We have been unable to generate such lists. The task of establishing general criteria for encouraging or excluding, that were not platitudinous and could actually be of use for rational policy, has not been performed. We are doubtful if such general criteria exist. It is likely that selective exclusion of substantial proposals for inward investment would be very largely arbitrary.

1.47 Similarly, one might think in terms of industries rather than firms. In and of themselves there may be little grounds for discrimination between potential candidates and successfully predicting the welfare effects on us of different firms, but we still might have rational grounds for limiting foreign participation in certain industries, or excluding it altogether. Again, we are not able to defend a list of special, or key industries, where a restrictive policy should be applied. (Military considerations have not entered into our work.) The text does not address itself to the inward investment counterpart of the infant industry argument, but our judgement based on several aspects of the work is unfavourable to this argument.

1.48 After choosing among firms and choosing among industries, a third possibility is setting some overall limit. This is the implication, though not the actual suggestion, of much of the literature mentioned in the Introduction section which worries about the multi-national firm. Obviously the choice of any precise number, like the safe alcohol level in the blood, is arbitrary in a range. But a general order of magnitude for a desirable upper limit is not obviously foolish. On pure economic grounds, narrowly defined, we see no case for such a limit. It is worth remembering that raising the proportion of foreign investment by allowing an inflow does not reduce, and probably augments, the volume of domestic capital. (Those perverse theoretical cases where inward investment hurts domestic income are cases where physical growth itself hurts welfare through adverse terms of trade effects.) But as the foreign proportion gets higher, say, over twenty per cent, the non-economic drawbacks may become more important. As to the political grounds of United States domination, we incline to the view that anti-Communism dominates American foreign policy rather than attempts to control developed countries where American interests have substantial investments. However, the multi-national firm may be forced to help an anti-Communist policy, through export embargoes for example, and there may be other less tangible grounds for an upper limit.

1.49 We have run through a hierarchy of policy stances, exclusion, discriminating by firm, discriminating by industry, and setting an overall upper limit. It is interesting to note that this last policy could be achieved by clever and flexible taxing of new investment. Of course, for the United Kingdom, this could bring about retaliation, not only on our new investments abroad but on those already there. Moving down the range of policy options we come to the matter of conditions. These tend to be of three kinds; financial, which mainly means whether capital is raised here in addition; regional, which is an aspect of local development policy; technological, which has to do with the extent to which foreign firms engage in research and development in this country. In other countries, required domestic equity participation has sometimes been a condition. We do not favour this, nor do we favour the existing technology conditions. However, a strong case can be made for conditions with respect to union recognition. Passing on, after various exclusions and conditions comes a neutral stance, treating foreign investment like domestic investment, and finally subsidy of foreign investment in the form of tax holidays and other inducements is possible. Less developed countries, for understandable reasons, have been prone to this extremely costly policy. A basic purpose of this study is to allow a more informed choice among the policy options which are open.

1.50 Clearly our knowledge is far from complete, and a close watch on inward investment is a minimal sensible policy. We have alluded to the small response to our postal questionnaire. (The number of forms returned is not a good index of the coverage due to the very skewed size distribution of foreign firms.) The holding company pattern of inward investing interest groups is very complex and hard to disentangle partly because of obscure reporting of take-overs by foreign firms already here. And not being publicly traded companies in the United Kingdom, information on wholly owned foreign subsidiaries, the typical case, is hard to acquire. We recommend a much intensified monitoring of the foreign activity in this country. Our study appears to take a rather sanguine view of inward investment. While asking for more information, we play down concern over balance of payments, monopoly, technology, and so on. We come out against selecting among applicants, and against keeping them out of certain industries, though we are sympathetic to the idea of an overall general limit. On economic grounds and grounds of national autonomy we express few arguments against inward direct investment. But the state of the discussion as we see it is this. Various observers and officials have pointed to certain statistics and expressed certain potential problems in a very general way. We have undertaken the investigation described in the text and have, on the whole, been unable to substantiate the case for intervention. For example, we find hardly any grounds for believing in a serious loss of national autonomy. That does not mean that such a loss does not exist, only that we have not found it. Others may be able to. We hope that our raking over the territory will stimulate a more rigorous search for disadvantages to the United Kingdom of inward investment. If such drawbacks exist, we hope they will be found. If they do not exist, we hope they will not be found.

1.51 It is hard to avoid the feeling that some of the objection to the growing success of the multi-nation firm is a dog in the manger attitude. Yet if it is particularly advantageous to a country to be the home base of a many country network (as opposed to being just advantageous to be a host), the United Kingdom is well placed to partake in this development. In terms of industry mix, commercial traditions, and general wealth, this country is a natural source country. Post-war restrictions on both equity participation in foreign multi-national firms and investment abroad by our own firms have hampered United Kingdom participation. Vigorous balance of payments policy to remove the necessity for restriction may be a more positive response to the growth of international investment than arbitrary regulation of the inward flow.

2. Inward investment and the balance of payments

2.1 Before examining the specific effects of inward investment on the balance of payments it may be useful to indicate the extent to which this particular effect is relevant to any question of policy connected with inward investment. It is clear that the balance of payments is not an ultimate goal of economic policy in the same sense as say, full employment, stable prices, a 'high' rate of growth, and so on. The balance of payments is the net result of the actions taken by individuals in attaining their economic goals, and the actions taken by policy makers to attain theirs. In a framework of fixed exchange rates, limited reserves constrain the options available to policy makers, and the balance of payments position becomes important to the question of whether the real economic goals can or cannot be attained.

2.2 If we look at the balance of payments as a constraint to the achievement of various economic objectives then we can only judge the balance of payments effects of a particular policy in relation to the balance of payments effects of other policies whose aim is to achieve similar objectives. A hypothetical example might make the problem clearer. Assume that an increase in the rate of growth of output is an objective of economic policy. Assume that this can be achieved in two ways, either by the use of investment grants or by encouraging inward investment. Both policies will have balance of payments effects (among other) which can be looked at as part of the costs (or gains) of attaining that particular objective. The knowledge of the balance of payments effects of any individual policy alone tells one very little about the desirability or otherwise of that policy. For this and other reasons (see below) our model examines the effects of inward investment on domestic income before going on to examine the balance of payments effects.

2.3 When examining the effects of inward investment on the balance of payments we have to distinguish between the initial, once and for all, effect of an inward investment and the continuing effects which arise because the firm is owned and operated by foreigners. Until section five of this chapter we shall be concerned only with the latter effects. Most of the previous work on the balance of payments effects of inward investment has concentrated on the relationship between parent and subsidiary in terms of the flow of funds between them—fees, royalties and repatriated earnings. Bell: 1962, for example, attempts to calculate the number of periods that it would take before an initial investment is covered by the remissions from the subsidiary to the parent. Moffat: 1967, uses a similar approach to examine both the balance of payments effects of inward investment and its effect on foreign ownership. This general approach implicitly assumes that the only effect of inward investment on the domestic economy is that part of the income now accruing to foreigners is taken out of the country and therefore represents a drain on the foreign exchange of the domestic economy. This approach seems highly dubious in the case of real foreign investment and not obviously valid even in the case of a takeover. In the case of real inward investment there must be an increase in total domestic output which has real macroeconomic effects or induces some policy to counteract these. These effects might very well have balance of payments effects which do not show up when looking only at the remissions from the subsidiary to the parent. An extreme example might make this clearer. A foreign firm builds a factory in the UK and uses only foreign factors to produce output. It exports all of its output. Then, even though we observe repatriated earnings of a 'large' amount this does not at all indicate that there is an adverse balance of payments effect. On the contrary, in our example, there may be a gain in the form of the taxation on the income of the foreign factors which would imply that not all the income (output) of the foreign factors was repatriated but by assumption all of the output was exported. The above example should make it clear that to ignore all but the flow of funds between parent and subsidiary can lead to totally misleading conclusions about the overall balance of payments effects of inward investment.

2.4 Even in the case of a takeover of domestic capital (e.g. a firm) it is not clear that the other effects can be ignored. The initial effect of the foreign investment in this case is to transfer income from domestic owners to foreign owners. The fall in domestic disposable income has presumably some repercussion on other economic variables, for example aggregate demand, which could affect the balance of payments. Also when a takeover occurs, it does not necessarily mean that the only change is the nationality of the owners. Foreign owned firms might use a different technology and thus affect output, or might have different exporting behaviour and thus affect the balance of payments directly. These effects might reinforce or offset the remissions effects on the balance of payments. It might be argued that if one is mainly interested in the balance of payments effects of inward investment one should start the analysis by assuming a specific government policy of demand management to maintain a given level of aggregate demand or domestic disposable income, and thus look at only the micro effects of inward investment. We believe that there are at least two objections to this. First, the macroeconomic effects of inward investment are of interest in themselves; it is an important question for any policy decision about inward investment to know its effects on aggregate demand, domestic income and other macro variables. As mentioned above the balance of payments is not in itself an ultimate goal of economic policy. It is therefore important to know the total effects of inward investment to see what the costs or benefits are, in terms of other desirable goals, of the balance of payments effect. Given that there are many policy goals and many tools with which to attain these goals, the choice can only be made if all the effects are considered. Second, as shown in section 4, different policies of maintaining aggregate demand at some specific level imply different balance of payments effects of inward investment. These differences can only be seen clearly if one examines the total macro effects of inward investment and traces out the interrelationships between the micro effects and the macro effects.

2.5 The model which we present below has been constructed in an attempt to overcome the above criticisms of the simple 'remissions' approach and to take account of other micro and macro interrelationships of inward investment, and their potential effects on the balance of payments. It is similar in approach to parts of the work of Hufbauer and Adler: 1968. An attempt was made to construct the model in such a way that it could deal both with the case of inward real investment and the case of a takeover, and in a way that could ultimately be estimated with the use of available data. Some of the seemingly complicated ways of expressing the variables are due to this fact. Wherever possible the concepts that were thought to be relevant were expressed in terms of such variables for which data were available. We also realize that no data are presently available for some of the variables which on *a priori* grounds would seem important to the balance of payments effects of inward investment, for example the degree to which the output of the foreign firm is used for import substitution. To ignore these in the model would only serve the purpose of incorporating our empirical ignorance in a model whose purpose is to shed some light on what empirical questions are relevant to the balance of payments effects of inward investment. We therefore incorporate these variables in the model in such a way as to allow a simulation experiment to be made giving us at least an idea of the range of possible answers. (See Appendix 2). We believe that the sacrifice in the elegance of expression is worth the increase in the potential usefulness of the model. For a more formal approach see Pearce and Rowan: 1966.

2.6 As the model is framed in such a way as to be used both for inward real investment and takeovers it may be useful to set out in general terms the basic difference of these two types of inward investment. More importantly, it is desirable to set out the implicit assumptions about the working of the economy that are made when evaluating the effects of these two types of inward investment on the balance of payments. The pure case of inward real investment occurs when a foreign company brings real capital into the domestic economy either directly, for example, a machine which is brought in and set up for the production of goods, or via an initial inflow of financial capital which is then followed by the importing of real capital (not necessarily from the same country), i.e. an outflow of the financial capital. In this case the initial balance of payments effects are zero; however total available resources of the domestic economy (the capital stock) has increased by the full amount of the foreign investment and therefore the flow of output of the economy has increased. The question is then how does this increase in the flow of output over time affect the balance of payments both directly in the form of exports, remissions, import substitution etc., and indirectly via its effects on aggregate demand and domestic income and the effects of these on the balance of payments. The pure case of a takeover occurs when a foreign company acquires ownership of an existing stock of capital (e.g. a firm) with no other changes occurring. This represents a pure transfer of a claim to a future income stream from domestic to foreign residents. The initial balance of payments effect is equal to the foreign investment; however there is no change in the total quantity of resources available to the economy and therefore in the flow of output over time. The question is then how does this change of ownership of an existing capital stock affect the balance of payments either directly via remission, changes in export behaviour etc., or indirectly via the change in the income stream accruing to residents.

2.7 However, most if not all inward investment does not fall neatly into the pure categories described above, but is some mixture of the two polar cases. If a foreign company takes over a domestic firm and because of the use of more advanced technology or better management the output of the firm increases, we have in essence a combination of a takeover of domestic resources (a change in ownership) and an inward real investment in the form of the new technology that is being used. And if we have real inward investment which also uses some domestic resources in the production process we again have a mixture of real investment and 'takeover'—not all of the output of the foreign firm can be attributed to inward real investment. A similar problem occurs in the case of an inward financial investment which is used to bid for current domestic output, for example a machine, as opposed to acquiring an existing capital stock (e.g. a firm) which is a pure takeover case. In this case the question must be asked as to whether the current output would have been acquired by a domestic firm or whether the resources used to produce the current output would have remained idle. If we have full employment or a policy to maintain the level of employment then the resources acquired by the foreign firm (and the future flow of output that these would produce) can be treated as a transfer from some other section of the economy and analytically treated as a takeover case. If, however, the resources would have remained unemployed then the foreign investment has the same effect on output as an inflow of real foreign capital, i.e. the increase in the output of the economy can be attributed to the foreign investment.

2.8 The above discussion should make it clear that the border line between takeovers and real investment, in terms of their respective economic effects, is quite blurred. In terms of the economic distinction between these two types of inward investment the available data are inadequate to separate out the proportion of one to the other. This is another reason why the model we have used is constructed in such a way as to deal with these two types of investment simultaneously, by including a variable which measures the proportion of total foreign output which can be attributed to the inward investment.

2.9 We shall examine the effects of inward investment on the economy in general and on the balance of payments in particular with the use of a simple income determination model and some specific hypotheses about the behaviour of the groups involved in the economic processes under discussion and the constraints facing them. The total effect on the balance of payments due to inward investment can be split up into four effects—the export effect, the import substitution effect, the import effect and the remissions effect. The second and third effects however are induced via the effects of inward investment on domestic disposable income. Therefore these have to be examined first. The model is presented in five sections. Section I examines the macroeconomic effects of inward investment, i.e. the effects of inward investment on aggregate demand and the disposable income of nationals. The former is important because the management of aggregate demand is an important goal of current economic policy and therefore if inward investment induces any changes in aggregate demand domestic policies might be undertaken to counteract these. The latter is important to the balance of payments question because we assume that domestic disposal income affects imports and therefore the balance of payments. In Section II we examine the relationship between the microeconomic effects of inward investment and the macroeconomic effects, and in Section III all of these are combined to examine the balance of payments effects. In Section IV we examine the effects on the balance of payments of various policies of managing aggregate demand and in Section V we incorporate the initial once and for all effect of the inward investment. After each section we examine the assumptions made in that section and some justifications for these are given.

I: Macroeconomic relations

2.10 The following symbols will be used:

$\bar{Y}$ = Aggregate demand on the output produced by domestic resources.

C = Domestic consumption.

E = Other domestic expenditures (investment, government expenditures and exports).

M = Imports.

Y_F = Total pretax income accruing to foreigners.

Y^E_F = Demand for domestic output specifically attributable to the fact that foreigners have a claim on domestic income.

$$\alpha = \frac{Y^E_F}{Y_F}$$

Y^D_F = The output of foreign firms which is used as import substitution.

$$\beta = \frac{Y^D_F}{Y_F}$$

T_D = Taxes on domestic income.

Y_D = Domestic disposable income, i.e. the disposable income of nationals.

$$Y_D = \overline{Y} - Y_F - T_D$$

We assume the following simple behavioural relationship

$$T_D = t(\overline{Y} - Y_F) + t_o \qquad (1)$$

$$C = a + b\,Y_D \qquad (2)$$

$$M = m_o + m\,Y_D + m'\,\overline{Y} - \beta\,Y_F \qquad (3)$$

However

$$\overline{Y} = \frac{Y_D}{1\text{-}t} + Y_F + \frac{t_o}{1\text{-}t}$$

$$\therefore M = m_o + Y_D\left[m + \frac{m'}{1\text{-}t}\right] + Y_F[m' - \beta] + \frac{m'\,t_o}{1\text{-}t}$$

Let $v = m + \dfrac{m'}{1\text{-}t}$

$$M = m_o + v\,Y_D + [m' - \beta]\,Y_F + \frac{m'\,t_o}{1\text{-}t} \qquad (3')$$

Equation (3) is stated in somewhat unusual form because ultimately we want to examine the potential import substitution effect of inward investment. Import substitution implies that imports are not only a function of domestic income but of something else also—people can be induced to substitute domestically produced goods for imports. βY_F the last term in equation (3) represents by definition such a substitution induced by foreign investment. How this is done, whether by changing prices or advertising or whatever is left unspecified and as a first approximation it does not matter for our purposes. Assume that product X has been produced by a foreign company in a foreign country and imported to the domestic economy, this would be included in M. Now assume that the foreign company takes over a domestic firm, or makes a real inward investment and starts to produce product X within the country. Consumers continue to consume product X but now because the output of X is part of domestic output imports have fallen. This is the effect we want to include in the last term of equation (3). The reason for including Y_D and $\overline{Y}$ in the import equation is that once there are foreign claims on domestic income, these are not uniquely related. However both can generate imports; m represents the marginal propensity to import consumption goods and m′ represents the import content of output as a fraction of the domestic resource content.[1]

2.11 Equation (1) assumes a simple proportional tax system on domestic income. Even though income taxes are progressive at higher income levels, the existence of various expenditure taxes and the relationship of these to income (via the relationship between consumption and income) makes it plausible to assume a proportional tax system. The analysis would be unduly complicated and the results only minutely changed if we were to postulate a progressive tax model.

2.12 Using the previous definitions

$$\begin{aligned}\overline{Y} &= C+E+Y_F^E - M \\ &= C+E+\alpha Y_F - M \qquad (4)\end{aligned}$$

and substituting the behavioural relationships, equations (1), (2) and (3′) into (4) and rearranging terms we have[2]

$$\overline{Y} = \frac{1}{s+v+t(b-v)} \times [Y_F(\alpha+\beta-m'-(1-t)(b-v))-t_o(b-m)+E+a-m_o] \qquad (5)$$

$$\text{Let } k = \frac{1}{s+v+t(b-v)} = \text{the multiplier}$$

$$\frac{d\overline{Y}}{dY_F} = k\,[\alpha+\beta-m'-(1-t)(b-v)] \qquad (6)$$

Equation (6) above shows the effect on aggregate demand of a change in the income accruing to foreigners.

Substituting the tax relationship [equation (1)] into the definition of domestic disposable income ($Y_D = \overline{Y} - Y_F - T_D$) we have

$$Y_D = (\overline{Y}-Y_F)(1-t)-t_o$$

$$\frac{dY_D}{dY_F} = \left(\frac{d\overline{Y}}{dY_F}-1\right)(1-t) \qquad (7)$$

$$\begin{aligned}\frac{dY_D}{dY_F} &= \{k\,[\alpha+\beta-m'-(1-t)(b-v)]-1\}\ \{1-t\} \\ &= k(1-t)[\alpha+\beta-m'-1] \qquad (8)^3\end{aligned}$$

(remembering that $k = \frac{1}{s+v+t(b-v)}$ and of course $s=1-b$)

Equation (8) above shows the effect on domestic disposable income of a change in the income accruing to foreigners.

[1] See Appendix 1A for the relationship between m′ and the import content when the latter is measured in terms of the value of domestic output.

[2] Where $s=1-b$. See Appendix 1B for the derivation of these equations.

[3] See Appendix 1C.

2.13 At this stage it may be useful to make explicit the economic assumptions implicit in the derivation of equations (6) and (8) which show the effects of inward investment (represented by changes in foreign income) on aggregate demand and on domestic disposable income. The use of the simple multiplier analysis in our model implies (as is true for all models of this kind) that there are no repercussions from the monetary sector.[1] If, for example, the initial change in aggregate demand, due in our case to a change in foreign income, were to lead to a change in interest rates and through this to a change in investment the ultimate effect would be less than that shown by equation (6). In the UK where monetary policy over the last few years has been aimed at fixing interest rates this assumption seems plausible in the short run; as long as inward investment does not lead to a change in the fixed rate of interest that monetary policy attempts to maintain. Our model also assumes that foreign investment has no effect on the demand by the rest of the world for domestic exports.[2] This is the same as assuming that foreign investment into the UK has no income and price effects on the capital exporting countries. This seems to be a very plausible assumption for the following reasons. First UK exports are presumably a function of total world income and the level of world prices, both of these would be only slightly affected by inward investment to the UK. Secondly, one can assume that most countries have some sort of demand management policies which would offset any 'large' income effects of outward investment. The omission of this effect would tend to bias the results of equations (6) and (8) downwards. If world income were to respond substantially to inward investment into the UK, which we do not believe, this would reduce exports from the UK and hence the response of aggregate demand to inward investment.

2.14 Another assumption which is important for the case of a takeover can best be seen by looking at equation (8) and for simplicity assuming the α and β are equal to zero, i.e. that the change in foreign income does not have any direct effects on aggregate demand or any import substitution effects. Equation (8) then reduces to

$$dY_D = -\, dY_F\, k\,(1 - t)\,[1 + m']$$

which says that domestic disposable income falls by some multiple of the rise in foreign income. In a takeover all that has happened is that domestic owners of an income stream (e.g. a firm) have exchanged the claims to the income stream for a capital sum—the initial capital inflow. If the initial capital inflow allows or induces outward investment of the same amount whose yield to residents is the same as the yield accruing to foreigners from the inward investment, then as a first approximation the inward investment would have no effect on domestic disposable income or for that matter on the balance of payments either initially or in the future.[3] The initial inflow is counteracted by an initial outflow of the same amount and future outflows, in the form of repatriated earnings etc., are counteracted by future inflows of the same amount. We assume however that this does not happen, i.e., that the inward investment does not lead to an outward investment. This is based on the assumption that government policy is such as to discourage outward investment either by working on interest rates or via other forms of controls, and that this policy is not affected by inward investment.

[1] This would imply either a perfectly elastic demand curve for money or a perfectly elastic supply curve of money.

[2] We assume that E in equation (5) is not affected by changes in foreign income.

[3] 'As a first approximation' because there might be differential tax, exports and other effects.

2.15 If the funds acquired by the owners of the firm which has been taken over are not used for outward investment (directly by themselves or indirectly by other residents) they can be used in two ways; either to acquire real domestic output (for example to make a real investment) or to acquire financial assets. The former of these if successful implies that there were some unemployed resources in the economy and that there is no policy to maintain aggregate demand. If this is the case we have exactly the same situation as the one discussed in paras 6-8 where an inward financial investment increased total output by inducing the employment of previously unemployed factors, except that in this case the inducement is indirect. From the point of view of the economic effects it is clearly immaterial whether the increase in the use of domestic factors occurs directly because foreigners via a financial investment bid for these or indirectly because domestics who have sold a capital stock (the firms) use the funds to bid for the resources. The other alternative is that the funds acquired are kept in the form of financial assets by the private sector of the economy and foreign cash reserves by the government sector. This occurs automatically via the operation of the Exchange Equalization Fund which issues Treasury Bills equal to the amount of foreign exchange used in the takeover. Thus even though domestics have exchanged one income stream for another after the takeover—the income stream yielded by the firm, for the income stream yielded by the Treasury Bills—the country as a whole has exchanged an income stream for a stock of foreign reserves.[1]

II: Microeconomic effects

2.16 The following symbols will be used:

P = Output per period time of foreign firms after takeover or after new investment.

O = Output per period time of domestic firm before takeover or of domestic resources in alternative use.

f = $\frac{P - O}{P}$ = % change in output due to foreign investment.

In case of real investment with no use of previously employed domestic factors

$f=1$; in case of takeover with no technical improvement $f=0$; we assume $o \leqslant f \leqslant 1$.

fP = Change in output due to existence of foreign investment.

$\frac{P}{1+m'}$ = foreign output less imported inputs.

$\frac{\pi P}{1+m'}$ = Pre tax earnings of foreign firms and factors. This is equal to total revenue *less* payment to domestic factors.

g = Proportion of foreign earnings $(\frac{\pi P}{1+m'})$ repatriated home (as profits, fees, royalties etc.)

γfP = Output of foreign firm used to substitute for imports.

x = Proportion of output exported by domestic firms pre takeover.

x' = Proportion of output exported by foreign firms.

[1] Because the interest payments made by the Government represent a transfer of income from somebody else.

2.17 The macro model in Section I made use of two variables α and β. The first represents the aggregate demand induced by foreign income as a fraction of foreign income and the second represents the import substitution induced by foreign income as a fraction of foreign income. The aggregate demand induced by inward investment is the change in exports. Using the previous definitions the change in exports is

$$P\,[x' - x\,(1 - f)] \qquad (9)$$

Using the above notation we have

$$Y_F^E = P\,[x' - x\,(1 - f)]$$

$$Y_F = \frac{\pi P}{1 + m'}$$

thus

$$\alpha = \frac{Y_F^E}{Y_F} = \frac{[x' - x\,(1 - f)]\,(1 + m')}{\pi} \qquad (10)$$

2.18 The import substitution induced by foreign investment is measured by γfP. This way of expressing this effect means that only if f is positive do we assume that there may be an import substitution effect. We recall that f is a measure of the change in output induced by the foreign investment. When $f = o$ we have the pure takeover case, in a sense the only difference between the 'new' firm and the old firm is the nationality of the owners. In this case we assume that the new firm will not use its output for import substitution to a greater extent than did the old. As f approaches 1 the new firm becomes 'really' new—it is producing output not previously produced by the domestic firm and therefore may use some of this for import substitution. What we are assuming here is that import substitution occurs when foreign firms who had been exporting to the United Kingdom decide for some reason or other (tariff barriers, transport costs, ease of marketing, etc.) to set up a subsidiary to produce in the United Kingdom. To do this they will either import real capital and set up a firm or take over a firm whose output can be increased to produce the import substitutes, by the use of better technology or management.

Using the previous notations

$$\beta = \frac{Y_F^D}{Y_F} = \frac{(\gamma f)\,(1 + m')}{\pi}$$

Substituting the values of α and β into equation (8) i.e.

$$dY_D = dY_F\,k\,(1 - t)\,[\alpha + \beta - 1 - m']$$

we have (as $dY_F = \frac{\pi \Delta P}{1 + m'}$)

$$dY_D = k\,(1 - t)\,\Delta P\,[x' - x\,(1 - f) + \gamma f - \pi] \qquad (11)$$

Equation (11) measures the effect on domestic income of an inward investment which changes foreign output by ΔP, taking into account all of the changes—both on the micro and the macro level—induced by the foreign investment.[1]

2.19 Before going on to the next section it may be useful to examine some of the problems of interpretation and estimation of two of the variables in equation (11) — f and γ. The former represents the fraction of the total

[1] We assume throughout that the marginal effects are equal to the average effects.

output of the foreign owned firm which can be considered as an increase in total domestic output. The latter represents the fraction of the increase of output which will be used by the foreign firm to increase import substitution. In the case of a takeover the interpretation of f is quite straightforward. If the change of ownership of the firm does not result in any technological improvement in its management the value of f is zero. If foreign ownership leads to a more efficient use of the firm's resources the value of f is positive and its size depends on the degree to which foreign firms are more efficient than the domestic firms. In the case of foreign real investment the problem of estimating f is more difficult, as is discussed above. If only foreign resources were used to produce the output of these foreign firms the value of f would be unity—all of the foreign output can be considered as an increase in total domestic output. However, even in the case of real investment it is seldom (if ever) true that no domestic resources are acquired and used in conjunction with the foreign resources to produce the output. If we stick with the assumption that aggregate demand is maintained via Government policy at a fixed level, or that the economy was fully employed before the influx of the foreign investment, then the domestic resources used by the foreign firm must be treated as a transfer from other domestic uses. This is in effect saying that the case of real investment also involves an element of 'takeover' by the foreign firm; in the sense that it acquires the domestic resources from other (domestic) firms. In this case we cannot treat the total output by the foreign firms as an increase in domestic output because somewhere else in the economy output has gone down. Presumably the most important domestic resource used by foreign firms is labour. Therefore one way of estimating the increases in output due to the foreign investment would be to deduct from total foreign output the wage share in output.[1] Another way of estimating f might be to take the foreign share in output as being the foreign pre tax earnings gross of depreciation.[2]

2.20 The interpretation of γ is quite straightforward but the problem of estimation is very difficult. The question comes down to how much of the increase in output of the foreign firm sold on the domestic market would have been imported by residents. It is clear that some firms whose parent companies export to the UK set up in the UK to overcome the tariff barriers and transport costs involved, and their output is used as import substitution (from the United Kingdom point of view). However the data available both from published sources and our own survey are not detailed enough to give much of an idea as to even the order of magnitude of this phenomenon.

III: Combining the Micro and Macro Effects on the Balance of Payments

2.21 The effect of inward investment on the balance of payments can be broken down into four categories—the export effect (X), the import substitution effect (MS), the import effect (M) and the repatriation effect (R). The first two improve the balance of payments; the last two worsen the balance of payments, i.e.

$$\Delta B = \Delta X + \Delta MS - \Delta R - \Delta M$$

[1] This might be estimated from the data on employment in foreign owned firms.

[2] This would only be valid for the case of real inward investment.

Using the concepts and the notations of the last two sections these four effects can be represented as follows:

Export effect (ΔX)	=	$\Delta P\,[x' - x\,(1 - f)]$
Import substitution (ΔMS)	=	$\Delta P \gamma f$
Repatriation effect (ΔR)	=	$\Delta P g \pi$
Import effect (ΔM)	=	$v dY_D + m' dY_F = v dY_D + \frac{m' \pi\, \Delta P}{1 + m'}$ (see eq. 3′)

Substituting

$$\Delta B = \Delta P\,[x' - x\,(1 - f) + \gamma f - g\pi - \frac{m'\pi}{1 + m'}] - v dY_D$$

$$= \Delta P\,[x' - x\,(1 - f) + \gamma f - \pi\,(g + \frac{m'}{1 + m'})] - v dY_D \qquad (12)$$

2.22 It may be useful to look at equation (12) on the assumption that $f = 1$ and $dY_D = o$; i.e. all of the output of the foreign firm can be considered as an increase in domestic output and that there is no effect on domestic disposable income. From equation (11) above we can see that when $f = 1$, $dY_D = o$ when

$$x' + \gamma = \pi \qquad (13)$$

From equation (11) when $f = 1$, and $dY_D = o$

$$\Delta B = \Delta P\,[x' + \gamma - \pi\,(g + \frac{m'}{1 + m'})] \qquad (14)$$

Substituting (13) into (14)

$$\Delta B = \Delta P\,[\pi - \pi\,(g + \frac{m'}{1 + m'})]$$

$$= \Delta P\,[\pi\,(1 - (g + \frac{m'}{1 + m'}))] \qquad (15)$$

However when $f = 1$, $\pi = 1$ because all of the earnings accrue to foreign factors

$$\therefore\ \Delta B = \Delta P\,[1 - (g + \frac{m'}{1 + m'})] \qquad (15')$$

Equation (15′) shows that in the case when $f = 1$ and $dY_D = o$ the balance of payments is improved by the full amount of the firm's revenue *less* the proportion of earnings repatriated and the import content of its output.[1] On our assumptions the result is eminently sensible. If $dY_D = o$, all of the output of the foreign firm must be used either for exports, or for import substitution. We can see this clearly from equation (13) where, when $\pi = 1$, the condition for $dY_D = o$ is $x' + \gamma = 1$. x' is the proportion of output exported, γ the proportion of output used for import substitution. In this case all of the firm's output represents an improvement in the balance of payments. To get the net balance of payments effect we must deduct from this repatriated earnings and the import content of the foreign output (shown in the last two terms of equation (15′).[2]

2.23 In the more general case we can substitute equation (11) into (12). Thus

$$\Delta B = \Delta P\,[x' - x\,(1 - f) + \gamma f - \pi\,(g + \frac{m'}{1 + m'})] - \Delta P v\, k\,(1 + m')\,(1 - t) \times$$
$$\times [x' - x\,(1 - f) + \gamma f - \pi] \qquad (16)$$

Let $z = v k\,(1 + m')\,(1 - t) = k\,(1 + m')\,(m\,(1 - t) + m')$

[1] See Appendix 1A.

[2] This example shows the danger of looking at only the flows between parent and subsidiary to estimate the balance of payments effects of inward investment. See the discussion in paras 3–5.

(remembering that $v = m + \frac{m'}{1 - t}$)

$$\Delta B = \Delta P [\{x' - x(1 - f)\}\{1\text{-}z\} + \gamma f(1 - z) - \pi\{g + \frac{m'}{1 + m'} - z\}] \quad (17)$$

2.24 Equation (17) thus shows the general balance of payments effect of inward investment taking into account all of the micro and macro relationships previously discussed.

IV: The use of Government policy to manage aggregate demand

2.25 Equation (17) in the last section showed the effects of inward investment on the balance of payments on the assumption that no government policy would be undertaken to offset any of the effects of inward investment on aggregate demand. In this section we examine the balance of payments effects of inward investment if the Government uses some domestic policy to counteract any discrepancy between the change in output and the change in aggregate demand introduced by the inward investment. Two policies are examined. First an expenditure policy, then a tax policy.

2.26 The change in domestic output induced by the foreign investment is $\frac{f\,\Delta P}{1 + m'}$. To maintain the same pressure on domestic resources as before the inward investment the change in total aggregate demand ($d\bar{Y}_T$)—consisting of the change in aggregate demand induced by the foreign investment ($d\bar{Y}_F$) plus the change induced by the Government policy ($d\bar{Y}_G$)—must be equal to the change in output. Thus $d\bar{Y}_T = \frac{f\,\Delta P}{1 + m'}$. If the Government uses an expenditure policy to affect aggregate demand, there is no change in the tax rate or the fixed taxes. Thus using equation (7) (para 12)

$$
\begin{aligned}
dY_D &= (d\bar{Y} - dY_F)(1 - t) \\
&= \left(\frac{f\,\Delta P}{1 + m'} - \frac{\pi\,\Delta P}{1 + m'}\right)(1 - t) \\
&= \frac{\Delta P}{1 + m'}(1 - t)(f - \pi) \qquad (18)
\end{aligned}
$$

equation (18) shows the change in domestic disposable income taking into account both the effect of inward investment and the Government expenditure policy to maintain a given level of pressure on domestic resources. Substituting this value of dY_D into equation (12) we get the balance of payments effect

$$
\begin{aligned}
\Delta B = \; & \Delta P [x' - x(1 - f) + \gamma f - \pi(g + \frac{m'}{1 + m'})] - \\
& - v\left(\frac{1 - t}{1 + m'}\right) \Delta P [f - \pi] \qquad (19)
\end{aligned}
$$

Let $z' = \frac{v(1 - t)}{1 + m'}$: simplifying and rearranging we have

$$\Delta B = \Delta P [x' - x(1 - f) + f(\gamma - z') - \pi\{g + \frac{m'}{1 + m'} - z'\}] \quad (20)$$

Equation (20) thus shows the balance of payments effect of an inward investment given that the Government maintains its aggregate demand management policy via the use of Government expenditures.

2.27 To show the effects of a tax policy we shall assume that the Government changes the fixed taxes to change aggregate demand.[1] From equation (5) (para 12)

$$\frac{d\overline{Y}}{dt_o} = -k(b-m)$$

$$\therefore dt_o = -\frac{d\overline{Y}}{k(b-m)}$$

the imbalance which has to be corrected via the tax policy is the difference between the change in output and the change in aggregate demand induced by the foreign investment, i.e.

$$\left(\frac{f\,\Delta P}{1+m'} - d\overline{Y}_F\right)$$

thus

$$dt_o = -\left[\frac{f\,\Delta P}{1+m'} - d\overline{Y}_F\right]\frac{1}{k(b-m)} \qquad (21)$$

2.28 The change in domestic disposable income resulting from *both* the inward investment and the Government tax policy is

$$dY_D = (d\overline{Y}_T - dY_F)(1-t) - dt_o$$

but as above $d\overline{Y}_T = \frac{f\,\Delta P}{1+m'}$ and substituting for dt_o

$$\therefore dY_D = \left(\frac{f\,\Delta P}{1+m'} - dY_F\right)(1-t) + \left[\frac{f\,\Delta P}{1+m'} - d\overline{Y}_F\right]\frac{1}{k(b-m)} \qquad (22)$$

$$\therefore dY_D = \frac{f\Delta P}{1+m'}\left[(1-t) + \frac{1}{(b-m)k}\right] - dY_F(1-t) - d\overline{Y}_F\frac{1}{(b-m)k}$$

but

$$d\overline{Y}_F = k\,dY_F(\alpha+\beta-(1-t)(b-v)-m') \text{ (see equation (6).)}$$

$$\therefore dY_D = \frac{f\Delta P}{1+m'}\left[(1-t) + \frac{1}{(b-m)k}\right] - dY_F\left[(1-t) + \frac{\alpha+\beta-(1-t)(b-v)-m'}{b-m}\right]$$

remembering that $k = \frac{1}{s+v+t(b-v)}$ and $v = m + \frac{m'}{1-t}$

$$dY_D = \frac{f\Delta P}{1+m'}\left[\frac{1+m'}{b-m}\right] - dY_F\left[\frac{\alpha+\beta}{b-m}\right]$$

but

$$dY_F = \frac{\pi\,\Delta P}{1+m'}$$

$$\therefore dY_D = \frac{\Delta P}{b-m}\left[f - \frac{\pi}{1+m'}(\alpha+\beta)\right] \qquad (23)$$

[1] It is less complicated than varying the marginal tax rate although the above framework can be used to analyse changes in the marginal rate also.

2.29 Equation (23) shows the effect on domestic disposable income of the inward investment accompanied by a tax policy to maintain the pressure of aggregate demand unchanged.

Substituting the values of α and β previously derived

$$dY_D = \frac{\Delta P}{b - m} [f(1 - \gamma) - (x' - x(1 - f))]$$

Substituting this value of dY_D into equation (12)

$$\Delta B = \Delta P [x' - x(1 - f) + \gamma f - \pi (g + \frac{m'}{1 + m'})] - \frac{v \Delta P}{b - m}$$
$$[f(1 - \gamma) - (x' - x(1 - f))]$$

Let $z'' = \frac{}{b - m}$

$$\therefore \Delta B = \Delta P [\{x' - x(1 - f)\} \{1 + z''\} + \gamma f (1 + z'') - z'' f -$$
$$\pi (g + \frac{m'}{1 + m'})] \qquad (24)$$

2.30 Equation (24) shows the balance of payments effects of the inward investment accompanied by a tax policy to maintain the pressure of aggregate demand.

Summary of results

2.31 We bring together below the three cases we have examined above. Let dY_D, dY_D^G, dY_D^T be the changes in domestic disposable income in the case of no policy, an expenditure policy and tax policy respectively. Similarly let ΔB, ΔB^T and ΔB^G be the balance of payments effects in the three cases.

Then

$$dY_D = k(1 - t) \Delta P [x' - x(1 - f) + \gamma f - \pi] \qquad (1')$$

$$dY_D^G = \frac{1 - t}{1 + m'} \Delta P [f - \pi] \qquad (2')$$

$$dY_D^T = \frac{1}{b - m} \Delta P [f(1 - \gamma) - (x' - x(1 - f))] \qquad (3')$$

Let $z = vk(1 - t)$

$$z' = \frac{v(1 - t)}{1 + m'}$$

$$z'' = \frac{v}{b - m}$$

then

$$\Delta B = \Delta P [\{x' - x(1 - f)\} \{1 - z\} + \gamma f (1 - z) - \pi \{g + \frac{m'}{1 + m'} - z\}] \quad (4')$$

$$\Delta B^G = \Delta P [x' - x(1 - f) + f(\gamma - z') - \pi \{g + \frac{m'}{1 + m'} - z'\}] \qquad (5')$$

$$\Delta B^T = \Delta P [\{x' - x(1 - f)\} \{1 + z''\} + \gamma f (1 + z'') -$$
$$- z'' f - \pi (g + \frac{m'}{1 + m'})] \qquad (6')$$

V: INCORPORATING THE INITIAL ONCE AND FOR ALL EFFECT ON THE BALANCE OF PAYMENTS

2.32 So far all our results were in terms of the balance of payments effect over time of an initial inward investment. We have ignored the initial inflow of funds used for the takeover which has a once and for all effect on the balance of payments. To make this effect comparable with the other we have to convert it into a flow concept and make some assumptions about how the foreign reserves acquired in the initial period are used by the Government.

2.33 Using the previous definitions $\Delta P(1-f)$ measures the flow of output produced by the firm which was acquired via the foreign investment. Let π_D be the profit per unit of output accruing to the domestic owners of the firm before the takeover; then $\pi_D \Delta P(1-f)$ is the income stream that has been sold to the foreign owners. For simplicity assume that this is a perpetual stream. Then the price paid for the firm (V), which equals the initial inflow of foreign reserves is

$$V = \frac{\pi_D \Delta P(1-f)}{R_D} \qquad (25)$$

where R_D is the domestic rate of interest.[1] Equation (25) thus measures the initial inflow of foreign cash reserves into the country. These reserves can be held by the monetary authority either in the form of cash or in the form of income yielding foreign assets (for example short term US Treasury Bills). Let R_F be the interest rate on foreign assets then

$$VR_F = \pi_D \Delta P(1-f). \frac{R_F}{R_D} \qquad (26)$$

measures the yield in foreign currency from the initial inflow due to the foreign investment. This amount has to be added to all the balance of payments effects previously discussed.

[1] The actual rate of interest to use for the discounting might be some concept of a world rate of interest if many foreign firms can compete to acquire the domestic firm.

Annex 1

A. Let Z = Value of domestically produced output

hZ = Import content of domestically produced output

$Y = Z - hZ = Z(1-h)$ = domestic resource content of output

In the text

$$m' = \frac{hZ}{Y} = \frac{hZ}{Z(1-h)} = \frac{h}{1-h}$$

Similarly

$$Z = Y(1+m')$$

and

$$m'Y = hZ = hY(1+m')$$

$$\therefore h = \frac{m'}{1+m'}$$

B.
$$\overline{Y} = C + E + \alpha Y_F - M$$

$$= a + bY_D + E + \alpha Y_F - m_o - vY_D - (m' - \beta) Y_F - \frac{m' t_o}{1-t}$$

$$= a + (b-v)Y_D + Y_F[\alpha + \beta - m'] + E - m_o - \frac{m' t_o}{1-t}$$

however

$$Y_D = (\overline{Y} - Y_F)(1-t) - t_o$$

$$\therefore \overline{Y} = a + (b-v)[(\overline{Y} - Y_F)(1-t) - t_o] + Y_F[\alpha + \beta - m'] + E - m_o - \frac{m' t_o}{1-t}$$

$$= a + (b-v)(1-t)\overline{Y} - (b-v)(1-t)Y_F - t_o(b-v) + $$
$$+ Y_F[\alpha + \beta - m'] + E + m_o - \frac{m' t_o}{1-t}$$

$$\therefore \overline{Y}[1 - (b-v)(1-t)] = a + Y_F[\alpha + \beta - m' - (b-v)(1-t)] +$$
$$+ E - m_o - t_o(b - v + \frac{m'}{1-t})$$

but

$$v = m + \frac{m'}{1-t}$$

$$\therefore \overline{Y}[1 - (b-v)(1-t)] = a + Y_F[\alpha + \beta - m' - (b-v)(1-t)] +$$
$$+ E - m_o - t_o(b - m)$$

C.
$$\frac{dY_D}{dY_F} = \{k[\alpha + \beta - m' - (1-t)(b-v)] - 1\}\{1-t\}$$

$$= k(1-t)[\alpha + \beta - m' - (1-t)(b-v) - \frac{1}{k}]$$

$$= k(1-t)[\alpha + \beta - m' - (1-t)(b-v) - s - v - t(b-v)]$$

$$= k(1-t)[\alpha + \beta - m' - b + v + t(b-v) - 1 + b - v - t(b-v)]$$

$$= k(1-t)[\alpha + \beta - m' - 1]$$

Annex 2

Simulation of the balance of payments effects of inward investment

The model we have developed in the text yields three equations showing the effect on the balance of payments of foreign investment in this country. The three equations refer to three different economic conditions and policies when the investment arrives here. The first equation gives the effects when conditions are such that the Government does nothing in the way of macroeconomic policy in response to the investment, and there is sufficient capacity to allow the multiplier effect. This is now re-numbered equation (1).

$$\Delta B = \Delta P\left[\{x' - x(1-f)\}\{1-z\} + \gamma f(1-z) - \pi\{g + \frac{m'}{1+m'} - z\}\right] \quad (1)$$

All variables are defined as in the chapter text. z is a composite variable introduced for convenience,

$$z = v K (1-t)$$

where the multiplier is K,

$$K = \frac{1}{s + v + t(b - v)}$$

and

$$v = m + \frac{m'}{1-t}$$

It can be seen that some of the relevant variables are reasonably observable, such as the overall import ratio, which sets a constraint on the size of m and m$'$, and the rate of taxation, t. And for some of the variables we can only guess at the magnitudes, such as f and γ.

The second and third equations call for government action. The second equation represents the case of a government expenditure policy to bring about full employment when there is inward investment.

$$\Delta B = \Delta P\left[x' - x(1-f) + f(\gamma - z') - \pi(g + \frac{m'}{1+m'} - z')\right] \quad (2)$$

where

$$z' = \frac{v(1-t)}{1+m'}$$

And finally, if full employment is maintained through a taxation policy,[1] we get,

$$\Delta B = \Delta P\left[\{x' - x(1-f)\}\{1+z''\} + \gamma f(1+z'') - z''f - \right.$$
$$\left. - \pi(g + \frac{m'}{1+m'})\right] \quad (3)$$

where

$$z'' = \frac{v}{b-m}$$

[1] Varying t_o in the expression $T = t_o + \bar{t}Y$.

We see that in all three cases the relationships are formulated in such a way that the changes in the balance of payments are expressed as some number, in the square brackets, times the output of foreign owned firms. Due to our assumption that margins equal averages, this can be looked at either as the overall effect on the balance of payments of total foreign output produced here, or as the extra effect on the balance of payments of extra foreign output. The question now is whether that bracketed number is positive or negative for the United Kingdom, and what is its magnitude?

The best answer we can give to the question of the sign and size of the balance of payments parameter is to consider a wide range of possible values of the determining variables. Theoretical considerations constrain all of them to being positive values betweeen zero and one. Statistical evidence and intuition further narrow the range of plausible variation, and some are mutually dependent due to our theory. Given an import ratio of .2 and a marginal tax rate of the same size, setting m′ at .10 implies a value of .13 for m. This implies a value of v of approximately .23. With a fairly high marginal propensity to consume out of disposable income, these values imply a multiplier of approximately 2. Varying m′ will have some small effect on the associated values of z, z′ and z″. The other six variables are in principle mutually independent, and π, f and γ are relatively unknown, or put another way, it is relatively difficult to guess at their magnitudes. In our simulation we therefore let them vary over quite a wide range.

The different effects on the balance of payments of allowing one of the independent variables to vary over a range will depend on the values selected for each of the other six (z being fixed when m′ is determined). Selecting a 'high' and a 'low' value for each of the six variables gives sixty-four possible arrangements as we allow the seventh variable to change. This is repeated for each of the six variables (it is quantitatively unimportant to allow m′ to vary over a range) giving 384 runs. Having selected a 'high' and 'low' for each of the other six, we allow the seventh to take on a new 'high' and new 'low' over a range which is broader than when that variable is part of the set of variables. As there are 384 cases to examine for each equation, with three equations we have in total 1,152 runs. Each run yields two answers, according to whether the variable under examination is at the 'high' or the 'low' end of its range. So we have a set of predictions as to what happens to the balance of payments as a result of inward investment, each prediction dependent on both what policy is being employed, and what are the values of the relevant variables. Table 2.1 below sets out the values used in this experiment. In addition, we made a 'best guess' for each of the six variables, again allowing the seventh to vary over its range. This generates another thirty-six runs.

Table 2.I

Simulation values

	Set value			*Range*	
Variable	*High*	*Low*	*Best guess*	*High*	*Low*
x′	.25	.22	.23	.30	.20
x	.22	.18	.20	.25	.15
f	.15	.05	.10	.20	.00
γ	.15	.05	.10	.20	.00
π	.50	.20	.35	.60	.10
g	.06	.12	.09	.20	.03
m′	.12	.08	.10		
z	.45	.40	.44		
z′	.18	.19	.18		
z″	.31	.33	.32		

Some quantitative impression of possible balance of payments effects may be gained by examining the three frequency distributions set out below, one for each equation. Each shows the 768 outcomes when x′, x, f, γ, π and g vary over their ranges for all possible combinations of the high and low set values for the other five plus m′ (and its associated z, z′ or z′′ as called for). Naturally, these are not to be taken as giving the probabilities of different outcomes. Rather, they are simply visual summaries of the outcome of systematically and mechanically exploring a wide range of possibilities. Obviously the choice of a different set of configurations of the values of the variables would yield different distributions.

We see that the two policy distributions become more peaked compared to no policy, especially the expenditure policy. If no action is taken under all reasonable assumptions as to magnitudes, a positive balance of payments effect is predicted by the model. Negative effects are plausible with the expenditure policy, and are the typical outcome with the taxation policy. Ignoring the tails of the distributions, two-thirds of the outcomes are between +.06 and +.20 for no policy, between .00 and +.07 for expenditure, and between .00 and —.09 for taxation. The range of plausible outcomes is not as narrow as one might have hoped for, and clearly depends on what the Government does.

The above uncertainty as to outcome is probably pessimistic as we are allowing quite a wide latitude for the seven variables. If we keep the set at their 'best guess' value, only allowing each variable in turn to vary over the range, a smaller, but still significant range of plausible outcomes results. Some characteristics of the outcomes are summarized in Table 2.II.

Table 2.II

Balance of payments simulation

	Equations	*Range (overall)* *High*	*Low*	*Means*	*Range (best guess)* *High*	*Low*	*Means*
(1)	No policy	.29	.03	.13	.23	.06	.14
(2)	Expenditure	.16	—.07	.04	.11	—.01	.04
(3)	Taxation	.05	—.17	—.05	—.01	—.10	—.05

It is interesting to examine the sensitivity of the balance of payments outcomes to changes in the various variables. These are set out in Table 2.III. The figures indicate the change in the balance of payments effects as a result of each variable in turn going from its low to its high end of the range, the other variables kept at their best guess values. We note that changes in f and γ, two very problematic variables, fortunately from the point of view of analysis have little effect. π is often quite big in its effect, but it could be argued that we have allowed it too wide a range.

Table 2.III

Sensitivity of the balance of payments estimates to changes in the levels of the determining variables

Variable	*Equation* (1)	(2)	(3)
x′	+.06	+.10	+.06
x	—.05	—.09	—.07
f	+.02	+.03	—.03
γ	+.01	+.02	+.01
π	+.13	—.01	—.09
g	—.06	—.06	—.06

While the effects on the United Kingdom balance of payments of foreign investment here could be adverse, these results suggest that it is unlikely, and that if no policy is employed, a favourable effect of, say, ten per cent of the output of foreign owned firms is the order of magnitude. If the Government maintains internal balance without regard to the balance of payments, foreign investment may well have little, or an unfavourable effect. Normally, we would assume that macro policy would operate with respect to internal and external balance simultaneously. This experiment gives some indication of the magnitude of change required.

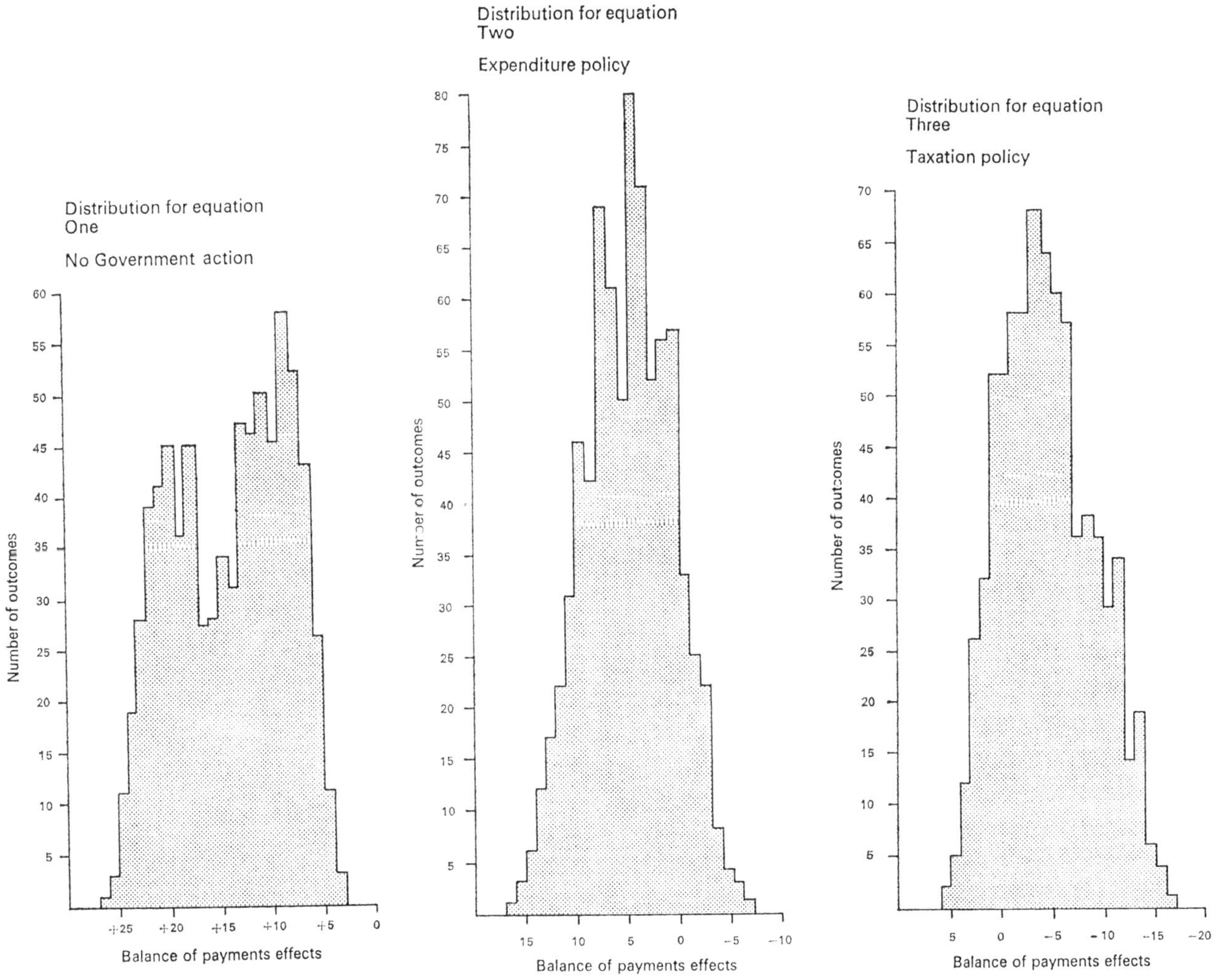

3. Inward investment and United Kingdom technology

3.1 The question of inward investment and its relations to United Kingdom technology is among the most elusive of the direct investment topics, and in the opinion of many people it is among the most important. Servan-Schreiber (1968) has dramatised the whole issue of United States domination and has expressed fears which are widespread in Europe. He quotes *The Guardian* as follows:

A European technological community is the real Europe of the future. To build it will be a test of nationalism versus rationalism . . . It will demand far-reaching psychological changes. *But the only alternative is economic decline, and probably complete domination by the United States.*

In this section our purpose is to carefully examine the evidence, such as it is, and the arguments which bear on the role of technology in the economy. Naturally, we will focus on the part direct investment plays in this relationship. The thesis we will defend is that the kind of statement quoted, and examples of similar sentiments abound, is wrong, and misleadingly over-simplified.

The profitability of producing inventions

3.2 Let us start by considering the activity of producing new knowledge as an industry, like any other. The inputs are qualified labour, sometimes highly qualified, and capital. And the output is a collection of ideas. Typically, these ideas will take three forms: *know-how*, i.e., skills and information possessed by individuals and embedded in teams of individuals; *records of a variety of kinds*, i.e., computer tapes, monographs, blue prints; *prototypes*, i.e., new products, once off plants, and so on. Conceptually, we may think of these forms as being for sale, even though in fact they may often be retained by the original investor in the research and development. In principle these ideas can be sold because they are transferable and capable of contributing to the profits of a purchaser when combined with a production process or a servicing process. Either they improve a product or the marketing of it, or they reduce the costs of production. Frequently the new idea will afford some monopoly power to its owner. These are all elementary and familiar points. But we should be quite clear initially about the distinction between the 'new knowledge' industry as such, and possible purchasers or users of the output of that industry.

3.3 One possible interpretation of the view that unless one is fully competitive with American technology, or put another way, unless one has a large and thriving amount of research and development activity owned by nationals, one is headed for economic decline, could be based on the proposition that this particular industry is extremely profitable in itself. If I design a better light bulb, the fee I can command from a light bulb producer for the right to use this design will be such that the transaction will add little to the manufacturer's profits and will constitute an enormous return on the investment in light bulb design. In this view, and we will of course come to other views, the importance of the technology industry as such is the very profitable nature of the activity. If commercial super-sonic passenger flight becomes a profitable reality, who will reap the benefit, the passengers, the airlines who run the planes or their employees, the manufacturer of the planes, or the developers of them, that is, the technology industry? Perhaps everybody, or nobody. Is there any particular reason to expect that the return to investment in technology will be much higher than the return to investment capable of employing the new technology? And do you have to produce the technology yourself in order to gain the profits from exploiting it?

3.4 Successes are remembered because they are gratifying *and* because there are so few of them. Failures are forgotten because they hurt *and* because there are so many of them. It would be a whole research project, and one which would take us far afield, to try to determine how the successes and failures balance out and what is the return to the technology industry as such. For present purposes it is sufficient to question, and it seems cast doubt thereby, on the view that the pay-off to developing improved techniques and products is a particularly high one. In most countries so much of this activity is carried on by, or subsidised by, the state. One wonders why private interests do not complain if potentially profitable activity is taken over by the public sector. Perhaps it may not be so profitable after all.

3.5 Again, it is a project in itself to determine the truth of the proposition, but casual information suggests that some countries, notably Japan, have been outstandingly successful in the struggle for economic growth while making only modest investments in developing technology, at least at the basic end of the research spectrum. This kind of observation is consistent with others, such as that private research organisations do not have an enviable record of profitability, nor are the people working for them able to command extremely high wages.

3.6 Poetic analogy is not normal procedure in scientific research, but one might consider, if only to dismiss, the situation in the arts. Serious film makers might be regarded as the research end of the cinema industry. The former part is not usually profitable, though providing a stream of developments to the latter part. Similar relations obtain in music, painting, the stage, *vis à vis* television, and so on. The use of invention can be profitable, and even essential to profit in many sectors, while the activity of producing inventions may not be.

3.7 Risk is an important factor which we have mentioned. Competition is another. No doubt the demand for the output of the 'technology industry' is, and has been, rising rapidly. But the growth of higher education, and other factors, have increased the supply of this service. Again, there is no presumption that super normal profits are the situation for this activity. With this background warning that producers of technology may not be particularly well rewarded in possible contrast to buyers of their output, let us enquire how inward investment might affect the size and profitability of the United Kingdom technology industry. By size we could mean an input or an output measure, in quantity or value terms, and by 'United Kingdom industry' we could mean located here or owned by nationals *and* located here. The latter is relevant for present purposes, and we can think of size in terms of numbers of qualified personnel so employed. There is little doubt that in this sense inward investment reduces the size of the United Kingdom technology industry. This conclusion follows from the following generalisations:[1] (1) There is excess demand for qualified personnel. If one research organisation releases scientists, engineers or technicians, they will quickly find employment elsewhere. A qualification to this arises because of highly specialized skills, which could in special cases markedly reduce the specific effectiveness of alternative employment. But broadly, the characterization in terms of ample vacancies is quite fair. (2) We can take it that the supply of qualified people is fixed in the short run, and in the medium run changes exogenously according to investments in education. (3) And the third generalization is that the staffing of foreign owned technology activity located here is done primarily, even almost exclusively, with British nationals. From these probably broadly correct generalizations it follows that the research efforts here of foreign owned subsidiaries reduces the size of the United Kingdom technology industry. In short, foreign subsidiaries in the United Kingdom when they engage in advanced technological activity hire people away from domestic firms and reduce the scale of domestic technological activity.

3.8 In times of slack demand and a high level of unemployment there may well be some unemployment even among technically highly qualified personnel. And it must also be acknowledged that the first generalization in the previous paragraph is a controversial one. Most observers agree that the extent of employment among scientists, engineers and technicians is low in the United Kingdom compared to other industrial countries. While this may suggest that there would be a substantial return to having a larger proportion of such personnel in British industry, it does not imply that there is excess demand for technically qualified labour at existing rates of pay. It could be that more research and development activity in foreign owned firms operating here would result in more scientific and technical employment in total with some of the now employed people coming from the formerly unemployed. But clearly this would not add to the size of the British owned technology industry. At best it would leave it unchanged.

3.9 Believing that the technology industry is a particularly profitable one, either because it extracts a lot of surplus value from its inputs or charges monopolistic prices for its outputs, and that inward investment reduces the size of the United Kingdom technology industry when it engages in research and development activity here, we might wish to discourage incoming firms from employing British nationals of a scientific and technical kind. The argument is analogous to brain drain arguments, (see Cmnd. 3417, 1967). What is the difference between a research engineer going to the States to work for Ford and the same man working for Ford in the United Kingdom if property rights in his output is the main concern? This is not to say that we support the brain drain position, with its emphasis on national as opposed to individual welfare, but rather to underline an inconsistency. It is inconsistent both to deplore the movement of highly qualified people abroad and to welcome the location of research activity here by foreign owned subsidiaries who employ largely British nationals.

[1] For a fuller discussion of the generalizations, and the relevant evidence, see M Peck, 'Science and Technology' in R E Caves and Associates, *British Economic Prospects*, Brookings Institution, 1968.

3.10 Oddly enough, post-war British policy has tended to classify as 'good' an incoming firm that does engage in research here.[1] It is regarded as bad if a new establishment does not engage in a characteristic amount of research here, according to the typical pattern in the industry. Professor Dunning (1968), for example, makes reference to the research and development activity here of foreign firms operating here, in addition to their ability to draw on the research of the parent, a topic to which we will be coming, and appears to see this activity as an unequivocable benefit to the United Kingdom economy. Our position is that there may be subtle benefits, but the straightforward effect, in terms of the profitability of the activity as such, is adverse.

Foreign takeovers of British research oriented firms

3.11 The same issue arises in the case of a takeover of a domestic firm by a foreign firm as in the new establishment case. The worry sometimes expressed here is that the foreign interest may choose to centralize research in the parent company country, disbanding an on-going research operation here. The Ministry of Health objected to the takeover of the Amalgamated Dental Co. Ltd., by the Dental Supply Co. of New York on this ground. Another comment-causing example, with the alleged removal of the more advanced work to the States, is the takeover of A C Cossor by Raytheon. But again, the act of disbanding, rather than retaining or expanding a research team in the case of takeover increases the supply of British scientists to domestic firms. Of course, this assumes that not all the technical personnel move to the parent company country, or some other country. Without any precise knowledge of how many people emmigrate in this way, we nevertheless have considerable assurance from our pilot interviews and the survey that the number is small.

3.12 There is an additional point on the disbanding of research teams which is convenient to make at this point. An integrated and experienced research organization is an asset to a firm which cannot be sold. If a parent company rationally decides to take this step of disbanding, we must ask why they give up an apparently valuable asset which cannot be sold. Intuition suggests that it is likely that they can achieve similar results at home at less cost, or perhaps better results. Indeed, they may *know* that the British effort is redundant, and that they already possess the material the British team is trying to produce. If this is the case, and if the takeover had been prevented, there is ground to feel that the benefit to the domestic firm, and to the United Kingdom economy, of that particular team would be small. In isolation it might look technically impressive, but in the light of its expendability from the point of view of a foreign parent, we may conclude that the competitive advantage it affords may be illusory.

3.13 So far we have been examining some of the implications of the notion that the technology producing 'industry', or activity, is particularly profitable *per se*, and important to the United Kingdom economy for that reason. But much more relevant is the question of the benefits to the users of improved and improving technology. The technology topic changes its aspect very radically if we introduce the realistic assumptions of a less than perfect market in 'inventions' (this term taken to mean the entire output of the technology producing activity). Let us take the case where firms produce inventions for their own use only. They do not buy or sell inventions. This opposite extreme assumption may be closer to the truth for many purposes, particularly if we

[1] See Chapter Nine, on the regulation of inward investment.

take account of the product and firm specific nature of some research, and the importance of a continuing tradition for efficient development and use of specialized research output. Under these circumstances it is not as relevant to separate out the pay-off to the research activity itself from the pay-off to the users.

3.14 As the users of ideas are likely to be the inventors of them, special concern has been expressed, by the former Ministry of Technology for example, at the prospect of foreign takeover of domestic firms with research traditions, and happily, with a stock of unexploited ideas. In this type of takeover, the user benefit would then accrue to the new owners. United Kingdom interests make the investment, and foreign interests purchase the company—Solartron is often quoted as a case of this kind—precisely to get the patented research output. The obvious policy question is should this country be on the look out for this type of case, and take appropriate steps to prevent it? Our position is that we need not be very concerned, and that this is an ingenious but not realistic concept of a potential danger of inward investment. Part of the reason for coming to this conclusion is that we have not come across cases which fit the description.[1] More of the reason rests on *a priori* argument.

3.15 Whatever the stock of ideas held by a research oriented domestic firm, there must be some price at which it would be in the national interest to sell, or more relevant, where we would be indifferent between foreign acquisition and domestic retention of the firm. So the problem, if it exists, must spring either from a systematic tendency on the part of private interests to undervalue research output or from a departure between social and private returns. Our task, then, is to see how these elements might arise.

3.16 First let us try to dispose of the point that some research ideas might be worth more to 'them' than to us. A foreign multinational firm might well be able to profitably exploit an invention which the domestic developer, or perhaps any British company, could not profitably exploit. At least, it is conceivable that the foreigner could do better with it, and therefore be willing to pay more for it. The invention might relate to other inventions in which they specialize, or have exclusive rights, and either in addition, or alternatively, it might be in a position to exploit economies of scale in production or marketing which are not open to anyone in this country. The simple answer to this type of situation where they can do better with an invention than we can is, why should we care? What matters to us is whether *we* can do better by retaining a stock of innovations or by selling them. What they can do with them is irrelevant.

3.17 There are two minor points which are just worth mentioning in connection with the above. It could be that there is something at fault with our general research stance if we consistently produce inventions which can be more profitably exploited by others. Imitation of American approaches may play too big a role. We have found no evidence of this, but it is a possibility. On a much broader front, there is a cluster of arguments that have to do with the scale of the British economy generally, economic integration, possibly with Europe, and the size distribution of British firms. Clearly it is a serious concern if these scale factors are tending to exclude the United Kingdom from

[1] The Cossor-Raytheon case is sometimes quoted in this connection. The Cossor management strongly denies the charges. See *The Sunday Times*, Business Section, 9 November, 1969.

sectors where markets are expanding most rapidly and productivity gains are most marked. But this observation, even if true, does not tell us what to do about inward investment.

3.18 If inventions are being, or might be, lost to the United Kingdom through foreign takeover at an uneconomic price, this must be interpreted as a sale below the value of domestic exploitation of them in this country. How might this come about? A stock of ideas can be thought of like any other portfolio evaluation problem in terms of the expected return and the variance of that expected return, i.e., the likelihood that the actual outcome will be a lot, or a little, above, or below, the expected value (Tobin: 1958). For a single enterprise, able to engage in a limited number of projects, the risk factor may be intolerable. While from the national point of view, the variances associated with various risky projects tend to cancel out. Consider two collections of inventions with equal expected value and equal variance. If we take the per unit expected value and the variance of the two collections taken together, the expected value is unchanged but the variance is lower. (This last conclusion follows if we can assume, which is reasonable, that the returns of the two sets of projects are uncorrelated.) A larger enterprise might be able to acquire both collections and thus enjoy the self-insuring aspect of the two taken together. We have here a possible divergence between social and private return. The nation, containing many collections of 'research assets', all with risks attached to their exploitations, might place a higher per unit value on the group as a whole than any one firm who has to bear all the risk of developing its own stock.

3.19 This tender argument is the main reason why we might expect private domestic interests to sell out to large foreign interests at too low a price, this price looked at from the national point of view. It is logically correct, but it rests on some empirically doubtful propositions. One of these is the proposition that the British enterprises are too small. Looking at the very biggest end of the scale, there are roughly eight times as many United States firms with assets of over a billion dollars as there are United Kingdom firms, but there are still ten of the latter. All of the top five industrials outside the United States are British, and over a quarter of the largest 200 companies outside America are British.[1] So it is difficult to defend this position on the grounds of a lack of large organizations here.

The product cycle and United Kingdom technology

3.20 In Chapter Five on the monopoly aspect of inward investment, passing reference is made to the product cycle theory of trade and investment. For a series of papers on the international aspects of technology, see Vernon: 1970. The subjects of technology and monopoly have important connections. Firms must feel that they can capture, at least for a period, sufficient extra returns to compensate them for the often high cost and high risk of undertaking research. If anyone can use the new inventions, there is little incentive for a private interest to create them. Also large firms, with very extensive markets and probably at least some monopoly position, are the ones who can support extensive research on a much larger turnover. At the same time, successful research tends to afford a company some monopoly position and help it to extend or maintain a commanding position.

[1] *Fortune*, 15 June 1968 and 15 September 1968.

3.21 The product cycle view holds that after establishing a new product in the United States, firms go on to exporting and where a large market exists, eventually undertake production abroad. By this time the research programme of the parent company has moved on, and the net result is that foreign subsidiary firms are always working on technologically backward products or production processes. In this sense inward investment is seen as an important link in a dynamic movement which keeps the United Kingdom, or any industrial host country, in an inferior position.

3.22 Is this really the case? Does advancing American technology tend to hold back the United Kingdom, with direct investment playing a critical role? It seems most unlikely. There are three especially important considerations here. One is that the parent company is not in competition with the subsidiary. It has every incentive to produce abroad in the most profitable way, to introduce new products and cost saving innovation. More and more the multinational firm is an integrated complex employing everywhere advanced techniques as rapidly as is efficient.

3.23 Certainly it is true that innovations of foreign firms compete with domestic efforts, but inhibiting direct investment does not stop this competition. (Nor is that desirable.) Exports are an alternative for the parent company, and these imports, from the host country point of view, are competitive with domestic efforts. We have here a special variant of the infant industry argument. For United Kingdom technology to get on its feet (across the board, or in selective areas?), foreign competition, it is argued, must be held off for a period. In this case the possible cost advantage to foreigners of producing here, and the avoidance of tariff barriers, are to be prevented through excluding direct investment. Of course the time horizon envisaged for this infant industry argument is even longer than for the traditional one, competitive production having to await the development of the prerequisite technology. Also, accurate prediction is even more of a problem. So we conclude that the policy of preventing direct investment would not afford a special advantage to domestic interests such as to encourage their progress, and that the product cycle view does not imply a retardation of British technology compared to the situation that would obtain with some foreign investment excluded.

3.24 Our third consideration is that excluding some direct investment would not have a favourable competitive effect in this country. It certainly would not improve our relative position with respect to foreign competition. American technology would go on developing in the home country and in third markets abroad.

Management technology and the foreign subsidiary

3.25 Many writers and observers take the view that the key feature of the direct investment phenomena, especially that from the United States, is superior management. The technological advantage of the foreign owned subsidiary lies not so much in products or processes, but in the organization of production and marketing. (To our knowledge, proponents of this view have tended to leave unexplained the reasons for applying superior management skills abroad rather than exporting.) This is of particular interest to host countries on two counts. First there is the question of the extent to which the superior efficiency of the foreign subsidiary as such works to the benefit of the host country. Second there is the question of whether the presence of foreign managers, or foreign management techniques, in this country raises the standards and performance of management in domestic firms.

3.26 The spirit, or setting, in which these questions are raised is important. Straightforward economic analysis would see foreign investment as adding to the capital stock, and draw the implications from this, and from the income going to foreigners. The management technology view says that the straight view is too narrow. It ignores the special qualities of the foreign capital, and looks to them for particular benefit to the host country. Admittedly, this type of benefit is hard to demonstrate. Nevertheless, we feel that there are certain considerations which should be raised, and that have the effect of dampening the uncritical expectations of host country gain which we have encountered, these hoped for gains resting largely on the ability of foreign managers.

3.27 Compare, for illustration, two cases. In the first the foreign manager gets more out of the domestic factors he employs because he combines them with his capital more skilfully. In the second he has no special skill. He gets more out of the domestic factors because he employs more capital. Which is better for our economy? Certainly a satisfactory solution to the puzzle would require more information than has been provided. But the puzzle does point up two interesting things. The first is that *superior* foreign management is a bit like simply having *more* foreign investment. Clearly from the world point of view the former is to be preferred, but from our point of view, the host country, there is not that much in it. The second is the question of how much of the extra efficiency accrues to the foreigner in higher profits, and how much comes to us in the form of better or cheaper products, higher factor payments, profits tax, or an improved atmosphere of competition. The simple fact that many foreign managements are superior (if they are) does not in itself automatically work to our benefit.

3.28 While granting the above, the second source of gain may be held to be the real one. Superior management, it could be held, is diffused throughout the economy due to proximity aiding imitation. On this count we are extremely doubtful. There are a number of reasons. Mobility between foreign subsidiaries and domestic firms does not seem to be of sufficient volume on a high enough level to be a good transmitter. Of course, this is not essential to imitation. But then, neither is proximity. Among the factors which have affected the growth of, and character of, the multinational firm are increased speed and ease of communication of all kinds. A determined domestic firm will find it little easier to learn from the practices of an American firm here than those in the States. With the growth of professional management training, often along American lines, in this country, the relative importance of informal contacts to the diffusion of knowledge and practices should decline. Scientific management literature and professional advice is also available on an international basis.

3.29 It could be pointed out, in rebuttal, that all firms buy from and sell to other firms, and that these contacts, particularly, transmit management knowhow. In our interviews with fifty, or so, foreign firms we have not been impressed with this possibility. We are not in a position to rule it out, but we cannot support the optimistic views sometimes expressed about the proximity factor.

3.30 Negative views on the management side are also to be found in the foreign investment literature. The argument is that potential domestic management talent in the employ of foreign subsidiaries gets less opportunity to develop. To us this also seems silly. Less compared to what? Usually the argument is put in terms of less compared to the alternative of the subsidiary being domestically owned. But that is, of course, not a meaningful comparison. The relevant comparison is more or less than if the foreign investment was excluded. Nevertheless, the argument holds that ultimate decision taking going on abroad stunts British managerial growth. Our interviews with firms strongly suggest the opposite; that multinational firms engage in more management training, are keen to promote, and have an excellent record with respect to looking at the man rather than his nationality. In any case, again the relevant comparison is not with a situation where the foreign subsidiary is now domestically owned, but where the inward investment is excluded by regulation. Then some men will probably be bigger fish in smaller ponds, which is not the same thing as increased scope for the development of management talent.

The exclusively research and development foreign investment

3.31 Early in our work for this project the former Ministry of Technology drew our attention to non-manufacturing subsidiaries of foreign parents who are engaged in this country in design and research activities only. The parent organization may be manufacturing in one or more countries, but the United Kingdom link in the network is purely a research unit. These polar cases at the opposite extreme from world organizations who happen to do no research in this country, are interesting in a number of ways. For one thing, they illustrate in quite a dramatic way a contradiction in current policy. These firms are looked at with some misgiving, along the brain drain lines, only here it is brain output which is going abroad. The contradiction lies in viewing these firms with some anxiety, while at the same time encouraging normal manufacturing foreign subsidiaries to engage in research here. Our view is that there is an insufficient case to warrant interference in either direction, either favouring or discouraging research here by foreign firms.

3.32 We decided to look at these research-only foreign owned firms in some detail, and found them to be quantitatively not very important. There are about a dozen of them, and they are all quite small. They are staffed by British nationals, and there seems to be no tendency for them to grow, either in size or in number, over time. In a way, this is mysterious. United Kingdom researchers in many fields are well trained, and reputedly can obtain employment in the United States, for example, quite easily. But salaries are markedly lower here, and there appears to be little mechanical reason to locate research, at least many kinds of research, close to company head-quarters or the main production centres. So one wonders why there is not more of this kind of activity.

3.33 It appears that rather special, and accidental, factors account for the presence here of exclusively research organizations. For example, a single individual of some standing may have a strong preference for the United Kingdom, and his team, due to the nature of their projects, may be able to carry on efficiently while being physically separated from the main research organization. In no case did the presence of foreign research activity here seem to be motivated simply by lower cost of scientific labour. We were told that non-wage cost, that is equipment, is about half of total cost, and tending to rise proportionately over time. Also, the non-wage cost is higher in the more advanced fields. These equipment costs are believed to be roughly the same here as in the States. In some instances they may be slightly higher here.

3.34 Probably the main reason for the small, and not growing, amount of this activity is that there are advantages in locating most of research in one place, as opposed to locating research and production together, and historically this is naturally in the country of the parent company. It is also likely that considerations of prestige and secrecy play roles in the location decision. We conclude, then, that this phenomenon is not very important quantitatively, not likely to grow, and not in principle different from the research activity of a foreign owned manufacturing subsidiary.

Access to parent company research

3.35 This inward investment report, in all its aspects, may be thought of as a cost-benefit appraisal of the impact on the United Kingdom of inward investment. As in many other studies, a particularly awkward problem is the possibility of very large but nevertheless intangible, or hard to measure, effects, which should nevertheless be added in on the appropriate side of the scale. Outstanding among these on the plus side is the assertion that the incoming firm, the foreign subsidiary, is backed up by the entire research programme of the parent organization. This is seen as a tremendous vehicle for raising the technological state of the host economy generally. In the United Kingdom this view is particularly associated with the work of Professor Dunning, but there are many other proponents of the view. It is pointed out, for example, that the expenditure on research by the parent companies of American owned subsidiaries exceeds total research expenditure of all kinds undertaken in this country. The implication being that when the subsidiary comes here, this research in some sense comes with it. The resulting benefit to the British economy is seen to be very large.

3.36 In our questionnaire survey we have attempted to gain some more information on such matters as subsidiary payments for research undertaken by parents, how subsidiary research is controlled by the parent and with what aims, and what the arrangements are for doing special research on behalf and at the request of the subsidiary. Other studies have attempted to gain information on such matters as the relevance of the parent company research programme to the activities of the subsidiary (Dunning and Steuer: 1969). Certain tentative generalizations may be made at this stage, not least among them the variety of parent-subsidiary arrangements on the matter of research.

3.37 Many subsidiaries estimate that much, if not all, of the research carried out elsewhere in the organization is relevant to their activity. And while many feel that, say, only a quarter of it is, none express the view that they are being deprived of possibly useful results. (This has some relevance to the 'product cycle' section above.) Quite a variety of arrangements are in evidence for the subsidiary to share the costs of research. But as one hundred per cent ownership is the typical case, and the parent has ultimate say as to product pricing (not always explicitly exercised; see Chapter Seven) differences in practice may have relatively little economic significance. Money returned to the parent as payment for R & D reduces potential profit for repatriation by an equal amount. Though there can be a difference to us in terms of corporate taxation. The basic point is that the multinational organization strives to earn a profit on its research investment, and one should not look at this research as coming free to us.

3.38 Generally research affords some monopoly advantage. This works to keep the technically possible diffusion of gain nevertheless within the multinational network. The mere fact of large research expenditure being undertaken in the parent firm is not of any automatic benefit to us. Some of that advantage must be competed away. We hold the view that additions to knowledge anywhere tend ultimately to benefit people everywhere. Some knowledge, at least, becomes part of the public domain. But this is independently of the direct investment phenomena. Analytically we may separate gains through investment from gains through parent company research. If, for example, IBM had no subsidiaries here, this country could still benefit from the research of that company. Knowledge made available through publications, and most of that available through less formal means, would still be here. Products could arrive as imports, and so on. It is much more difficult to make a plausible case for technological spill-over of great magnitude through direct investment as such.

The role of inward investment in the technology acquisition process

3.39 It is sometimes suggested that where British firms, that is domestic firms, produce foreign developed products under licence, the payment is often uneconomically high. As direct investment and production under licence are frequently viable alternative ways of introducing a product or process into this country this charge is of relevance to this chapter. One may attempt to focus on the gain and losses of a particular phenomenon, i.e. inward investment, but it is always necessary to allow that there may be close substitutes. This observation cuts both ways. In fairly finding gain one must consider the next best alternative, and also if one avoids a particular cost, one must take account of what will happen as a result.

3.40 The charge that licensing is expensive carries an implication in favour of direct investment. There is, of course, a serious problem in what this charge means. Does it mean that the foreign firm would let us have it for less, if competition among potential British users of the patent was less keen? Does it suggest a departure between social and private returns? (No doubt many imports would come into this country at least somewhat cheaper if the Government prevented domestic middlemen from competing.) Is it suggesting that we could do the research more cheaply ourselves? It is not really our job to answer these questions, but rather to draw the relevant implication of the view for direct investment, while pointing out that it is not a well established view.

3.41 Much of this chapter has been in a debunking vein. Yet clearly the force of the chapter is not to suggest that new techniques and improved products are unimportant to the British economy. They certainly are. But that is not the same as saying that in all instances it is profitable for us to do the research. Research comparative advantage should be pursued like any other comparative advantage. We believe that in the past there has been an unwise emphasis on completeness of invention, on favouring large recognizable projects. Whereas it may be in only certain aspects of these projects that we actually have an advantage. And in research, of all areas, the goal of autonomy is likely to be a particularly costly one. In many areas it will pay to leave the activity alone altogether and buy the products. In many inward direct investment is to our advantage. Then there are cases where production here under licence makes sense, and finally in some areas it will be efficient for us to do research. The success of civil servants and politicians in deciding which is which has not been great up to now.

3.42 To summarize, a closer look at the inward investment implications for United Kingdom technology suggests that the familiar *a priori* arguments, both for gain and for loss, are not very persuasive. Where hard work on a particular case may show that one or the other favourable or unfavourable effects has indeed taken place, generalizing from this work across the economy is not warranted. The kind of view quoted in the first paragraph, that an independent technology is essential to our prosperity and the avoidance of American domination, is romantic nonsense. It is often more profitable to apply an invention than to create one. The United States steel industry is not dominated by Austria though it employs in a fundamental way a technique first used there.

4. Industrial relations, labour disputes, and labour utilisation in foreign owned firms

4.1 A number of studies appear to find that the foreign owned subsidiaries of multinational firms are more efficient than comparable domestic firms in the host country. This is true of American firms operating in Britain, and of direct investment in other industrial countries. Superior performance is thought of in terms of higher profitability, greater output for the same total input, more advanced technology, and sometimes simply as higher labour productivity. This last, of course, need not in itself be a sign of either efficiency or profitability. There is some literature, and the expressed opinions of managers of foreign owned firms, to the effect that managerial skill, particularly in more careful and intelligent utilisation of labour, is largely responsible for better performance.

4.2 At the same time, there is some general recognition that the presence of foreign owned firms in host country labour markets constitutes something of a problem. Oddly enough, this potential problem area is not usually considered, or even mentioned, in the direct investment literature as such.[1] Explicit discussion arises more in statements by governments, unions, and the labour economics literature (Barkin: 1967). In 1971 a ten weeks stoppage at Ford plants in the UK brought the industrial relations of the foreign owned companies into popular discussion. The TUC has held a conference on this question, and some observers have stated it to be the major issue of the 1970s, (*Evening Standard:* 25 March 1971).

4.3 In this chapter we set out some statistical and institutional information bearing on the industrial relations and labour utilization of foreign owned firms in the United Kingdom, and attempt to derive some implications. The chapter is in three parts. The first part outlines the pattern of British industrial relations, and the special situations which arise as a result of foreign firms coming into this environment. It ignores the new situation that the Industrial Relations Act (1971) may create since our study is concerned solely with the pre-Act situation. Emphasis is on the contrasts between British and American industrial relations, trade union recognition, the nature of agreements between employers and unions, and plant personnel practices. We attempt to appraise the impact of the foreign firm on United Kingdom industrial relations. The second part examines the industrial disputes of foreign firms. A basic question is, are they more or less strike prone than domestic firms, and are the stoppages which occur in them different in kind? In the third section the electrical engineering industry is taken as a case study to compare some aspects of labour utilization in domestic and foreign owned firms. The emphasis here is on the use of more highly skilled labour.

[1] For example, the industrial relations of multinational firms in host countries is not discussed with respect to any of the many countries examined in the recent volume edited by Litvak, Israiah A. and Maule, Christopher J., *Foreign Investment: The Experience of Host Countries*, Praeger, New York, 1970. Nor does the topic occur in the well-known work of Brash, Dunning, Kindleberger, Safarian, and so on.

I: Industrial relations and the foreign owned firm

Introduction

4.4 The foreign firm investing in the United Kingdom is coming into a country where there is already an established industrial relations system with its own structures and values which may differ radically from those of the parent company country. The foreign subsidiary has the option of accepting completely the main features of the British industrial relations system, or alternatively, it may attempt to adopt by evolutionary means some of the features of its home country. It is unlikely to totally reject the system here for fear of generating an intolerable level of industrial conflict. But the incentive to modify the system is strong, particularly in cases where its views on labour utilization differ markedly from those of domestic firms.

4.5 Prior to the Industrial Relations Act the prevailing ideology of the British industrial relations system was one of voluntarism in that there was an absence of legal regulation over the main features of collective bargaining. There was no legislation compelling employers to recognise and negotiate with trade unions; arbitration and state intervention were a minor mechanism in the system. Agreements made between trade unions and employers' organisations were not legally enforceable contracts and were considered to be binding in honour only.[1] British agreements tend to have no set termination date, and cover a small number of matters. Often these are only wages and hours, in contrast to the American system where many aspects of employment are subject to formal agreement.

4.6 Apart from the voluntary nature of our system, which Allan Flanders (1965) sees stemming from the value placed by the British on economic freedom (freedom of contract, freedom of association, freedom to strike and lock out and freedom of self government) and industrial peace, the foreign firm is faced with other peculiar features of our industrial relations system. There is a high degree of centralisation of collective bargaining. This is centred at the national level and takes place between national trade union officials and national officials of employers' associations and agreements reached are for the industry concerned and apply at the national level. In many industries, especially in the private sector, a second tier of negotiation takes place at the workplace between shop stewards and individual management, and is on an informal basis. Some industries have formalised national negotiating machinery, which takes the form of National Joint Industrial Councils, or statutory wage fixing bodies known as Wages Councils while other industries have *ad hoc* negotiating arrangements. The Department of Employment estimates that there are over 500 pieces of negotiating machinery at the national level covering some 14 million out of the 16 million manual workers in employment (Royal Commission on Trade Unions and Employers' Associations: 1965). Collective bargaining machinery is increasing among non-manual workers but at the present time less than 50 per cent of such workers have their wages and conditions of employment settled through joint negotiating machinery.

[1] This chapter summarizes the industrial relations practices of foreign owned firms in the post war years, a period which was dominated by voluntarism. The Industrial Relations Act (1971) which became completely operative on 28 February 1972, extends the law into most areas of industrial relations. However, the government sees this legal extension as a support to the voluntary system, and not as a replacement of it.

4.7 There is also a high degree of unionisation in this country. Approximately 44 per cent of the British working population is in trade unions and how this compares with other European countries is shown in Table 4.1. The British trade union structure is untidy, consisting of craft or occupational unions, general unions and industrial unions, and there has been little attempt until recently to rationalise the structure. This has led to problems of multi-unionism bringing jurisdiction demarcation and wage differential problems. There is also the shop steward movement which has grown up outside the formal trade union structure of government. The Trades Union Congress is the central body of the unions but is a relatively weak organisation only having the power which its affiliated unions are prepared to give it.

Table 4.1

Trade union membership as a percentage of the labour force

Sweden	70
Denmark	65
Norway	63
Belgium	60
UK	44
Holland	40
Western Germany	38
USA	28
France	25

Source: Windmuller, J P, *Labor Relations in the Netherlands*. Cornell, UP, 1969.

4.8 The industrial relations system of the United Kingdom with its unique features presents problems for foreign owned companies operating in Britain. For the Western European companies the problem of adapting to the main features of our system are not as difficult since there are similar features in their parent countries; for example, industry-wide bargaining, a degree of organisation among employers, and multi-unionism. (In France, Belgium, Holland and Italy there is the additional problem of religious and ideological splits in union movement which happily is not a feature here.) However, a major difference is that on the continent, in the majority of countries, collective agreements between employers and unions are legally enforceable contracts.[1] For companies from the United States the acceptance of the British system requires a radical departure from the practices used in their parent companies.[2] American employers are used to dealing with unions that accept the 'free enterprise system' and which are mainly concerned with improving wages and working conditions rather than unions that want to make fundamental changes in society and in the structure and the role of the enterprise within it. In some ways this makes it easier for employers here. The American union expects to get virtually all improvements for its members from the company. The British union directs a much larger proportion of its pressure on the Government, particularly in the field of social security, for example, pensions, unemployment benefits and redundancy payments. USA firms at home have not had to face the jurisdictional and demarcation problems of multi-unionism because the National Labor Relations Act provides that the union selected by the majority of workers in a bargaining unit 'shall be the exclusive representative for all employees in such bargaining

[1] The notable exception is Belgium but this country legislated in 1969 to enable agreements between unions and employers to be made legally enforceable if both sides desire it. In the UK the Industrial Relations Act makes all written agreements presumed to be legally binding, unless *both* parties state otherwise.

[2] For a discussion of the problems facing American companies investing in Europe and the UK see J C Shearer, 'Industrial Relations of American Corporations Abroad', in Barkin, S. *et al*, *International Labour*, *op. cit.*

unit for the purposes of collective bargaining.' Collective agreements with unions are legal contracts and operate for a fixed time period. Disputes arising during the period of contract are usually settled through voluntary grievance procedures. Agreements made in the United States are much more comprehensive than the usual British agreements and the level of negotiation is at the place of work (the plant) and not the industry.

4.9 Lloyd Ulman has argued that the major characteristics of the British industrial relations system have a tendency to build in restrictive practices which have implications for the labour utilisation of firms (Ulman: 1968). He considers the legal obligation of employers in the UK to observe Wage Council Awards and by the Terms and Conditions of Employment Act (1959) to observe terms and conditions of employment not less favourable than those which have been established by Agreement as well as award to be a depressing influence on productivity. In the States many employers keep unions out by paying above the union rate and thus giving them complete managerial prerogative in the use of labour. This in turn influences efficiency levels in the plants of their unionised competitors. The British system gives less opportunity for the American types of trade off between pay and labour efficiency. He considers the untidy trade union structure to have adversely affected labour utilisation through its contribution to skill shortages through restriction of supply, inappropriate wage differentials, and overmanning and restrictive practices. The larger the proportion of the work force segregated into craft unions, the more opportunity for duplication of work restrictions on work assignments and similar practices. National industry-wide bargaining has tended to weaken the ability of management to handle problems at plant level where the weapons in the hands of the shop-stewards (for example the unconstitutional strike, the ban on overtime and the work to rule) can exercise a depressing influence on productivity because the uncertainty as to when unofficial action may take place can result in management delaying or refusing to instal new capital equipment.

The level of negotiation

4.10 The level of negotiation in the UK has tended to be industry-wide rather than plant or company based. The employers in a particular industry combine together to form an association to negotiate with the unions and achieve a uniform basic wage rate for the industry. There are estimated to be 750 autonomous employers' associations.[1] National based bargaining resulted in industrial relations in the UK companies being seen as something outside plant management and an aspect of business to be hived off to an external body. However, there are clear signs that the picture is changing. Nationalised industries have always engaged in company bargaining but in the private sector the number of domestic firms that have developed company bargaining is increasing (Cmnd. 3888: 1969, and Roberts and Gennard: 1970). A small number of privately owned domestic firms, for example, the Lancashire Cotton Corporation and ICI, have always undertaken company bargaining. The recent trend towards plant and company bargaining in domestic firms has not been mainly the result of management initiative but has been a response to demands from shop stewards that companies engage in plant bargaining and from the Government that wage increases should only be given in return for productivity concessions, which by necessity involves the workplace.

[1] See the *Royal Commission on Trades Unions and Employers' Associations*, Evidence of the Ministry of Labour, HMSO, 1965, p. 12. If one includes local employers' organisations affiliated to the nationals the figure is over 13,500.

4.11 A certain number of foreign owned companies have always negotiated on a company basis with British unions. For these firms company bargaining has not been a response to trade union pressure but has been the deliberate policy on the part of the management concerned. They have preferred to retain an autonomy over their industrial relations policies and practices. This fits in with the well-known reputation of the foreign firm to try to utilize labour more effectively. There are numerous examples of foreign owned firms negotiating independently of employers' associations, and this may or may not involve plant bargaining. These include in vehicles Chrysler (UK) Ltd. (Rootes), Fords and Vauxhalls; in oil refining Esso, Shell and Mobil Oil; in food manufacture Brown and Polsons, Heinz and Kellogs; in engineering Alcan, Massey-Ferguson, Kodak and International Nickel; and in retail distribution Woolworths. The foreign firms that have deliberately opted for plant bargaining are predominantly American owned. Massey Harris and Rootes are examples of British firms who, on being taken over by North American companies, withdrew from employers' associations to have autonomy in industrial relations. The foreign firms of Western European origin have tended to join employers' associations for their particular industry and to be partners to industry-wide agreements. This is to be expected since employers in Western Europe are highly organised into employers' associations. Although one Dutch company, Philips Industries, has questioned the usefulness of such associations, it has not withdrawn from the Engineering Employers' Federation. It has suggested that the Federation be broken down into smaller groups on an industrial basis (Royal Commission on Trade Unions and Employers' Associations: 1966[1]). However, a number of foreign companies from the continent have moved towards company bargaining under pressure from shop stewards and the Government's productivity, prices and incomes policy, for example, British Olivetti and Electrolux. But most of these companies have remained in membership of employers' associations.

4.12 Not all of the movement has been in the direction away from employers' associations. There are American owned firms who have made a deliberate policy decision to join, even in cases of take over where the previously British firm was not a member. In March 1968 there were 186 American owned firms, comprising 283 establishments, in membership of the Engineering Employers' Federation. The Census of Production (1963) showed 18 USA owned rubber firms and all were in membership of the British Rubber Manufacturers Association. There have been no withdrawals since this date. In food manufacturing the Census revealed 57 American owned firms of which about a half were members of the Food Manufacturers Industrial Group. Within the jurisdiction of the Soap, Candle and Edible Fats Trades Joint Industrial Council there were 63 American owned firms of which only two were members of the relevant employers' association. However, these two firms accounted for a very high percentage of the foreign output in the industry under the jurisdiction of this employers' association.

4.13 Domestic firms appear to employ a smaller amount of management input into industrial relations than the foreign firm, especially the American ones. In the UK the role of personnel departments in top management is only just emerging. Such departments have traditionally been seen as performing a welfare function in industry and having little executive authority in industrial relations because such matters have been dealt with by the employers' association to which the company belongs. USA firms have viewed the

[1] We are indebted to the Employers' Associations who have helped us with this part of the study.

personnel manager as providing an essential service to management so that human resources can be used most effectively and thus help labour efficiency and production stabilisation. The personnel director is ranked in importance with other specialised management functions, e.g. production, research, sales and accountancy. The task of selection, training, promoting and servicing the personnel employed in a large enterprise is seen as one that can only be carried out by experts. USA companies operating in the UK tend to employ more scientific methods of selection of personnel than domestic firms, e.g. the use of personality and intelligence tests.

4.14 Where the foreign firm conducts its own industrial relations it tends to appoint industrial relations directors, who in many cases are answerable to the parent headquarters. This may take the form of regular reports on labour matters in the plant and general industrial relations developments in the UK. At the same time, many parent company headquarters send back periodic reports to the subsidiary showing the relative performance of its establishments on the basis of certain economic efficiency indicators, for example, labour productivity and work performance standards.[1] The purpose of these reports is to 'shame' managements to improve their position in the league table. To do this may involve a review of existing labour utilisation and in the light of such a review an improvement in labour productivity. Interplant comparison was important in the development of productivity bargaining in the UK, one of the results of which was hoped to be an improvement in labour utilisation so that wage increases could be self-financing. We return to this later. It has not been possible for us to discover on a systematic basis to what extent the parent company interferes with personnel policy in the UK. The foreign owned firms submitting written evidence to the Royal Commission argued that they had autonomy in labour matters, although they sometimes had to justify their actions to headquarters.[2] When there has been a dispute between British unions and a foreign owned company the unions have often argued that the company has taken a particular course of action because of instruction from parent headquarters.

4.15 In 1969 when the Ford Motor Company took legal action against the Transport and General Workers' Union and Amalgamated Engineering and Foundry Workers over the enforcement of its company procedural agreement, some unionists argued that the company was acting on the instruction of Detroit, but this has never been substantiated.

Trade union recognition policy

4.16 Prior to the Industrial Relations Act, there was no means whereby a trade union could force any employer, whether British or foreign, to recognise and negotiate with it over the terms and conditions of employment for its members.[3] This was in marked contrast to the situation in the United States, Canada, Australia and parts of Western Europe. The question of union recognition can be divided into two parts, manual workers and staff workers. The failure to recognise and negotiate with manual trade unions does not appear to be a problem with foreign firms from Western Europe. However, it

[1] See Chapter Seven.

[2] See, Minutes of Evidence to *Royal Commission on Trade Unions and Employers' Associations*, Massey-Ferguson, Kodak, Esso, Mobil Oil and Phillips. This evidence is also interesting for the views of some foreign companies on the values of membership of British employers' associations.

[3] See the footnote on page 49 of this chapter.

has been suggested in some quarters that some USA owned firms are anti-union and have refused to recognise British trade unions. One can point to examples of non-recognition. International Business Machines do not recognise unions, preferring instead to adopt a paternalistic approach to their employees and attempting to check demands for unionisation by paying relatively high rates of pay and giving generous fringe benefits. In this company, communication with employees takes place through an Advisory Council elected from various levels and which has a chairman who is in turn elected by the representatives. There have been no demands at the company for union recognition.

4.17 An American company that has withstood demands for recognition of unions by its employees is Kodak. At its Hemel Hempstead factory there was a one-day stoppage for recognition. Ten unions have been attempting to get recognition from the company arguing that, although membership was not high in the company, this was the outcome of the anti-union attitude of the company. Kodak conducts relations with their employees through the Kodak workers' representative committees which the company claims have not expressed a desire for trade unionism. The usual anti-union devices of high pay and generous fringe benefits are used.[1] The TUC General Council has attempted to persuade the company to recognise the unions but has had little success, other than a suggestion from the firm that they would give serious consideration to any demand for recognition coming from the majority of their employees. Kodak does not recognise unions in the United States and has attempted and, so far, succeeded, in importing this policy into its British establishment.

4.18 The Amalgamated Engineering Union has complained of recognition problems from foreign owned firms. In 1966 the union was refused recognition at the west of Scotland establishment of the Caterpillar Tractor Company, an American firm. Several approaches were made to the company but when these proved fruitless, 1,200 employees came out on a strike which lasted for 13 weeks. When the union withdrew 600 of its members from another factory of the same company where recognition had been granted, the company agreed to recognise and negotiate with the union. The AEF also had recognition difficulties at the Stockport factory of Roberts-Arundel. This was originally a British textile machinery firm that negotiated with the union, but when it was taken over by a USA company union members were dismissed and replaced by female workers, and later recognition of the AEF was withdrawn. Eventually there followed a 12 months strike beginning November 1967 for the reinstatement of the union members and the recognition of the union. Although the company conceded in 1968, in January 1969 it closed down and withdrew its capital to the United States.

4.19 These incidents of refusal to recognise British unions by foreign firms have resulted in two motions being debated on the matter at the TUC. In 1965 the Association of Cinematography, Television and Allied Technicians proposed:[2]

> Congress can no longer tolerate foreign companies operating in Britain which deny their employees collective bargaining rights . . . Meanwhile the General Council are instructed to mount a campaign to help affiliated unions experiencing difficulties with foreign companies operating in Britain and to draw public attention to the attitude of such companies who are guilty of anti-trade union behaviour.

[1] For some of the devices used see *Report of Annual Trades Union Congress*, 1965, p. 405.

[2] *Annual Trades Union Congress Report*, 1965, p. 405.

In 1968 the AEF proposed and succeeded in getting carried the motion:

Congress calls upon the Government to make it a condition that foreign firms recognise the British trade union movement and the rights of organised workers before they are allowed to operate in this country.[1]

4.20 While there clearly is a problem of recognition with respect to foreign subsidiaries, the scale of this problem may not be very great. During 1967 the General Council of the TUC conducted an inquiry into the issue of trade union recognition and recruitment. Five hundred firms covering 39 unions and $6\frac{1}{2}$ million trade unionists were surveyed, and although the majority were British there were a number of foreign firms. The survey revealed that the areas in which trade union organisation was noticeably difficult were characterised by:[2] (a) the prevalence of small firms; (b) a relatively high proportion of female employees; (c) a high incidence of labour turnover; (d) non manual employment. Attention was drawn to particular difficulties in firms under foreign ownership and control. These foreign firms were found to be larger than British companies in which similar difficulties were encountered, although there were several large British companies who were shown to refuse to recognise trade unions. The inquiry did not conclusively suggest that the foreign firm was more anti-union than the British owned firm. Recognition problems are far greater amongst the small British firm with a paternalistic attitude. The TUC *Economic Review* for 1970 (Chap. 3, para 85, p. 35) did suggest that with the foreign owned firm there was a problem of determining where decisions were taken and how attitudes were formed over such problems as trade union recognition.

4.21 Esso provides an example of a company with an anti-union attitude in the United States, but who have accepted and recognised national unions in their British establishments. During the first World War the company installed an Industrial Representative Plan which became a model for other large employers wishing to avoid the recognition of trade unions. The employees were discouraged from joining unions by an elaborate welfare programme. This was challenged under the Wagner Act but when the Act's constitutionality was upheld by the Supreme Court in 1937, a legalised version of much the same arrangement was produced whereby the companies negotiated with local, so called independent unions. These arrangements have endured and have recently survived the onslaughts of large national unions (Flanders: 1964, Chap. 1, pp. 27-28). In its UK establishments, however, the company has always accorded full negotiating rights to the appropriate British trade union and those recognised include the Transport and General Workers Union, Amalgamated Engineering Union, the former Plumbing Trade Union and former Electrical Trades Union, the Boilermakers and Amalgamated Society of Woodworkers and Carpenters.

4.22 The Commission on Industrial Relations, established in January 1969, is empowered to examine cases where a company is withholding recognition from trade unions. References to the Commission are made by the Secretary of State for Employment after consultation with the Confederation of British Industries and the TUC. Up to September 1971 the Commission had received six manual workers non-recognition references of which only one involved a North American firm; the others were all British.[3] The four reports concerning non-recognition of manual unions covered domestic firms. None

[1] See *Annual Trades Union Congress Report*, 1968, p. 429.

[2] See *Annual Trades Union Congress Report*, 1967, pp. 129-132.

[3] None of the references to the CIR since September 1971 concerned recognition problems with foreign owned firms.

of its pending references on recognition are concerned with foreign owned firms. Since its inception only six foreign companies have been referred to the Commission. For four of them it was on the grounds of defective industrial relations procedure and for two on the grounds of non-recognition.

4.23 The general conclusion is that non-recognition of manual worker trade unions by foreign owned firms is no worse than amongst domestic firms. Where recognition is withheld the company tends to pay high rates of wages and give generous fringe benefits relative to the companies that recognise unions in their particular industry, e.g. Kodak, Mars and Heinz. Where trouble arises over non-recognition by an overseas company it tends to get a lot of trade union and press attention and gives the impression that foreign firms are more reluctant to recognise manual unions.

4.24 Information provided by five employers' associations indicates that the foreign firm, like the domestic firm, appears to have a fear of white-collar unionism, not only amongst middle and lower management, but also amongst clerical workers. In the UK in the public sector staff unionism is widespread and encouraged. In local and national government over 80 per cent of white-collar employees are unionised. In the private sector staff unionism is not very widespread but is nevertheless increasing. In the United States unionism amongst staff employees in 1964 was about 11 per cent and USA owned companies have shown a similar reluctance to accept a demand for unionism amongst staff ranks here, even though they have been prepared to accept manual unions without much difficulty. The Ford Motor Company have recognised manual unions since the early 1940s, but only concluded recognition agreements in 1970 for their supervisory staff, although they had earlier recognised the Professional, Technical, Administrative, Clerical and Supervisory section of the T & GWU for clerical staff. The policy of many of these companies is to speak with union officials but not to grant formal recognition. The Association of Scientific, Technical and Managerial Staffs complained in its evidence to the Royal Commission about such companies, and argued that foreign owned companies were hostile to white-collar unions (Royal Commission on Trade Unions and Employers' Associations, Minutes of Evidence No. 53: 1968).

4.25 The first report of the Commission on Industrial Relations concerned non-recognition of staff unions at the foreign owned Associated Octel Company Ltd., which is also a firm with a history of satisfactory factory relations with the unions representing craft and process workers on its payroll. The reasons given to the Commission for the withholding of recognition were those common to most firms whether domestic or foreign, namely, unionism would destroy a direct relationship between management and employee and thus weaken loyalty and restrict the scope of management discretion (Commission on Industrial Relations, Report No. 1: 1969).

4.26 The attitudes of companies of West European origins to staff unionism are less well known than those of American firms. In rubber manufacture Pirelli (Italian) and Michelin (France) are both reluctant to accept staff unionism, although they have always accorded negotiating rights to manual unions. In engineering, Philips Industries, a Dutch company, has been reluctant to concede recognition to staff members, but being members of the Engineering Employers' Federation, they go along with that body's recognition of the draughtsmen union, Draughtsmen and Allied Technicians Association. (This Union is now the Technical and Supervisory section of

Amalgamated Union of Engineering Workers.) In oil refining, all the well-known foreign owned companies recognise manual worker unions, but they have shown a reluctance to accept claims for ASTMS to negotiate on behalf of technical and middle managerial staffs. The policy of Shell (UK) Ltd. is to recognise a union for staff where the majority of staff in a common grade decide by ballot that they wish union representation. However, the common grades are so broad that it is difficult to get a majority. A ballot was held in two of the company's establishments for recognition of ASTMS but a majority was not secured. A further ballot was held in 1971 and this time a majority was obtained, and ASTMS granted recognition. In companies where staff unions have been recognised the attitude of management could be summed up as a grudging acceptance of an unavoidable, but rather unpleasant necessity (Roberts *et al:* 1972). Some foreign companies have encouraged the formation of staff associations as an alternative to unionisation but the true extent of this has been difficult to assess.

The nature of agreements

4.27 Before the change in the presumed legal status of collective agreements brought about by the Industrial Relations Act such agreements in the UK were not legally binding contracts and were considered to be binding only in honour. Even before the Act it was possible for an individual company and a trade union to conclude a legally binding contract if both sides desired it. However, foreign companies in the UK negotiating on a company basis had not taken advantage of this legal provision, and only entered into 'morally' binding agreements. Agreements between employers' associations and trade unions were not legally binding because by legal definition they were both trade unions and the Trade Union Act of 1871 precluded legally binding agreements between two such bodies. Foreign firms who are members of employers' associations were thus voluntary partners to a 'gentlemen's agreement'. Hence the foreign firms in the UK can find themselves facing a problem of unconstitutional industrial action, that is action in breach of an agreed procedure, without any form of legal redress. However, in 1968 and 1969 two foreign firms attempted to achieve a revolutionary breakthrough. Henry Wiggins, a subsidiary of International Nickel, succeeded in 1968 in negotiating what they thought to be a legally binding agreement, and in 1969 the Ford Motor Company sued two British unions for allegedly breaking agreed procedural arrangements.

4.28 The Henry Wiggins agreement was made at the Hereford establishment and is unique in British industrial relations. Both the management and the union involved, the AEF clearly intended on signature that the provisions of the agreement should bind them in law. The deal was to last for two years and there were to be no strikes or lock-outs during the course of the agreement. Any employee involved in unconstitutional strike action was to lose the performance rate component of their basic hourly rate. This rate was made up of two components—the basic rate and the performance rate. However the agreement had been concluded in an area where unemployment is high and little trade union tradition exists and attempts by the company to secure a similar agreement at its Swansea establishment resulted in a prolonged strike.

4.29 In February 1969 the Ford Motor Company succeeded in getting the majority of unions in its National Joint Negotiating Committee to accept a proposed settlement which would have given increases in basic rates, an incomes guarantee plan covering a holiday bonus and guaranteed pay for lay-off due to disputes in suppliers' establishments, and improved fringe benefits in return for which employees would lose some of the holiday and lay-off payments if they were involved in unconstitutional action. Also in any week there was an unconstitutional strike as in Ford establishment the management would not make payments with the lay-off and holiday bonus funds. There was also a reform to the company's disputes procedure. When shop-floor pressures built up to oppose the deal the T & GWU and the AEF declared the strike action official. The company insisted there was an agreement and if there were a dispute about its terms settlement should be through the company's procedure agreement of 1955, and the 1967 amendment. On 27 February the company sought and obtained injunctions against the two unions. Fords sued the unions alleging that the calling of official action constituted a breach of the procedural agreements which had laid down circumstances in which strikes could take place during the course of an agreement. The Judge concluded that the procedural agreements were not legal contracts because it had not been the intentions of the parties at the time to create legally binding contracts. On 6 March the injunctions were discharged and when the strike action ended the company dropped its intention to appeal against the decision or to take the matter to a full trial. The Court had thus upheld a tradition of the UK industrial system, that is, agreements were legally enforceable only if this was the intention of the parties. In 1970 the Vauxhall Motor Company attempted to obtain a greater degree of conformity to procedure by offering the trade unions a 100 per cent union shop in return for an adherence to agreed procedure.

4.30 Procedural agreements lay down a procedure to be followed where there is a dispute over the application and interpretation of any existing substantive agreement, i.e. the price list aspect of an agreement. In the UK industry-wide agreements generally have an industry-wide disputes procedure stating the number of stages in attempts to settle differences that have not been solved within establishments. Domestic firms tend to be parties to such procedures as do foreign firms that are members of employers' associations. British firms that negotiate on a company basis often follow industry-wide disputes procedures, but foreign owned firms who are involved in company bargaining have their own company procedures which tend to be shorter and more speedy than industry-wide ones. Ford and Vauxhall are not members of the Engineering Employers' Federation and have their own procedural agreements. Industry-wide procedures usually stipulate that there shall be no strike or other form of industrial action while a grievance is being processed. In return employers pledge not to lock-out employees until all the stages of procedure are exhausted. The Royal Commission on Trades Unions and Employers' Associations saw breach of procedures, and thus unconstitutional strikes, as a major problem in British industrial relations. The Commission suggested that before legal regulations were to be brought into our system to make procedural agreements legally binding there should be a reform of existing procedures. An examination of 160 agreements made between 1966 and 1969 indicates some reform is in progress. In 1968 in twelve agreements some kind of procedural reform was present as opposed to only three before 1968 (Roberts and Gennard: 1970). Of the twelve agreements, four concerned foreign owned firms. For two the reform was of the plant procedure but as members of the appropriate employers' association the industry-wide procedure operated in cases not settled at the plant. For another the reform was a modification to an existing company procedure but for the fourth, which had just withdrawn from an employers' association, it amounted to a new company disputes procedure. The other eight were concerned with domestic companies and the main direction of change was a speeding up of the processing of grievances within the plant.

4.31 Although domestic firms are having to give more attention to procedural reform they have not been as inventive as some of the foreign owned firms, two of whom have given their employees a financial incentive to observe an agreed procedure. Foreign firms have not attempted to obtain legally enforceable disputes procedures and have accepted the British system, and there have been few attempts to challenge it. The fact that foreign owned firms operating in the UK and negotiating on a company and/or plant basis have not gone in for legally enforceable agreements illustrates the extent to which foreign firms abide by accepted customs and practices in industrial relations. It is nevertheless significant that a Canadian and United States firm have in the one case achieved what is thought to be a legally enforceable agreement and in the other tested the legal status of procedural agreements in the British Courts.

The duration of agreements

4.32 The typical UK industry-wide agreement has no set duration and negotiations for a new agreement can be started at any time. On a number of occasions unions have given notice of a new claim within a week or two of signing an agreement on the grounds of the length of time taken to negotiate the agreement just reached. For many foreign firms, and especially Canadian and United States companies, the pattern in their parent country is to negotiate fixed term agreements which state clearly the number of years for which the agreement is to run, the period of notice required to terminate the agreement, and the circumstances that apply when a new agreement has not been negotiated at the expiry of the original agreement, and a commitment not to strike, or to engage in other forms of industrial action or lock-outs during the term of the agreement. Fixed term agreements alter the approach to bargaining since they carry with them the concept of exchanging peace and co-operation on specific terms for a definite period. This gives rise to two problems: (1) what to do if there is any major change which alters the basic assumptions on which the agreement has been made, and (2) resolving disputes over the application of the provision of an agreement during its term.

4.33 Since 1962 a number of UK industry-wide agreements have been concluded with set termination dates, lasting on the average about three years. Between 1962 and 1965 twenty-two such agreements were signed covering over 7 million workers. The most important of these was the engineering agreement and foreign firms who were members of the Engineering Employers' Federation were thus operating with a fixed term agreement. Disputes over the agreement were to be resolved through the industry's disputes procedure, and the wage increase awarded was to be spread over the three-year period. However, fixed-term company agreements have been rare among UK firms, although by 1969 there were signs that under the influence of productivity, prices and incomes policy and the Royal Commission Report the position might be changing. Nationalised industries have concluded company agreements with fixed termination dates, e.g. the airlines, the electricity and gas supply and railway sectors; but in 1968 some private British companies concluded agreements for a fixed duration, for example, Ilford and Parkinson-Cowan and in 1969 it appears an even larger number were involved in such agreements, such as Ansell's Brewery, Swan Hunter and Tyne Shipbuilders, Perkins Engines, the Scottish and Newcastle Breweries and GEC/AEI.

4.34 Foreign owned companies have been involved in fixed term company-wide agreements since the early 1960s, but as among domestic firms the trend appears to have accelerated in the last few years. In 1960, Esso, at its Fawley refinery, negotiated a two-year agreement with its employees. In 1962 Massey-Ferguson concluded a four-year agreement; at the end of 1965 Alcan concluded an agreement with its production and service workers to take effect in 1966 having concluded a similar agreement with its process workers in 1964, while in 1968 Henry Wiggins signed a two-year agreement. In 1969 a number of foreign owned firms concluded company agreements with a termination date, for example, Chrysler (two years), Otis Elevator, International Harvester and Vauxhall.

4.35 Although company-wide fixed term agreements are at present more prevalent among foreign firms than domestic, the former have not developed voluntary grievance arbitration for the settlement of disputes over the application and interpretation of the agreements during their duration. Such disputes are usually processed through the agreed company procedure and, should no agreement be reached, third party intervention by the Department of Employment is generally only used if specifically requested by one or both parties, or in some cases, the matter may be referred to arbitration, which may involve the Industrial Court. The Henry Wiggins agreements, however, come close to the typical USA type of fixed agreement. The 1970 agreement clearly states the length of the agreement; the circumstances in which negotiations can be re-started during the term of the agreement; the conditions in which industrial action is acceptable during the agreement, and provides a claims procedure as the means of raising and resolving claims that the company has breached the provisions of the agreement. The procedure lays down time limits for each stage of the procedure and provides for a Board of three arbitrators, and a separate board sits for each 'alleged' company breach. The union and company each appoint one arbitrator and if they cannot mutually agree a third, one or more of the parties may ask the Secretary of State for Employment to submit lists of arbitrators and from this a third person will be selected. Any Arbitration Board is to deliver its decision in writing thirty days after the end of any hearing.

Productivity bargaining

4.36 Productivity bargaining has probably been the major innovation in UK industrial relations during the last decade, and foreign firms have had a large influence on this development. Among American owned firms comparison of performance between UK and US establishments is crucial. In engineering, rubber manufacturing, food processing, soap making and chemicals, comparability appeared very influential. The personnel director of the UK foreign firm usually has to write monthly reports to the Vice-President of the parent company covering such matters as wages and conditions of employment, recruitment, and developments in industrial relations in the country as a whole. In return, the parent company sends reports showing how particular establishments compare with others and there are also visits from the Vice-President to see operations at first hand.

4.37 The first known productivity agreement in the UK was that signed at Esso's Fawley plant in 1960. However, the seeds of this agreement have been traced back to 1956 when its parent company, Standard Oil, showed a new interest in manpower utilisation in an attempt to survive an intensification of competition in the United States and in international oil markets and so prevent falling profits (Flanders: 1964, chapter 2). The company introduced a new statistical basis for judging comparisons of manpower utilisation and the Fawley plant made a comparatively poor showing. As a consequence, pressures built up on the Fawley management to do something about its use of manpower, and in particular the excessive amount of overtime worked. In 1960 an agreement was reached with the unions giving pay increases in return for which the elimination of overtime, flexibility between jobs, changed manning levels (in particular the ending of craftsmen's mates) and shift working were accepted.

4.38 It can be seen from the above that a productivity agreement is one in which workers agree to make a change, or a number of changes, in working practices that will lead to more efficient production. In return, the employer agrees to a higher level of pay or to other benefits. The idea is that the pay increase will be self-financing through the savings made by the work-force accepting and operating the agreed changes in the way in which a job is performed. Productivity agreements can be comprehensive or partial. The former cover a number of related changes in working practices and affect all, or nearly all, of the manual workers in an undertaking, whereas the latter normally affect only one practice and often only a single group of workers. Comprehensive productivity agreements are to be sharply distinguished from conventional wage settlements in the UK. These latter agreements generally relate pay to matters external to the plant, for example, changes in the cost of living, disturbances in comparative wages, profit levels and labour recruiting problems in the industry as a whole. Productivity agreements are related to the workplace itself.

4.39 It is difficult to discover the relative proportion of productivity agreements in domestic as against foreign firms because there is no register of such agreements before January 1967, and as firms submit the information in confidence there is no access to the register for research purposes. However, the first companies involved in the pre-1967 era were foreign owned. Table 4.II below shows the dates when negotiation for a productivity agreement began, the degree of comprehensiveness and whether the company is foreign or domestic. Of the 14 agreements, 8 concerned foreign owned establishments, and six domestic firms.

Table 4.II

Productivity agreements

Date of start of negotiations		*Company*	*Comprehensive (C) or Partial (P)*	*Ownership of company*
	1960	Esso (Fawley)	C	USA
April	1962	Esso (Fawley)	C	USA
	1963	Petrochemicals	P	Dutch
	1963	Mobil Oil	P	USA
June	1964	Esso (Milford)	C	USA
June	1964	Alcan (Rogerstone)	C	Canada
July	1964	Central Electricity Generating Board	C	British
July	1964	British Oxygen	P	British
	1964	Mobil Oil (Distribution)	C	USA
	1964	BP (Kent)—Isle of Grain	P	British
Sept.	1964	Esso (Distribution)	C	USA
May	1965	Imperial Chemical Industries	C	British
	1965	Co-operative Insurance Society	P	British
	1966	Stanton and Stavely (Derbyshire)	C	British

Source: National Board for Prices and Incomes, Report No. 36, *Productivity Agreements*, Cmnd. 3311, Appendices A to H inclusive.

4.40 The growth of productivity bargaining offers a challenge to the traditional British system of industrial relations. Since it is concerned with workplace matters, industry-wide negotiation is clearly being attacked as it would be impossible with this type of agreement to work out at national level the details for each individual plant. Although the 'pioneering' firms were mainly non-federated, they did represent a challenge since the rates of pay agreed upon were generally well above those for federated firms and there was a feeling that workers in such companies would demand parity with workers covered by productivity agreements but without the corresponding productivity concessions. Some of the companies involved in productivity agreements were at one time federated but felt it desirable to resign from employers' associations when they began to engage in productivity bargaining, and so free themselves from any need to observe industry level agreements. Esso withdrew from the Employers' Panel of the Oil Companies Conciliation Committee after concluding its distribution workers agreement. Alcan, who concluded a productivity agreement, also withdrew from the local employers' association. Employers' associations were afraid that the supra-marginal firms might withdraw from association and conclude productivity agreements rather than be held back by the marginal firms in an association. However, the associations have dropped their initial opposition to productivity agreements and the chemical, rubber, and electrical contracting associations have taken steps to assist member firms in negotiation of such agreements. The rubber industry employers' association negotiates national minimum earnings levels which firms in membership can exceed through productivity bargaining. The Engineering Employers' Federation has also come to terms with productivity bargaining and has established a research department to assist its member firms.

4.41 On the trade union side the union officials, who are involved in nationwide bargaining, opposed productivity bargaining because its concentration on the workplace might give more power to shop stewards. As stewards would become the main agents in the determination of pay, they might be able to undermine the authority of the full-time officials. However, trade union opposition has tended to subside as the realisation of the benefits to be gained from such operations became clearer.

4.42 Between 1 January 1967 and 31 December 1969 the then Department of Employment and Productivity considered nearly 4,200 productivity agreements, the majority of which were accepted. However, few of these agreements were of the type concluded pre 1967 and many were accepted although they were not genuine in the Fawley sense with the result that the idea of productivity agreements has become somewhat weakened. In January 1970 the incomes policy became more flexible and the 'something for nothing agreement' appeared to re-establish itself among the domestic firms and foreign firms. As the rate of inflation and unemployment increased throughout 1970 and 1971, so the unions became more and more reluctant to enter into productivity negotiations, preferring to go for large wage increases to maintain the real wage levels of those remaining in employment.

Plant personnel practices

4.43 Inter-plant comparisons between parent and foreign establishments are important in wage payment schemes. In the UK the majority of manufacturing firms employ workers on some form of incentive payment schemes which in tight labour markets tend to become undermined. Few domestic firms employ schemes like measured daywork and cost reduction plans which require work measurement through the application of industrial engineering techniques, but the position showed some change under the influences of the productivity, prices and incomes policy. American, and some Dutch-owned firms, in the UK have used inter-plant comparison within their own organisation of worker performance and have demanded that comparatively poor UK establishments improve. The National Board for Prices and Incomes in Report 123 studied 40 productivity agreements. A number of the agreements chosen for study tried to ensure, through tighter measurement of performance, that the increase in pay did not exceed the expected increase in productivity, and the Board argued that comparison with higher American performance was sometimes an influential factor getting subsidiaries to undertake reform in the case of firms with American parentage (NBPI, Report 123: 1969).

4.44 There is a feeling among observers of industrial relations that measured day work has been growing as a form of wage payment, but R B McKersie argues that a major trend to measure daywork is not under way at present and the impression has only been created because of the publicity given to the abandonment of piecework by a small number of firms, for example, Vauxhall Motors, Pet Foods Limited and Glacier Metals (McKersie: 1968). The term 'measured daywork' covers many variations within the general theme of hourly wage payments accompanied by the use of performance standards. In the motor car industry there is still a contrast (although this is declining), between the payment systems used in the domestic companies and those used in the foreign owned company.[1] There is now only one major domestic motor car assembly firm, British Leyland Motor Corporation, and this still employs conventional payment incentive schemes although in some areas it has succeeded in introducing measured daywork. The three foreign owned motor car firms, Ford, Vauxhall and Chrysler, have changed from piece rates to measured daywork. Vauxhall's abandoned piecework in favour of straight time in 1956, Fords in 1967 and Chrysler in 1968. It would be useful to see whether this has had any effect on the relative strike frequency and type of strike experienced in the domestic and foreign firm. One would expect there to be more wage issue strikes at the domestic firm than at the foreign one, and this appears to be the case.

4.45 Philips, a Dutch company, uses a measured daywork system which has a very direct link between effort and earnings. Each employee works under a contract that enables him over a long-term period to generate more take-home pay by fulfilling the performance standards. The approach envisages the periodic adjustment of a worker's pay in accordance with his performance. It has been estimated that only 8 per cent of the workers in the Philips plant have failed to fulfil their bargain with the company (McKersie: 1968, para. 103, p .51). Successful results suggest that the practice will spread.

The impact of the foreign firm on UK industrial relations

4.46 Writing in 1957 Allan Flanders remarked, 'The recent history of collective bargaining in post-war Britain is, perhaps, most remarkable for its lack of innovations. The traditional pattern has been extended—although this took place mainly during and immediately after the war—but it remains

[1] But McKersie points out that outside the traditional automobile areas none of the new plants has been established on daywork.

substantially the same in form and extent' (Flanders: 1957). Since that date a number of innovations have taken place in the industrial relations system and the leaders in this respect have been foreign owned firms. The majority of the foreign firms have accepted the traditional features of the UK system and while attempts at radical departure by importing practices from the parent country have been rare, one can point to clear innovations stemming from the foreign firm.

4.47 Productivity bargaining—where workers are given wage increases in return for changes in working practices so that the increase is self-financing is an example. Esso, a UK subsidiary of Standard Oil, USA were the pioneers in this field, being followed by other foreign and British firms. Productivity bargaining, by concentrating on the plant, challenged the industry-wide basis of the industrial relations system and was opposed by employers' associations and trade union officials. However, the system has adjusted to the change and unions and employers now accept productivity bargaining. The idea of productivity bargaining has been a central plank in the Wilson Government's productivity, prices and incomes policy and the Roberts and Gennard study has shown that company bargaining is becoming more of a feature of the British system.

4.48 Two foreign firms have made revolutionary attempts to overcome the unconstitutional strike problem by offering financial incentives to employees to honour the disputes procedure. Ford has offered payments into a lay-off and holiday bonus fund on the condition there is no unconstitutional action. Henry Wiggins have introduced a penalty of loss of performance rate if employees assist or take part in any industrial action that is in breach of agreement. Employers' associations are beginning to reform industry-wide procedures, but an attempt by the Engineering Employers' Federation has met difficulties with the unions over the number of external plant stages to the procedure, and the status quo provisions. In addition Vauxhall have attempted to reduce the incidence of unconstitutional strikes in their plants by giving the unions a 100 per cent union shop in return for seeing that their members kept procedure and that no industrial action will be taken if management takes disciplinary action against employees who breach procedure.

4.49 The foreign firm has been in the lead in the making of fixed terms company agreements. This stems from the practice of some USA and Canadian firms in the conduct of their own industrial relations. In the early 1960s some industry-wide agreements were made with a fixed termination date. Some domestic firms are now beginning to make company agreements because of a more flexible approach to such agreements by employers' associations.

4.50 Ford and Henry Wiggins have challenged the UK system in another aspect. The latter company have achieved a unique agreement in Britain with its alleged legally binding agreement at its Hereford plant, backed with a voluntary grievance procedure to examine allegations of management's breach of the agreement. The Ford Company sued two unions in the Courts for an alleged breach of a disputes procedure. The suit was rejected by the Courts, but had it been successful it could have changed the whole environment of British industrial relations and seriously questioned the voluntary basis of the UK system.

4.51 There are other areas where the foreign firms appear to have been innovators. International Business Machines and Shell (UK) Ltd. have pioneered uniform fringe benefits for staff and manual workers. Philips Industries have been among the leaders in introducing work structuring and the application of industrial psychology to plant industrial relations. In the motor car industry the foreign owned firms have introduced stricter measures of performance of the workforce, by the use of measured daywork, than the domestic firm which typically still relies on the traditional conventional payment by results schemes.

Trade union response to the foreign firm in the UK

4.52 The British trade union movement has made little response to the foreign owned firm operating in the UK, but recent trade unions literature shows that much thought and discussion is presently being devoted to such companies, for example, the TUC *Economic Reviews* for 1970, 1971 and 1972, and the initiation by the trade unions of discussion in the National Economic Development Council on possible public policy to international companies. This small response has been due to the fact that some of the implications of such companies have not yet been realised and because the foreign companies have on the whole accepted the main features of the British system. Anti-foreign feeling amongst some unions has been aroused on occasions through a failure of a small number of foreign companies to recognise and negotiate with manual trade unions. British unions are aware of the ability of the foreign owned company to withdraw its operations from Britain and continue business in another area, but up to the present they have suffered little from such moves. One example however, is the AEF experiences with Robert Arundel when the company removed its operations back to the States following a 12-month strike for union recognition. In addition, in February 1970, shop stewards at the Ford plant at Halewood, Liverpool questioned Henry Ford, chairman of Ford of Detroit, about rumours of a possible build-up of car production in Germany at the expense of Britain. They were afraid that the company's replacement for their Escort model would be built at a new factory at Saarlouis, Germany. The unions feared not a run down in existing plants, but, a large proportion of future investment might be diverted to Germany at the expense of the UK. Similar threats were made by Henry Ford during the 10-week stoppage in early 1971. The American management of Ford, Detroit, is known to be shocked by the attitude to industrial relations in the UK, but the UK plants of the company have dismissed fears of a run-down in investments in the UK as nonsense. The TUC *Economic Review* for 1972 refers to other instances of work previously performed in the UK now being undertaken overseas. Unions have seen the power of the foreign firms in their ability to withstand strike action by supplying customers from establishments in the parent country or other countries of operation. American owned rubber companies in the UK have used this tactic.

4.53 British trade unions have developed international contacts by affiliating to the appropriate International Trade Secretariat. There are 16 International Trade Secretariats (ITS), the biggest of which is the International Metalworkers' Federation. However, these contacts have not been the direct result of the upsurge of foreign-firm operations in the UK but rather spring from a desire for international trade union co-operation on all matters of interest to trade unionists. The contact between British unions in foreign owned firms and unions in the firms' parent country or other countries of operation is small. Sid Harraway, for example, the shop steward convenor at Ford's Dagenham plant, admits that there is too little contact with his European opposite numbers.[1]

4.54 Action to meet the threat of multi-national companies is being instigated by the United Automobile Workers, an American union. In 1969 it sent a delegation over to Britain to have talks with the Amalgamated Union of Engineering and Foundry Workers and the Transport and General Workers' Union. A conference of the three unions met to study each others' constitutions, problems and working methods, and to examine in considerable depth the agreements and negotiating procedures and timings as they stand at present and to see what sort of co-ordination might take place to bring progress and benefit to all three unions' members in the motor industry. At the end of the conference a statement acknowledged that there was a need for regular contact and an exchange of agreements and information on a consistent basis, and that it was likely that eventually there would be co-ordination of some aspects of agreements in the two countries, particularly so far as terminal dates for wage agreements were concerned (Gennard: 1972). A further meeting of representatives of the three unions was held in the USA in March 1971. The UAW initiatives stem from Walter Reuther[2] (former UAW President) who was a strong advocate of international co-operation and argued that in the negotiation of company agreements the unions should ensure that all agreements with supra-national car manufactures end at the same time. This was seen as a precondition of international bargaining.

4.55 Individually the British unions have not been as active, but as affiliates to the International Metalworkers Federation have joined its World Automobile Council, which was also the outcome of a UAW initiative. In December 1969 a Paris conference concerned with the development of the motor-car multi-nationals was attended by 11 British trade unions, including the AEF, the T & GWU, and the Vehicle and Sheet Metal Workers. At the meeting consideration was given to a study of wage rates and earnings paid by motor manufacturers to their employees in different countries. The union leaders in the Council Conference voted for a policy which aims to ensure that, for instance, all Ford workers in Europe have parity of real wages. The object of this, apart from improving wages, is to ensure that international companies do not run down operations in one country and build them up in cheaper labour markets. However, the first priority in host countries is for the unions to get parity of earnings in their own factories, for example, the British unions in the motor-car industry are attempting to negotiate the same rates for all plants as those paid to the highest paid workers at motor-car assembly plants in Coventry and district.

4.56 At the Paris conference the unions also agreed that they should try to stop companies transferring work from one country to another during strikes and that they should aim for a guaranteed annual wage, a forty-hour week

[1] L. Turner—*Politics and the Multinational Company*, Fabian Research Series 279. However on 24 April 1970 the *Financial Times* reported that convenors from Ford Motor's Plant in Britain were hoping in June 1970 to strengthen unofficial contacts made recently with Ford workers in Belgium and Germany. There were plans to hold a conference in Britain to discuss comparative Ford pay rates in the three countries and to examine whether 'parity' could become an international issue and a basis for wage demands. In 1971 at a meeting of the International Metalworkers Federation, Belgium workers agreed in principle not to substitute continental cars for lost United Kingdom production.

[2] Since this paper was written Walter Reuther was killed in an aeroplane disaster on 10 May 1970 in the USA.

(this has already been achieved in the UK) and security of employment. The union leaders set their sights on achieving equal pay for women without conditions, for example, that women should now work shifts and that factory legislation giving certain protection to females should be withdrawn. A further conference was held in London in 1971 and called for more Government control over the activities of multi-national companies. Another example of British participation occurred in June 1970 when a world conference of unions with workers employed in the Shell Oil Company was held in Istanbul. This conference noted that dwindling employment in the petroleum industry was one of the most disquieting aspects of recent developments. A study committee was appointed to examine the broad range of workers' relations with the Shell Company. The 6th World Congress of the International Federation of Petroleum and Chemical Workers decided at its June 1970 meeting on important structural innovations to enable its member unions (which include British ones) in various countries to make more uniform, for workers employed by the same international company, wages, working hours, collective agreements and other issues. To this end the Congress recommended the convening of trade union council meetings covering Standard Oil, Du Pont, ICI, and other world enterprises.

4.57 The main action undertaken by British trade unions with respect to foreign firms has been in the form of demands that overseas companies should give an undertaking, as a condition of being allowed to operate in the country, that they will give recognition to British trade unions, and proposals to the Government that foreign companies should provide more information for collective bargaining purposes. The Trade Union Congresses of 1965 and 1968 debated motions concerned with foreign firms and union recognition and these have been discussed elsewhere in this paper. The TUC *Economic Review* for 1970 called for more information on international companies arguing:

Trade unions thus have a common interest with governments in obtaining increased information about the activities of international companies, and defining guidelines for their operation . . . (Chapter 3, para. 100, p. 39)

The *Review* said there was a clear need for obligations to be placed by governments on subsidiaries to provide information for collective bargaining purposes from companies' central accounts. More information was needed about how such companies worked and how they affected major questions like a country's balance of payments and how they paid or avoided paying tax. However, at a press conference on the *Review* the General Secretary of the TUC discounted international trade union operations against international companies in the near future, feeling at the present time the most useful work to be done was the exchange of information between countries. In October 1970 the TUC held a conference on International Companies to consider what union action is needed to cope with the problems posed by the operation of such companies. The conference felt that more information was necessary about such companies and the unions most active in the conference were those representing white-collar workers and those employed in the motor industry. It was suggested that the British Government should adopt a series of guidelines to regulate the activities of international companies operating in the UK.

4.58 To conclude this part, one can say that the British trade unions have made little response to the foreign firm because such companies have accepted the main tenets of the UK industrial relations system and because the ability of the foreign firms to switch operations from one establishment to another has not been widely experienced. Foreign firms have on occasions refused to recognise trade unions and this has resulted in a number of motions at annual Trade Union Congresses calling for recognition of unions as a necessary condition of being allowed to operate in this country. The growth of policies to counter the foreign firms has come from the United Automobile Workers and the British Unions have been approached by the Union for co-operation. The result has been two conferences with the AEF and T & GWU. The TUC has shown an awareness of the problem by devoting sections of its 1970, 1971 and 1972 *Economic Reviews* to the problems of obtaining more information on the multi-national firm to help restore the balance of power in collective bargaining. British unions have participated in the activities of International Trade Secretariats in connection with multi-national corporations.

II: Industrial disputes in foreign owned firms: 1963 and 1968

4.59 There are four main reasons why we might expect the foreign subsidiaries of multi-national firms to generate more disturbed industrial relations than is typical for a host country generally. One is the issue of ultimate decision taking going on abroad. Power lies with people who are removed from the local host country work force and have no history of, or present experience of, involvement in the community. This could, in principle, give the multi-national organization a lower sense of responsibility to its employees and a consequently greater willingness to risk a strike. At the same time, foreign ownership could generate greater suspicion and hostility on the part of the workers because of either actual or presumed callousness or insensitivity due to actual or presumed remoteness. The possibility of longer and more complex lines of communication opens up the potential for misunderstanding and protracted friction over differences that might be more directly resolved by domestic firms.

4.60 Greater distance, bearing in mind the *proviso* if it exists, is a source of difficulty in itself apart from the question of substantive, genuine economic conflict. That economic conflict might be heightened in the case of the foreign subsidiary is also a real possibility. Briefly far wider economic factors impinge on the foreign subsidiary than on the domestic firm. It is not unreasonable to suppose that it would be experiencing swings in prosperity that would be less in step with the host country economy than would be true of most domestic firms. Doing well when other firms were doing less well would not be a problem, but the converse would be a source of extra tension bearing on its industrial relations.

4.61 In the previous section of this chapter we have discussed some ways in which the industrial relations traditions and practices of foreign parent companies, particularly United States companies, differ from those of the United Kingdom, and the general tendency for inward investing firms to import at least a part of the labour relations structure of the source country to the host country. Particularly in the initial phases of direct investment, but indeed all the way along, there is a potential source of conflict due to the imposition, or the attempted imposition, of a different system of industrial relations which could lead to more, and more intense, industrial disputes. Of course, there is nothing necessary about this. The foreign system may be a better system in the sense of leading to fewer strikes.

4.62 Finally, there is the related factor that the foreign subsidiary, again particularly the American owned firm, is alleged to utilize labour more effectively, which could be a nice way of saying work people harder. Here also this need not lead to industrial disputes. Better motivated workers, whose special talents are more quickly recognized and productively employed may not only be paid more, but may find the work itself more satisfying and identify more closely with the interests of the employer. More and more intelligent supervision, including more flexibility in promotion, can contribute to industrial peace. However, different standards of work intensity can be a disruptive factor.

4.63 The four factors we outline above—distance, economic conflict, different industrial relations traditions, more intense labour utilization—establish some plausibility for adding in labour relations tension on the cost side of direct investment. However, the latter two factors have at least the potential of operating in the other direction on balance, that is, towards industrial peace. The primary purpose of this section is to determine if stormier industrial relations in the United Kingdom are, in fact, a cost for this country of inward investment.

4.64 We direct our attention to strikes because of a lack of other kinds of data on industrial unrest. This is a limitation. Industrial tension can exist without reaching the stage of strike action. Indeed, in isolated cases, the foreign firm may have an effective policy which does not allow unions in the subsidiary. This could raise tension without leading to strikes. Even with unions, it may be possible to avoid strikes while paying a higher price in terms of other forms of conflict. Ideally, one would like to examine a spectrum of discontent in which actual strikes were one important element. Analysis of turnover figures and of absenteeism would be relevant, but it was not practical to obtain such information. But while strike figures are not the whole story, they do have certain advantages. They are relatively hard information and they are an important index of personal and social cost.

4.65 We do not want to imply that the optimum amount of industrial disputes in the form of strikes is zero. There certainly are worse things, such as passive acceptance of a substandard work environment which is dangerous, unjust, arbitrary and spiritually debilitating. The national cost of strikes generally is often over-estimated. But it is interesting in itself to know if foreign owned firms have more or less of them than domestic firms, and it sheds some light on the four propositions discussed above.

4.66 In appraising whether or not inward investment entails extra industrial disputes we make two simple assumptions. The first is that industrial unrest due to foreign subsidiaries is not external to the firms themselves. In other words, setting aside for the moment the question of how to quantify strike activity, we assume that the relative amount of striking to peaceful relations in domestic firms would be the same whether the foreign firms were in the United Kingdom or not. The second assumption is that the relevant comparison is the norm for the industry, rather than, say, the region, size of firm, age of firm or some other category. As it happens, the results are quite strong and the conclusions would tend to stand up under considerable relaxing of these assumptions.

4.67 Information on stoppages is given to the Department of Employment. No distinction is drawn between strikes and lock-outs, though the latter are held to be very few in number. The coverage of the data is believed to be very good, affording a virtually complete picture of industrial disputes. Very small stoppages, that is, those involving less than ten workers and those lasting less than one day are excluded from the statistics, unless the aggregate number of working days lost exceed one hundred.[1] The figures include the workers indirectly involved, i.e. those out of work at the establishment where the dispute is taking place who are not party to the dispute. But workers laid off at establishments outside the one in which the stoppage takes place are excluded. This can lead to an understating of the costs of a strike.

4.68 In principle it would be possible to extract the strike figures for foreign firms for a large number of years, but given the sheer volume of material we settled for two years, 1963 and 1968.[2] The choice of years followed fairly naturally from three considerations. We wanted a pair of reasonably recent years; the general consensus is that these two are rather 'normal' years, apart from a special one day stoppage in 1968; being Census years the strike figures can be related to other industrial information.[3]

4.69 The choice of 1968 does, however, entail a potential problem which requires comment. On 15 May of that year there was a one-day stoppage involving 1,500,000 workers in the engineering and several related industries. This was a token stoppage in support of a claim for an all round pay increase. From the data, no foreign subsidiaries appear to have reported being involved in that dispute. As the total number of working days lost in the year was 4,690,000, the 1,500,000 days lost through this single action is very significant in the total, being thirty-two per cent. One can make a reasonable case for either keeping it in or for taking it out of the figures; where possible, we try to indicate the role of this dispute in the strike picture which emerges.

4.70 Table 4.III below shows the overall proportions of foreign firm disputes to the total, with the surprising result that the foreign subsidiaries are less subject to strikes than the domestic firms.

Table 4.III

Aggregate comparison

			Number of stoppages	*Workers involved*	*Working days lost*
1963	1.	Foreign	70	21,046	58,077
	2.	Domestic	1,998	434,154	1,938,923
	3.	Total	2,068	455,200	1,997,000
	4.	Ratio of (1) to (3)	.033	.046	.029
	5.	Ratio of foreign to total sales	.104	.104	.104
1968	6.	Foreign owned	208	75,532	454,437
	7.	Domestic	2,170	1,998,468	4,264,563
	8.	Total	2,378	2,074,000	4,719,000
	9.	Ratio of (6) to (8)	.087	.036	.096

[1] The total strike statistics, drawing no distinction between domestic and foreign, are reported and discussed annually in the May number of the *Employment and Productivity Gazette*.

[2] We are much indebted to the DE at Watford for making the annual volumes available, and the considerate help provided.

[3] At the time of writing the 1968 Census showing proportion of foreign ownership by Minimum List Headings was not available. This forced us to use the 1963 sales figures as a rough guide for 1968 as well.

While the results are much stronger for 1963 than for 1968, for both years the contribution of foreign owned firms to total stoppages, whether measured by number of stoppages, number of workers involved, or working days lost is less than their proportionate contribution to total output.[1]

4.71 Inevitably, this result calls for some qualification. Our list of foreign owned firms may not be complete.[2] Errors in extraction would be more likely to misclassify a foreign firm as domestic than the other way around. However, it is reasonable to expect that errors, if they occur, would be confined to the small firms. This means that the effect on the number of stoppages might be significant, but it would be much less on the number of workers involved and working days lost. As to row 5, the ratio of foreign to total sales, there are two reasons to regard this figure as being too high. One is that certain service and transport categories are included in the strike figures but missing from the output figures, and these are ones where foreign participation is very small or non-existent.[3] Secondly, an employment comparison, unfortunately not possible on a comparable basis, would be more appropriate and would lead to a smaller foreign proportion. For 1963 these changes could conceivably raise row 4 to the order of six per cent and lower row 5 to the order of eight per cent. This still supports the conclusion that on aggregate, the foreign owned subsidiaries are more peaceful. For 1968 we lack, at the moment, firm figures for foreign participation, but are safe in presuming that it was higher than for 1963. The foreign strike proportion is also higher for 1968, except in terms of workers involved, but still supports the conclusion that foreign subsidiaries generally are equally or more peaceful compared to domestic firms. Since this work was undertaken, David Forsyth at Strathclyde has made a comparison of industrial disputes in foreign and domestic firms in Scotland. His results, covering each year of the sixties, suggest that foreign firms are more strike prone, with the possible exception of the years 1963 and 1968! Of course, it could be that his generalization for Scotland and ours for the United Kingdom are both correct. But his result does suggest that the choice of 1963 and 1968 may be misleading. The chances of drawing two unrepresentative years out of ten are one in forty-five; nevertheless, in the light of his results it seems advisable to check a run of years for the United Kingdom. This is being done and the results should be available for journal publication.

4.72 The aggregate comparison of quantity of disputes in foreign owned and domestic firms is not the most searching one. It is well known that some industries are more strike prone than others, this persistent differential tendency to strike activity showing up in both international comparison and

[1] Removing the one day token engineering stoppage alters Table 4.III as follows:

		Workers involved	*Working days lost*
1968	(6) Foreign owned	75,532	454,437
	(7) Domestic	682,068	2,735,523
	(8) Total	757,600	3,190,000
	(9) Ratio of (6) to (8)	.10	.14

While removing the token stoppage reverses the above conclusion with respect to working days lost, there are two points to bear in mind. The main one is that the proportion of foreign to total sales in 1968 may well have risen five per cent over the five years. And secondly, of course, there is no clear reason to remove this stoppage.

[2] It is the official Department of Trade and Industry List and while no doubt the best available, it is also generally regarded as quite reliable.

[3] See note to Table 4.IV for industries where we lack figures on foreign owned proportion.

in examining a single country over time (Kerr and Segal: 1954, chapter 14, pp. 189-204, and Knowles: 1952). As foreign investment is not evenly distributed across sectors, a better comparison could be made holding the industry mix equal. The available data do not allow us to normalize for other factors such as region and firm size, but the industry factor is by far the most important one. For example, coal mining is generally very strike prone and, of course, in the United Kingdom there is no foreign investment in that industry. The procedure we have adopted to deal with this problem is, for each industry, to multiply the domestic quantity of strike activity by the ratio of foreign to domestic sales, and sum.[1] This figure can be compared to the total foreign strike activity directly, as it gives the volume of domestic strike activity, with given propensities, that would occur if the domestic sector was the same size as the foreign owned sector in each industry. The results are shown in Table 4.IV.

Table 4.IV

Disputes comparison normalized by industry

			Number of stoppages	*Workers involved*	*Working days lost*
1963	1.	Foreign owned (actual)*	55	19,905	48,855
	2.	Domestic (normalized)	162	109,494	271,357
	3.	Ratio of (1) to (2)	.36	.19	.18
1968	4.	Foreign owned (actual)*	175	97,368	385,003
	5.	Domestic (normalized)	276	420,815	821,018
	6.	Ratio of (4) to (5)	.63	.23	.47

* Rows (1) and (4) in this Table show smaller numbers than rows (1) and (6) in Table 4.III because certain industries had to be excluded from the comparison here for lack of industry breakdown on foreign and domestic proportions. The excluded industries are: construction; gas, electricity and water; railways; road passenger; road haulages; sea transport; port and inland water; other transport and communication; distributive trades; insurance, banking and finance; professional and scientific services; miscellaneous services; public administration and defence. Most of these have no foreign component and the exclusions do not bias the results.

4.73 This more appropriate comparison suggests very strongly that the foreign owned firm is less strike prone than its domestic counterpart. For both years there was less of a difference in number of stoppages compared to the other measures, but still a very marked one. In 1968 total strikes were well up over 1963, and the foreign proportion rose. But broadly put, there was in excess of twice as much strike activity in domestic firms compared to foreign owned firms, after allowing for differences in the distribution of foreign to domestic proportions across industries.

4.74 For the above comparison, in our view the critical one, we are working with thirty-three industrial categories. In fact, most industries make only insignificant contributions to the total volume of disputes, however measured. Taking only those eight or so industries making the biggest contribution in either year (usually an industry is big in both years if it is in one year), gives a very large proportion of the total. Motor vehicles and non-electrical engineering are important contributors to total strikes as are certain

[1] Where : S_{Di}; volume of strikes in domestic firms in the ith industry.
S_{Fi}; volume of strikes in foreign owned firms in the ith industry.
O_{Di}; sales of domestic firms in the ith industry.
O_{Fi}; sales of foreign owned firms in the ith industry.

We compare:

$$\sum_i \frac{O_{Fi}}{O_{Di}} \cdot S_{Di} \gtrless \sum_i S_{Fi}$$

heterogeneous categories such as 'Other manufacturing industries', 'All other metal manufacture', and 'Metal goods not elsewhere specified'. It is only in these last three categories that, on a normalized comparison, the foreign subsidiaries tend to be more strike prone than the domestic owned counterparts.

4.75 Because of the heterogeneous nature of the industries where the foreigners are more strike prone, it is difficult to generalise about them. One point can be made, however. The 'Other manufacturing industries' category includes rubber, and it is this sub-sector which accounts for all the foreign strike contribution. It is interesting to note that in this case the foreign firms are all members of the employers' association, though the strikes were in fact with individual companies.

4.76 There is some interest in comparing the magnitudes of the stoppages in foreign owned and domestic firms, as well as the aggregates and their industrial distribution. Totals, of course, may be made up of lots of little strikes, strikes involving few workers and short duration, or the opposite. This comparison is made in Table 4.V. To economise on time and effort, only proportions are given. (The absolutes are readily calculated from Tables 4.III and 4.IV.) The comparison is a little faulty on three counts. The foreign proportions are compared to the total, not the pure domestic contribution (again, to save on computation effort); there is no normalization as to the size distribution of the foreign owned compared to the domestic firms, and particularly in 1963, with the small total number of strikes in foreign firms, the categories of the distributions tend to be a little fine, which introduces some meaningless variation. None of these points appears to be of great significance.[1]

4.77 The comparison suggests that very big and very small strikes are more important in the domestic total. The foreign owned firms are more given, in these years, to medium sized disputes. To highlight some of the aspects, many more of the domestic strikes than foreign involve less than two days, under twenty-five workers, and less than two hundred and fifty man days lost. At the other end, sixty-eight per cent of the domestic workers involved in any strikes were in strikes where over fifty thousand man days were lost. This is true of less than five per cent of the 'foreign' workers. Nearly half the man days lost by domestic firms were in these big strikes, with less than a fifth for foreign owned firms. Again, for 1968, three quarters of the workers were involved in one-day disputes, with only a quarter for foreign owned firms. That did not

[1] We can readily correct part of Table 4.V for the token one-day stoppage. The duration percentages, taking out this dispute are as follows:

		Percent of workers involved—Domestic (total)	*Per cent of working days lost—Domestic (total)*
Not more than one day		28.1	5.0
1<	≤2	15.0	4.8
2<	≤3	13.3	6.9
3<	≤4	9.6	5.5
4<	≤5	6.2	5.7
5<	≤6	4.0	4.3
6<	≤12	10.2	15.7
12<	≤18	5.9	13.6
18<	≤24	3.7	11.8
24<	≤36	2.0	7.5
36<	≤60	0.5	4.2
60<		1.5	15.0

Again, this does not appear seriously to alter the conclusion in the text.

Table 4.V

Comparison by magnitude of domestic and foreign stoppages 1963

		Per cent of total number of stoppages Domestic (total)	Foreign	Per cent of number of workers involved Domestic (total)	Foreign	Per cent of total working days lost Domestic (total)	Foreign
Duration in working days							
Not more than one day		38.9	27.1	25.1	34.3	5.8	8.8
1<	≤ 2	23.0	20.0	22.1	14.4	10.0	8.8
2<	≤ 3	13.4	8.6	10.9	3.1	6.6	2.3
3<	≤ 4	7.2	12.9	9.8	8.1	7.9	7.0
4<	≤ 5	4.2	8.6	7.2	4.2	7.0	7.2
5<	≤ 6	2.7	4.3	13.2	2.4	19.5	2.4
6<	≤12	5.6	10.0	5.9	17.3	10.5	42.6
12<	≤18	1.8	2.9	0.8	1.5	2.9	3.2
18<	≤24	0.8	2.9	1.2	14.0	5.1	10.8
24<	≤36	1.7	1.4	3.4	0.1	22.5	0.9
36<	≤60	0.4	1.4	0.3	0.6	1.5	6.2
60<		0.3	0.0	0.1	0.0	0.7	0.0
Number of workers directly and indirectly involved							
Under 25	Workers	25.7	5.7	1.5	0.4	1.5	1.3
25≤	< 50	19.4	11.4	2.3	1.4	2.2	1.2
50≤	< 100	15.7	21.4	3.8	4.7	3.6	5.4
100≤	< 250	16.5	28.6	9.1	12.9	9.0	22.6
250≤	< 500	11.0	12.9	13.6	13.5	10.4	11.8
500≤	< 1,000	6.3	14.3	14.8	29.1	11.4	26.7
1,000≤	< 2,500	4.0	4.3	20.0	24.8	17.4	26.5
2,500≤	< 5,000	0.8	1.4	10.1	13.2	5.1	4.7
5,000≤	< 10,000	0.4	0.0	10.4	0.0	6.9	0.0
10,000≤		0.2	0.0	14.4	0.0	32.5	0.0
Number of working days lost							
Under 250	Days 250	64.9	44.3	12.9	9.6	5.2	6.1
250≤	< 500	11.4	20.0	10.2	20.8	4.2	8.3
500≤	< 1,000	9.8	17.1	11.7	17.8	6.9	13.8
1,000≤	< 5,000	11.7	17.1	31.1	43.0	24.8	47.6
5,000≤	< 25,000	1.8	1.4	15.9	8.9	16.6	24.1
25,000≤	< 50,000	0.3	0.0	6.2	0.0	11.8	0.0
50,000≤		0.1	0.0	12.0	0.0	30.5	0.0

Table 4.V

Comparison by magnitude of domestic and foreign stoppages

1968

		Per cent of total number of stoppages		Per cent of number of workers involved		Per cent of total working days lost	
		Domestic (total)	Foreign	Domestic (total)	Foreign	Domestic (total)	Foreign
Duration in working days							
Not more than one day		28.6	18.3	75.9	23.7	35.2	4.9
1<	≤ 2	20.5	21.2	5.0	15.9	3.3	4.5
2<	≤ 3	11.9	13.9	4.5	15.2	4.8	7.6
3<	≤ 4	8.0	8.7	3.2	8.8	3.7	6.7
4<	≤ 5	6.0	8.2	2.1	8.7	3.9	9.1
5<	≤ 6	4.3	3.4	1.3	4.9	2.9	5.0
6<	≤12	11.1	18.3	3.4	14.1	10.7	27.0
12<	≤18	4.0	2.9	2.0	2.0	9.2	3.8
18<	≤24	2.0	3.4	1.2	5.3	8.1	21.3
24<	≤36	1.7	1.9	0.7	1.6	5.1	10.2
36<	≤60	1.1	0.0	0.2	0.0	2.9	0.0
60<		0.8	0.0	0.5	0.0	10.2	0.0
Number of workers directly and indirectly involved							
Under 25	Workers	15.8	6.25	0.3	0.2	1.0	0.4
25≤	< 50	15.8	12.0	0.6	0.8	1.2	1.0
50≤	< 100	17.4	15.9	1.3	2.1	3.1	2.0
100≤	< 250	23.4	24.0	3.9	7.2	7.5	8.9
250≤	< 500	12.3	12.0	4.4	7.4	7.7	6.7
500≤	< 1,000	9.2	17.8	6.5	23.6	11.9	21.7
1,000≤	< 2,500	4.1	7.2	6.6	21.4	17.4	25.5
2,500≤	< 5,000	1.3	4.3	4.7	28.8	10.7	31.9
5,000≤	< 10,000	0.5	0.5	3.5	8.5	7.6	2.0
10,000≤		0.2	0.0	68.2	0.0	31.9	0.0
Number of working days lost							
Under 250	Days						
	25	50.4	31.7	3.9	4.7	2.6	1.5
250≤	< 500	16.2	18.3	3.4	6.6	2.9	3.1
500≤	< 1,000	13.2	16.8	5.2	12.8	4.6	5.2
1,000≤	< 5,000	15.4	21.6	9.6	27.9	15.8	19.9
5,000≤	< 25,000	4.2	10.6	9.0	42.7	21.0	45.7
25,000≤	< 50,000	0.3	0.5	0.8	1.1	5.1	7.2
50,000≤		0.3	0.5	68.1	4.3	48.0	17.4

hold for 1963, but if we compare the biggest and smallest categories, for the three by three classification, for both years, that makes thirty-six comparisons. Of these, in thirty-one the domestic component is bigger than the foreign at the extremes of size, big and small.

4.78 The difference in strike patterns between domestic and foreign firms may be related to the bargaining structures and procedures in these firms. Domestic firms tend to be involved in national bargaining for increases in basic wages and conditions of employment. As a result any stoppage will involve large numbers since all firms in the employers' association will be involved. Procedures for dealing with grievances involve a large number of stages and employees become frustrated that their grievances are not being dealt with quickly enough and unconstitutional action takes place in order to force the issue. The foreign firms, on the other hand, tend more to plant and company bargaining and have shorter and quicker procedures for negotiating a new agreement and settling grievances. This encourages a greater adherence to procedures but it must not be thought that the unconstitutional strike is not a problem to the foreign firm although it would appear less so than to the domestic firm.

4.79 The different pattern of strikes in the foreign owned firms suggests they have personnel policies and industrial relations procedures that somehow avoid a large number of small unforeseeable strikes and terminate large strikes before either too many people are involved or the stoppages go on too long. There is a body of opinion that considers the short small unplanned-for strike to be more damaging than the longer, larger, but more predictable strike in the sense that the former type of strike may result in management failing or delaying to introduce new working methods and capital machinery for the fear that employees may down tools without warning. If this argument has any validity then the different strike pattern in the domestic and foreign firms may account for some of the greater efficiency in the latter firms over the former. The foreign firm appears to be less affected by the problem of the continuous unscheduled interruption of production lines through stoppages and may therefore be less inhibited in introducing new capital investment.

4.80 Apart from industrial relations, the differences in strike magnitudes may have to do with the causes of the strikes, and it is to these that we now turn. Any student of industrial relations is familiar with the problem of determining the major cause of an industrial dispute and the possible difference between stated and actual causes. While being aware of this, it would be a mistake to go to the other extreme and regard the official classification of disputes according to causes as meaningless. The official figures use a broad, eight-way, industrial classification. For our purposes we have eliminated Mining and Quarrying which has no foreign component, and two other sectors, Shipbuilding and Marine Engineering and Transport and Communication, all of which have tiny foreign contributions to total strikes. We then divide the causes into two groups, wage and non-wage. The wage category includes claims for increases and other wage disputes. The non-wage category consists of hours, demarcation, employment or discharge, personnel questions, other working arrangements, union status and sympathetic action. It is possible that hours would be better classified with wages, but the numbers are so small as not to affect the overall result. Table 4.VI compares foreign and domestic proportions of total disputes.

4.81 Without formal significance testing, one nevertheless feels more confidence that there is no difference as to causes of disputes between domestic and foreign owned firms when we look at number of stoppages. But in terms of workers involved and man days lost, three generalizations seem well supported. In general wage disputes are quantitively more important than non-wage. This is more marked in 1968 than in 1963. And the difference is bigger in domestic firms than foreign owned firms. None of this need be too surprising. The points raised at the beginning of this section suggest a relatively greater involvement of foreign owned firms in disputes over such things as union status and working arrangements.

Table 4.VI

Comparison of causes of disputes (wage and non-wage) in foreign owned and domestic firms

		1963		1968	
		Wage	*Non-wage*	*Wage*	*Non-wag*
Number of stoppages	Domestic	47.6	52.4	52.0	48.0
	Foreign	43.5	56.5	56.8	43.2
Workers involved	Domestic	61.6	38.4	90.4	9.6
	Foreign	52.7	47.3	57.9	42.1
Man days lost	Domestic	76.0	24.0	80.6	19.4
	Foreign	53.4	46.6	68.3	31.7

4.82 With respect to the above comparison, the removal of the one day token stoppage in the engineering industries (broadly constructed), now does seriously affect the results. It will be recalled that this action was over wages. Table 4.VII sets out the relevant wage-non-wage information taking out the national one day stoppage.

Table 4.VII

Comparison of causes of disputes (wage and non-wage) in foreign owned and domestic firms, taking out the one-day (15 May 1968) national engineering stoppage

		1968	
		Wage	*Non-wage*
Workers involved	Domestic	43.5	56.5
	Foreign	57.9	42.1
Man days lost	Domestic	64.1	35.9
	Foreign	68.3	31.7

With this one strike removed there is now nothing to choose between domestic and foreign owned firms. Indeed, there is a slightly greater tendency of the domestic firms towards the non-wage dispute. More detailed examination in terms of industry mix may be revealing. But pending this one must conclude that the issue of causes sheds little light on the relative number or magnitude of domestic and foreign disputes.

4.83 To summarize the statistical findings, we conclude that foreign owned firms have fewer disputes than domestic firms, especially after allowing for differences in industry mix. There are only one or two industries where this is not true. Disputes in the foreign firms tend to be in the middle size range, without either many of the very small strikes or the very big ones. And finally, disputes in foreign subsidiaries are hard to distinguish as to cause from domestic firms. These findings relate to and are broadly consistent with, other aspects of the labour market, the industrial relations structure which is outlined in Part I, and the question of labour utilization to which we now turn.

III: Labour utilization in domestic and foreign owned firms in the electrical engineering industry

4.84 The industrial relations and strike experience of foreign owned firms can differ from those of domestically owned firms for reasons to do with foreignness as such. Several of these reasons are discussed in Parts I and II, above. In addition, it may be the case, and is often alleged to be the case, that foreign subsidiaries generally have a different labour policy compared with their domestic counterparts. The most popularly held views as to differences may be summarized as follows. The foreign firm uses relatively (a) more capital, (b) more people in the higher skill categories, (c) better qualified people in comparable categories, and (d) pays higher wages per man hour. As indicated above, this may or may not be the same thing as paying more for labour services. One rational reason for paying more for comparable labour services might be a greater reluctance on the part of the foreign owned firm to experience an industrial dispute. If the foreign firm is more efficient in the utilization of labour services it can afford to pay more for them. And a subsidiary which is a part of an integrated multi-national complex may be reluctant to interrupt production when that could harm the whole complex. However, in cases where the firm is producing duplicate, or near duplicate, items in more than one country, it may be a stronger bargainer, being able to play one union off against another. Along with these views, it is often suggested that the management of a foreign subsidiary devotes relatively more resources to labour management and utilization, employing and deploying its labour with considerably greater expertise and care.

4.85 This set of views is interesting on several counts. One of them is that collectively they are often offered as an explanation of the superior performance of the foreign owned firm. Of course, they constitute an explanation of better performance which is flattering to the subsidiary management, in contrast to some alternative explanations such as exclusive access to technical advances undertaken by the parent organization, or the exploitation of a monopoly position. Secondly, this set of views implies different behaviour in the labour market on the part of foreign owned firms which has implications for the appraisal of the impact of inward direct investment on host countries.

4.86 The purpose of this last section is to present some data which will afford us no more than a glimpse into these labour utilization propositions. A glimpse into a significant and little explored area may be better than nothing, but at the same time we should be cautious in attaching too much importance to the results. Rather the familiar rubric of treating them as suggestive must reluctantly be applied.

4.87 We are indeed fortunate that the Higher Education Research Unit at the London School of Economics has for some time been engaged in a research project on the effect of educational experience on industrial productivity, and that an unintended consequence of their remarkable effort at data collection is to provide some figures which shed light on our problem. That project, which is nearing completion, is based on unusually solid statistical information, most of it generated by the project itself. Though intended for other purposes, the detailed information generated on sixty-eight firms in the electrical engineering industry, some of whom are foreign owned, can be re-worked in an effort to get some insight into our particular concerns. Do the foreign owned firms get more output out of their labour?

Do they pay more? Do they use more skilled people? Do they use trained people in different ways? The Unit, while maintaining complete confidentiality of the data, has extended some analysis for us so that we can at least make a start on these intriguing questions. The choice of the electrical engineering industry is a particularly happy one from the point of view of direct investment. Foreign owned firms are important in it, and it is a science based industry. As such it is an important employer of highly qualified labour. Where just over one per cent of workers in British industry are qualified scientists and engineers, the proportion is two and one half times as high for this industry (Committee On Manpower Resources for Science and Technology: 1966).

4.88 A complete description of the data would extend a lengthy chapter beyond reasonable bounds (Layard: 1971). Briefly, the industry can be divided into six categories: electrical machinery (mainly for electricity generation and related activities); cables; telephone apparatus; electronics (a very heterogeneous category covering radio, radar, cathode ray tubes, computers, television transmitters and receivers and much else); domestic appliances (all the more simple electrical home equipment); other goods (obviously a catch all, but mainly 'car electrics', sparking plugs, batteries, lamps and so on). The data refer largely to 1968, the unit of analysis being the factory rather than the firm. A stratified random sample, with replacement for non-responders, was adopted for all factories employing over two hundred men. This resulted in a sample of about twelve per cent of all factories. The foreign factories are not proportionately distributed across activities within the industry, as can be seen from Table 4.VIII, which gives a cross-categorization by size, and shows the foreign and domestic contributions to the sample. The question of the comparability of domestic and foreign factories arises in other ways than the distribution across activities, and we will be turning to some of these.

Table 4.VIII

Electrical engineering factories (England and Wales, 1968)

Numbers employed		*Electrical machinery*		*Cables*		*Telephone apparatus*		*Electronics*		*Domestic appliances*		*Other goods*		*Total*	
		For.	*Dom.*	*For.*	*Dom.*	*For.*	*Dom.*	*For.*	*Dom.*	*For.*	*Dom.*	*For.*	*Dom.*	*For.*	*Dom.*
2,000 to	In sample	—	7	1	2	1	2	1	5	1	1	—	2	4	19
2,000 plus	Population	17		9		9		26		6		10		77	
1,000 to	In sample	—	2	—	1	—	—	—	7	—	—	—	1	—	11
1,999	Population	21		7		7		46		9		15		105	
500 to	In sample	—	7	—	2	—	—	1	3	1	1	1	3	3	16
999	Population	29		14		7		65		15		26		156	
200 to	In sample	—	5	—	1	—	—	1	3	1	1	1	2	3	12
499	Population	70		10		14		116		15		77		302	
TOTAL	In sample	—	21	1	6	1	2	3	18	3	3	2	8	10	58
	Population	137		40		37		253		45		128		640	

4.89 Taking no account of the fact that foreign owned and domestic factories may be making very different types of products, and in general be in rather different economic circumstances, Table 4.IX gives an overall view of the basic economic data describing the sample factories. On average, the foreign and domestic factories turn out to have broadly similar sizes of output, the foreigner having a somewhat higher value added as a proportion of output. The data lend some support for some of the views expressed above. The foreign factories have more capital per head, with the difference being in fixed rather than working capital. In fact the domestic firms appear to use relatively more working capital. We also see a higher net output per head in the foreign owned factories, and a higher labour cost per head. Total factor productivity appears to be almost identical.[1] With the figures also indicating a nearly equal rate of return on capital, the domestic and foreign owned factories give the impression of being equally efficient, with the latter using relatively smaller amounts of labour, and paying its work force relatively more. If we look just at the highly trained part of the work force, either by education, i.e. Higher National Certificate and above, etc., or by occupation, i.e. technicians and technologists, the foreign owned and the domestically owned firms appear to be paying roughly the same annual salaries. It is interesting, however, that in the same category the foreign owned factory is inclined to employ a significantly younger man. This, of course, is the same thing to the individual as being on a generally higher pay schedule, as is the case for less trained workers. The fact that the foreigners pay better, in the sense of promoting more quickly, in income terms keeps their wage bill in the higher training and occupational categories the same as for domestic factories. They may even have the advantage of having more recently, and hopefully therefore better, trained people. And maybe the trade-off between experience on the one hand and more drive, flexibility and so on is also in their favour. At the lower levels of the employment structure they simply pay more. As yet we cannot say whether this higher pay has to do with hiring a different kind of workforce, or paying more for the same man. The sales of the foreign factories are growing faster than those of domestic factories, with the numbers employed in each growing equally quickly.

Table 4.IX

Basic economic data on sample factories

(Thousands of pounds—Means)	*Domestic*	*Foreign*
Gross output	6,648	6,324
Net output	2,714	2,912
Numbers employed	2,074	1,640
Labour cost	2,003	1,943
Total capital	4,795	5,929
Fixed capital	2,642	4,301
Working capital	2,153	1,629
Total capital per head	2.37	3.48
Fixed capital per head	1.34	2.32
Net output per head	1.43	1.86
Labour cost per head	0.98	1.12
(Pure numbers)		
Total factor productivity	1.11	1.12
Rate of return on capital	0.20	0.21
Growth of sales	1.06	1.15
Growth of numbers employed	1.03	1.03
(Pounds)		
Mean salary of Higher National Certificate employees and above	1,682	1,646
Mean salary of Ordinary National Certificate employees and above	1,510	1,516
Mean salary of technologists	1,841	1,854
Mean salary of technicians and above	1,522	1,581
(Years)		
Mean age of HNC and above	38	34
Mean age of ONC and above	37	34
Mean age of technologists	40	38
Mean age of technicians and above	37	37

[1] This is value of output per unit cost. Labour cost is the wage, and capital cost was calculated by amortizing machinery at 12.5 per cent over ten years, and buildings and land at 10.0 per cent in perpetuity. Clearly this method can introduce a bias in evaluating the domestic and foreign capital input though we have no *a priori* reason to assume it goes one way or the other due to systematic differences in capital structure.

4.90 So, as is indicated above, the general picture to emerge is one that lends some support to many of the widely held views, namely, that the foreigners go in for a more expensive labour force and a more capital intensive operation. These greater costs, compared to domestically owned operations, are offset by higher productivity. What these figures seem to reject is the view sometimes put forward by managers of foreign owned firms themselves that they achieve higher labour productivity *solely* through better labour utilization and not through a larger capital input.

4.91 On all these conclusions a warning must be emphasized on the question of the comparability of the domestic and foreign owned factories. Take the question of the larger capital input per man and per unit output on the part of foreign owned factories. It could be that this reflects, more than anything else, a difference in the mix of type of product, or line of activity, and that the domestic factory is like the foreign owned one when they are doing the same things, but in our sample of factories there is a significant difference on average, in what they are doing. The heterogeneity of the industry is, after all, very great. Some of the products are very new, others have long histories. The industry ranges from mass production to large once-off jobs. It produces simple, and complex, capital goods, as well as simple and complex, consumer goods.

4.92 Table 4.X gives a further breakdown of some of the information contained in Table 4.IX on the basis of whether the factory is producing newer or older products, taking 1955 as the cut-off year. This is the most practical breakdown for the sake of checking on general economic comparability, and it does yield some interesting extra information. While the general impression from the above material is confirmed, we note that the foreigners have a markedly higher total factor productivity and rate of return on capital when it comes to the newer products, and the position is reversed with the older ones. Also, the domestic factories are smaller than the foreign owned factories when it comes to the older products, the situation being reversed on the newer ones. On the basis of these numbers, however, one would not be wise to infer decreasing returns to scale. What holds up nicely under this breakdown is the higher net output per head of the foreign owned factories along with a greater input of fixed capital.

Table 4.X

Age of product, pre- and post-1955 breakdown

(*Units as in Table 4.IX*)

	Pre- 1955		*Post-* 1955	
	Domestic	*Foreign*	*Domestic*	*Foreign*
Net output	2,559	3,813	4,103	809
Net output per head	1.44	1.67	1.25	2.28
Capital per head	2.20	3.49	2.07	3.46
Fixed capital per head	1.43	2.59	1.10	1.69
Total factor productivity	1.10	1.10	1.06	1.56
Rate of return on capital	0.21	0.14	0.18	0.36

4.93 Without dwelling too long on the point we should mention again the problem of intrafirm pricing in these, and indeed other comparisons, and even with perfectly accurate pricing, the foreign owned subsidiary is more likely to be a specialist link in an integrated production process than the domestic factory. One might, for this reason, want to compare foreign multi-nationals to domestic multi-nationals. But again, this would be a comparison of parent operations to subsidiary operations. The key point is, of course, that without more theory, no particular comparison is the right one and the interpretation of any observed difference is very open ended. At best, some new and possibly suggestive information is made available, and some popular myths, rather than theories, are exposed to a limited range of data.

4.94 It is still interesting and significant in appraising the effect on host countries of inward direct investment, and especially the industrial relations aspect, to enquire if the foreign owned subsidiary uses a more highly educated workforce. The Higher Education Unit data enables us to examine this question only at the top end of the training scale. The figures are grouped in terms of four education categories. First come Graduates with university training. The next is called Professional, which consists of training as an engineer. And then comes Higher National Certificate and Ordinary National Certificate. Table 4.XI gives the broad picture, without taking account of how these trained workers are used, or how the aggregate are affected by the industry mix in the foreign owned or the domestic sectors.

Table 4.XI

Proportion of educated employees in the total electrical engineering workforce

	Domestic	*Foreign owned*
Graduates	1.26	0.67
Professional	0.99	0.93
Higher National Certificate	2.13	2.84
Ordinary National Certificate	2.03	2.05
Professional and above	2.25	1.60
HNC and above	4.33	4.44
ONC and above	6.41	6.49

4.95 Overall, the proportion of educated employees in the total electrical engineering workforce is remarkably similar, 6.4 as against 6.5 per cent in the domestic compared to the foreign owned factories. The overall equality masks the tendency for the foreigners to use fewer Graduates and more Higher National Certificate trained employees, with very close similarity, domestic and foreign, in the other two categories. There is a suggestion in these numbers that the foreign owned subsidiary gets some of its required input of knowledge from being a member of the international network as such, without embodying that input in labour in the subsidiary factory. But below the highest two levels, it uses correspondingly more people who have the Higher National Certificate. Taken together, the figures certainly question rather strongly the view that foreign owned firms employ a markedly better educated workforce.

4.96 This last conclusion rests very critically, of course, on the comparability in terms of activity, or product mix, of the foreign owned and domestic factories. Ideally one might want to compare product and process, only grouping closely similar enterprises. Even here there would remain the problem of the efficiency factor in multi-product factories. But given the small number of foreign firms it does not pay to do a very detailed breakdown. Most of the cells would be empty, and one would really be asking about the performance of individual factories rather than about the characteristics of foreigners generally. It is, however, of some interest to try a two way split into Heavy and Electronic as against the rest, the former tending to represent the more technically advanced sectors of the electrical engineering industry.

Table 4.XII

Proportions of educated employees

	Heavy and electronic		*Other*	
	Domestic (27)	*Foreign* (4)	*Domestic* (23)	*Foreign* (6)
Graduate	1.89	1.17	0.49	0.34
Professional	1.36	1.10	0.56	0.82
HNC	2.87	3.02	1.26	2.72
ONC	2.77	2.58	1.22	1.44
Prof. plus	3.25	2.27	1.05	1.16
HNC plus	6.12	5.29	2.31	3.88
ONC plus	8.89	7.87	3.53	5.32

4.97 The main conclusions with respect to use of highly educated labour hold up under the normalization set out in Table 4.XII. In addition, we see, as might be expected, that both domestic and foreign owned factories employ more educated people in the more complex and advanced activities. What appears also to be the case, and certainly is in line with widely held views, is that the foreigners use a significantly more educated input, comparatively, into what are presumably the more prosaic activities. Some further check on this possibility may be made by regrouping the above figures along product lines.

Table 4.XIII

Proportion of educated employees by product groups

	Machinery and cables		*Telephone and electronics*		*Domestic appliances and other*	
	Domestic	*Foreign*	*Domestic*	*Foreign*	*Domestic*	*Foreign*
Graduate	0.84	0.70	2.13	0.36	0.56	0.36
Professional	1.10	0.68	1.14	0.89	0.57	1.05
HNC	2.05	1.55	2.83	2.71	1.57	3.32
ONC	2.15	1.50	2.58	2.50	1.09	1.26
Prof. plus	1.94	1.38	3.45	1.80	1.13	1.41
HNC plus	3.99	2.93	6.28	4.51	2.70	4.73
ONC plus	6.14	4.43	8.86	7.01	3.79	5.99

4.98 Table 4.XIII gives interesting support to the possibility that the domestic firm is less aware than the foreign subsidiary of the potential use and economic benefit of employing educated labour in what might be termed ordinary economic activity, as against the obvious need to employ such people in the technically more advanced and more rapidly advancing sectors. Where it is possible, rather than optimal, to make a product in a more traditional way using a less skilled input, the domestic firm may be inclined to do so. The data are consistent with the view that the foreign owned subsidiary is more alert to opportunities for employing more educated labour. This leads naturally to our final topic, namely how, or in what jobs, the more educated workers are being used. Before going on to this question we should note that taken together Tables 4.XI, 4.XII and 4.XIII suggest that overall, and in some detail, the differences between the domestic and the foreign owned factories on the score of proportion of educated input are not very great, if we look at work places themselves. Unfortunately, our information is restricted to the very upper end of the education scale.

4.99 The remaining tables are intended to provide information on two points; how the foreign and domestic factories deploy educated labour in different activities, namely research and design, production, and sales, and what is the comparative education input into broad occupational categories. The collection of data bearing on these questions involved considerable discretion and on the spot judgement on the part of individual researchers.

Using rather broad categories avoids some of the problem and does afford an indication of broad tendencies. The general criteria applied were that if a job involved the skills and knowledge typical of a pass degree in science or engineering, or passing the examinations for the main professional institutions, it was classified as a 'technologist' occupation. At a lower level, if the job involved substantial scientific or engineering knowledge, at least of the 'A' level or ONC curricula, but not as high as the technologist requirements, then it was classified as a 'technician' occupation.

4.100 Table 4.XIV shows the education input into the occupational categories of technologists, technicians, and management. The figures show some tendency for the foreign owned factories to employ roughly ten per cent more formally qualified people in the technologist and technician categories than the domestic factories. This difference does not emerge at the Graduate and Professional levels, but at the National Certificate levels. It is an interesting finding, in line with the view of a number of observers that British industry tends to play down the importance of education below the university level. A similar tendency can be seen in the figures with respect to management, that is, slightly smaller proportions in the foreign factories at the upper levels offset by a larger proportion at the Higher National Certificate level. But this is slight. What is striking with respect to management is the very equal education input in the domestic and foreign factories. This challenges the myth that management in foreign subsidiaries is better educated, and again raises the point that the knowledge input into the subsidiary of a foreign parent company need not all be embodied in men on the spot.

Table 4.XIV

Educational input into selected occupations: proportions of people with given qualification

	Technologists		*Technicians*		*Management*	
	Domestic	*Foreign*	*Domestic*	*Foreign*	*Domestic*	*Foreign*
Graduates	22.3	22.6	2.1	2.1	15.3	12.4
Professional	21.6	18.8	4.9	5.7	13.1	11.9
HNC	24.7	31.8	20.4	22.1	18.4	26.2
ONC	9.9	14.5	22.8	26.2	8.9	5.6
Prof. plus	43.9	41.4	7.0	7.8	28.4	24.3
HNC plus	68.6	73.2	27.4	29.9	46.8	50.5
ONC plus	78.5	87.7	50.2	56.1	55.7	56.1

4.101 Our final table takes up the question of where the highly educated labour is being used. It is often emphasized that British industry would benefit from greater use of more qualified people in the less obvious areas, such as sales. This raises the question of whether the existing qualified workforce is optimally deployed, as against the need for greater numbers of educated employees. The present chapter, of course, cannot contribute in that area, being only concerned with practices in foreign owned and domestic owned factories.

Table 4.XV

Proportion of educated employees by activities

		Research and design	*Production*	*Sales*
Machinery and cables	Domestic	3.05	1.30	1.52
	Foreign	0.89	1.43	0.82
Telephone and electronics	Domestic	5.22	2.03	0.71
	Foreign	2.23	4.65	1.32
Domestic and other	Domestic	1.56	1.46	0.56
	Foreign	2.76	3.13	0.57

4.102 Clearly the comparison in Table 4.XV would be meaningless without an industry, or product, breakdown. Even so, the usual caveat of significant product differences across firms within a category applies strongly here. More interestingly, the comparison with respect to research and sales calls for particular comment. For both of these activities are likely to be very different for a link in a multi-national complex compared to a more self-contained business unit. This is probably why, for both of these activities, the foreign proportions are strikingly low. Once again, the point that the foreigners do not employ more educated people in sales in this country is being made. The production comparison is probably the most meaningful. It supports the finding discussed earlier of greater use of knowledge in more prosaic activities.

IV: Summary and conclusions

4.103 The impact of the inward investing foreign firm on the host country economy may have important components due to indirect, or spill-over effects. We examine here one locale of such effects, namely the labour market in the United Kingdom. The emphasis is on United States direct investment because it is quantitatively large and because industrial relations practices in that country differ more from British practices than do those of most European countries. This chapter undertakes a three-pronged attack on the topic by looking at foreign subsidiary industrial relations as such, labour disputes in foreign subsidiaries, and labour utilisation in foreign firms in the electrical engineering industry taken as a case study. This work is at an early stage, and while some effort will be made here briefly to draw the threads together, we will also indicate gaps in understanding and further areas for investigation.

4.104 On the issue of union recognition by employers, our investigation suggests that though there are foreign subsidiaries who display a markedly anti-union policy, such an attitude is no more characteristic of foreign firms generally than domestic firms generally. However, there is a difference in the two situations. When the foreign firm comes here, backed by a powerful parent company organisation, it is not like a domestic company starting from scratch. And the balance of power could well be such as to make organisation of the workers and subsequent recognition more difficult to achieve. This suggests a possible need for legislation. Some of this need may be met by the Industrial Relations Act of 1971, which sets out a procedure whereby registered trade unions can obtain bargaining rights. No special account is taken of the special power position of the foreign subsidiary.

4.105 The main innovation stimulated by foreign subsidiaries here is productivity bargaining. This practice, and other considerations, raise the general issue of the impact of foreign firms on wage movements in this country. In the case of duplicates where the foreigner is capable of producing in many countries, the subsidiary could be a tougher bargainer than its domestic counterpart. Conversely, where the subsidiary is a link in an integrated international production complex, it might be especially unwilling to risk a strike that could damage the whole complex. So we have reasons to expect departures in both directions. As to the spread of productivity agreements, the inflationary danger is that parity considerations could force wage increases without the full accompanying changes in output per man taking place. Earlier work suggesting that the foreign firm, while often paying higher wages, has not been an important stimulus to domestic firms paying more, tends to be questioned by some recent unpublished work. At this stage we can only point to this interesting question in the transmission of inflation without providing any answer.

4.106 There is a clear indication in our work that the foreign subsidiary is an innovator here in industrial relations in ways that can lead to greater flexibility and higher productivity. Casual evidence would suggest that the general extent of such an impact through spill-over has not been large. However, it remains an important possibility for the future. In the short run, concern with general legislation on industrial relations is likely to take precedence.

4.107 We have pointed out in the text a number of responses on the part of trade unions to the multi-national firm. At the moment the emphasis seems to be on better exchange of information. There is, however, some discussion of the question of international parity. Apart from the practical difficulties of implementing this policy, it should be noted that it receives its major support from high wage areas. This is natural, of course, as the burden of such a policy is likely to fall on the lower wage areas and keep capital in the areas where productivity and wages are currently higher.

4.108 An interesting finding in this part of our study is that foreign subsidiaries do not appear to suffer more labour disputes than domestic firms, particularly on the basis of a comparison normalised by industry mix. There are *a priori* reasons to expect more strikes in foreign firms, and the opposite outcome is probably due to a combination of factors. Among them may be more and better management input into personnel problems, a high wage and high productivity policy, less willingness to risk strikes, and in some cases a stronger and more successful anti-union policy. Perhaps the most important factor is less use of industry wide bargaining.

4.109 Claims that foreign management achieve higher productivity solely through better utilisation of labour are not supported in our data, which on the contrary suggest larger fixed capital inputs as playing a significant role. Nor do the figures suggest that the foreign subsidiaries employ a significantly better educated workforce, at least at the upper end of the skill scale. Two points immediately suggest themselves. One is that differences in the quality of labour need not necessarily be readily measurable in terms of formal qualifications. The other is that the knowledge input of a multi-national company in host country production need not be entirely embodied in the workforce in the host country.

4.110 Our work suggests that inward investment in the United Kingdom has a tendency to bring the source country (which is primarily the United States) industrial relations practices with it. The foreign firms have been, on the whole, cautious with respect to introducing change and flexible with respect to adjusting to British conditions. Some subsidiary firms have enviable records in their dealings with British trade unions while refusing to recognise unions in the United States. Apparently this caution and flexibility has been rewarded. While organised American workers are markedly more strike prone than their British counterparts, foreign subsidiaries here are less troubled by disputes than domestic firms. This is not to suggest the absence of problems, and in particular there remains the issue of the balance of power between labour and management which is raised by the multi-national firm.

5. Monopoly power and the inward investing firm

5.1 The operations of multi-national firms raise a serious question of monopoly power for host countries. The purpose of this chapter is to examine some of the implications following from the nature of this type of competition. The economics of inward direct investment cannot be based on the theory of perfectly competitive markets because the assumptions of this theory are violated by the size and market share of many foreign owned subsidiaries, and the implications of this theory are in important respects not consistent with the evidence. For example, under the assumptions of perfect competition, a country either receives or sends out direct investment capital, but not both. Capital migrates in order to take advantage of differing rates of return in different countries, and in equilibrium the flows exclusively into or out of a single country have the effect of equating returns everywhere. But for the United Kingdom, direct investment is characterized by 'cross-freighting'; the in and out flows are simultaneously substantial. In his recent book, *American Business Abroad*, Professor Kindleberger states flatly, 'Direct investment belongs to the theory of monopolistic competition' (Kindleberger: 1969). While most investigators of direct investment would agree with this statement, the question of whether on balance the multi-national firm widens or restricts competition is much more problematical.[1]

5.2 To form a judgement in this area it clearly is not enough simply to document the role of giant firms in total direct investment. While the present chapter will go some way towards doing that limited task, the central analytical point is that competition in the United Kingdom is not perfect in the absence of the foreign owned firms. American, European and other large foreign subsidiaries may be operating in British markets which would be even more monopolistic in their absence. An over simplified dichotomy of more or less leaves out of account such questions as whether one is referring to product or factor markets, whether one is referring to the short or the long run, and other dimensions of the problem, which are hard to evaluate. Our present preliminary point is that the typically large scale of the multi-national firm is consistent with both favourable and unfavourable effects on competition in the host country.

5.3 Professor Dunning's pamphlet, *The Role of American Investment in the British Economy*, affords a brief and relatively up-to-date picture of the United States' contribution to the inward stock and flow of foreign capital (Dunning: 1969). In it he discusses six problems, or potential drawbacks, of direct investment. These have to do with such issues as effects on technology here, conflicts between subsidiaries and national economic and political policies, tax avoidance, export restriction and so on. Though he does not list monopoly power as a problem as such, this aspect is implied and involved in

[1] Professor Kindleberger's judgement is a favourable one. '. . . its main impact is in widening the area of competition'. *Ibid.*, p. 32. Not surprisingly, journalists have tended towards the opposite conclusion, e.g. Williams: 1962, Macmillan and Harris: 1968 and Servan-Schreiber: 1968.

the other problems. Indeed, this is almost bound to be the case. Under perfect competition the other problems would not arise. Traditionally, economists place little emphasis on questions of ownership, or who controls a particular productive unit. The theory of profit maximization calls for the same behaviour regardless of who is the owner, so it is of little interest. The monopolist behaves differently from the perfect competitor, but not because he is foreign rather than domestic. However, staying within the traditional framework, the profit maximizing foreign monopolist may behave differently in the host country compared to a domestic firm because being a unit in a multi-national company alters the constraints. We will devote some attention to the traditional monopoly problems, higher price, smaller output, unexploited economies of scale, monopsonist buying behaviour, in the setting of the multi-national constraints. It is particularly important to do so because the benefits of inward investment to the host country depend on not all the extra efficiency being captured by the foreigner.[1] Some must be competed away. But it is also important that we step outside the traditional framework. We will also devote attention to the neo-technology monopoly problems.

5.4 Generally, exporting is an alternative to investing abroad. Which is more profitable depends on tariffs, transport costs, taxes, factor costs, advantages of proximity and so on. In appraising the significance for competitiveness of direct investment, we must assume that the alternative, in most cases, is imports, and not that the product does not arrive at all. This leads us to direct special attention to the role of tariffs and the effects of monopoly on factor markets.

5.5 Professor Vernon, and others, emphasise the role of innovation and uncertainty in the explanation of direct investment (Vernon: 1966). An important part of the explanation of why firms invest abroad, why the firm becomes multi-national, is related to monopoly. Large firms can support more extensive research programmes in America, and the benefits of the research can be applied from a commanding market position. If a new product succeeds, sales may begin abroad. As exports expand, the innovator feels sufficiently confident to undertake investment in sales, and perhaps light assembly, in foreign countries. As sales expand further, more and more production is undertaken abroad. Note that the shift to production abroad does not result from changed cost conditions. Indeed, if it was profitable to produce abroad in the end, so it was in the beginning. But was the market there, and what were the cost conditions? The role of uncertainty is a critical justification of this process of feeling one's way along. It also means that the direct investor begins in a position of some monopoly power at home and arrives in a monopolistic position abroad. Some investment more clearly seems to be of this kind. Considerable empirical investigation, so far largely favourable to the view, is in progress (for a recent example see Wells: 1969). It suggests the importance to the direct investment phenomenon of a continually maintained monopoly position which is achieved in part by a continually advancing research and development programme.

5.6 There are other theories of direct investment which depart from the traditional arguments in terms of rates of return on capital. One is the view that managerial spare capacity is itself a key factor in firm growth. Growth of output is one dimension, along with growth of plant, number of employees,

[1] Aspects of this proposition are discussed at several points in the Watkins Report. See in particular the section 'Diffusion of Net Benefits', *Foreign Ownership and the Structure of Canadian Industry*, Report of the Task Force on the structure of Canadian Industry, Privy Council Office, Ottawa, January 1968, pp. 65-109.

and similar indices of scope of control. Where the firm cannot expand at home because of market saturation or anti-monopoly legislation, expansion abroad is a possibility. Professor Penrose, for example, has emphasised this role of managerial capacity (Penrose: 1956). What should be clear by now is a fair presumption in the direction of the importance of monopoly power in the direct investment phenomenon.

5.7 Of course, even if the multi-national firm is a monopolistic firm, it does not follow that such firms have an adverse effect on competitiveness in the host country, as we mention above. An incoming giant may add to the number of competitors, even bringing about some competition where there was little before. A policy of growth through acquisition may have the opposite effect. We agree completely with Professor Kindleberger that generalisations on the level of new establishment vs. take-over, manufacturing vs. distribution, and other simple tests, will not help us to distinguish helpful from harmful direct investment. 'Direct investment is, then, a subject in which it is necessary to judge case by case' (Kindleberger: 1969, p. 36). But what, we might ask, are the criteria? Would reasonable men tend to agree that a particular investment proposal was good or bad for competitiveness in the host country? We hope to make some progress with these questions.

5.8 A salient feature in examining the monopoly effects on the United Kingdom economy is its points of resemblance to the American economy. From the point of view of concentration the two countries are similar in outline. 'The United Kingdom evidences a tendency toward approximately the same (as the United States) or a slightly lesser degree of concentration of control of industries by a few large firms' (Bain: 1966). This view of Professor Bain is supported by a range of interesting comparative material across countries. It tends generally to suggest greater similarity of the United Kingdom and the United States than is true of the other countries he examined. (The drive of many countries towards greater industrialization and towards higher income per capita suggests that the current effects of direct investment on the British economy may apply more broadly to other countries over the coming years.)

The importance of company size in direct investment

5.9 In this section we hope to document the role of large firms and industrial concentration in the growth of direct investment. The first question is which of the foreign firms are doing the direct investing. Do the largest firms in foreign countries tend to establish subsidiaries here? The answer to this question is yes. That is not to say that the medium size, and even smaller firms in some cases, are not also engaged in foreign direct investment. But the large firms definitely are. Professor Vernon notes that, 'The number of companies involved in the overseas movement has proliferated. International direct investment is no longer the special preserve of a small number of very large US enterprises' (Vernon: 1968). He goes on to note the difficulty, from the point of view of statistical sources, of tracing trends over time. Elsewhere he observes that, '. . . nearly half of *Fortune's* 500 largest US companies today have extensive overseas investments' (Vernon: 1967). The definition of 'extensive' is not given, but presumably it is framed from the point of view of the parent company.

5.10 Looked at from the United Kingdom point of view, the evidence tha the largest United States companies typically engaged in investment here is overwhelming. Of the 500 largest industrial corporations and the 50 largest merchandising firms, both ranked by sales, 302 have some overseas interest in this country, though not necessarily a controlling interest (*The Fortune Directory:* 1968). This amounts to 59 per cent of the industrial firms and 12 per cent of the merchandising firms (*Who Owns Whom:* 1968). These figures, and others following, are intended to apply to the year 1967, and in spite of referring to a phenomena undergoing rapid change, should be broadly accurate for the present. Much economic activity is also undertaken here by the 50 largest American banks, transportation and life insurance companies. These are omitted from this compilation because of the difficulty of obtaining relevant information on a basis comparable to the industrial and merchandising firms.

5.11 While 302 of the largest 550 United States merchandising and industrial firms have an interest in one or more United Kingdom located firms, not all of the 302 enjoy a parent-subsidiary relationship or have a controlling interest, though most of them do. A few simply have a portfolio interest, such as Hart, Schaffner and Marx holding some shares in the Austin Reed Group Ltd. In some cases a minority interest, even a small minority interest, may be accompanied with licensing and other technical arrangements which could involve control over some aspects of the British firm's activity. For example, United Glass Ltd. has some technical arrangements with Owen-Illinois Inc. involving, among other things, a small amount of exchange of personnel. The American firm has some portfolio interest, but the British firm is not a subsidiary or an example of foreign control. At the other extreme, Esso Petroleum Co. Ltd. is a wholly owned subsidiary of The Standard Oil Co. (New Jersey), yet it would be a mistake to think of the channels of control as a simple one-way flow from the States to here. Links in an international complex exert their influence on the complex as well. Alternatively, subsidiaries of United States companies, such as F. W. Woolworth & Co. Ltd., may in turn have overseas sub-subsidiaries, such as that company's holdings in Barbados, Jamaica, Trinidad and Tobago, and Rhodesia. In some instances this type of formal arrangement may involve direct control of the sub-subsidiary by the American parent, and in other cases the control may lie with the British firm. There are also simple parent-subsidiary links in which the subsidiary is left entirely alone and is virtually autonomous, though this is less common today than in earlier periods. These examples are mentioned here for illustrative purposes in order to indicate the variety and complexity of questions of control.[1]

5.12 The most difficult problem in counting the number of large foreign firms with direct investment here is not the question of minority interest, but the question of whether they are actually engaged in production or services in this country. For example, airlines maintain ticket offices here, but one would not want to count that as a direct investment. Some American firms maintain a 'paper' company here simply to insure no one uses their name. Others maintain an importing office which receives orders and does book-keeping. But when they engage substantial numbers of salesmen, or engage in warehousing and perhaps packaging, it begins to look like a direct investment. There is an element of judgement involved in deciding when the degree of merchandising and product modification constitutes a direct investment in the sense of significant economic activity undertaken abroad.

5.13 Bearing in mind all the problems of interpretation surrounding the concepts of control and of significant foreign activity, a more careful check

[1] See Chapter Seven.

of the largest 550 United States industrial and merchandising firms reveals that 263 have ownership interest in one or more British firms. This is made up of 6 merchandising and 257 industrial, which is 12 per cent and 51 per cent respectively. We will be looking at the larger European and other foreign non-American firms, but for the present it is clear that a very significant number of United States giant corporations engage in direct investment in this country.

5.14 It is also the case that the British subsidiaries of the largest American firms are in turn large firms among our subsidiaries. Confidentiality of returns to the United Kingdom Government precludes identifying these firms by name. However, 300 foreign interest companies, excluding oil, had profits of more than £100,000 or losses of more than £500,000 in the year 1966[1]. Of these 300 firms, 140 are owned by the largest American firms. This rough and indirect indication that 47 per cent of the largest British foreign owned subsidiaries are owned by one of the largest American firms is probably broadly correct. Apart from the mismatching of years and the inappropriateness and mismatching of size criteria, there also is the problem that most United States parent firms have more than one subsidiary here.[2] In some cases one of the subsidiaries is a holding company for all the others, reducing the problem, but not in all cases. So the total size of all the subsidiaries of a single American parent might place that group, as a group, among the largest foreign owned British subsidiaries, while no one of them qualifies on its own. In spite of these considerations, it is still a well supported generalization that the British subsidiaries of the largest American parents are generally large firms compared to other foreign subsidiaries here.

5.15 Probably more interesting is to compare these American owned subsidiaries to British firms generally. Here we find that 45 of them are among the 500 largest United Kingdom firms (*The Times* 500: 1968). The accounting year varies company by company, but the ranking, by tangible assets less current liabilities and sundry provisions, centres on the year 1967. *The Times* list includes merchandising along with industrial companies. A frequency distribution can be expressed as follows:

Table 5.I

Company rank in United Kingdom	*No. of subsidiaries with large US parent*	*No. of subsidiaries with large non-US parent*	*Total*
1-100	8	3	11
101-200	8	3	11
201-300	13	4	17
301-400	7	3	10
401-500	9	0	9
	45	13	58

Source: *The Fortune Directory* and *The Times 500, op. cit.*

[1] Figures based on the Board of Trade Annual Inquiry into Inward Investment.

[2] A frequency distribution according to number of subsidiaries of the large US parents can be seen as follows:

No. of subsidiaries	*No. of parents*
1	75
2–3	81
4–7	56
8–15	27
15+	18

Source: *Fortune Directory* and *Who Owns Whom, op. cit.*

The spread of numbers of subsidiaries is quite even, with some clustering in the 201-300 range. Of course there are other non-American foreign owned firms among the largest British 500. They also are evenly distributed, but not represented in the lowest, 401-500, range.

5.16 One way of looking at the overall importance of large companies, from the United States side, is in terms of numbers of firms in given categories. Additional insight can be gained by examining net asset figures. Unfortunately, official figures do not readily allow a calculation of the proportion of foreign assets in the United Kingdom which are owned by large parents. But a crude approximation suggests strongly that they are of the order of 75 per cent.

5.17 With respect to the non-American large firms, there is a problem of coverage. One could, in principle, cull over the largest firms in each country, as we have done with the States. That would imply a relative approach, treating the largest in every country as comparable. It would give an answer to a slightly different question than the present one: do the larger firms in other countries invest here, larger defined in terms of relative size in each country. Our present interest is in the larger firms abroad taking the world as the unit. For this purpose we have again used *Fortune* magazine for, 'The 200 Largest Industrials Outside the US.' (15 Sept., 1968, pp. 130-136). Of these 200, fifty-three are British firms. We find a significant proportion of the remainder, as with the Americans, 38 out of 147, have subsidiaries here. And of the 38 companies, 19 are among the largest 300 United Kingdom based foreign owned companies, and 13 are among the largest 500 United Kingdom companies.[1]

Table 5.II

	United States		*Non-United States*		*Total*		
	Excluding oil	*Including oil*	*Excluding oil*	*Including oil*	*Excluding oil*	*Including oil*	
1. Large foreign firms, number of, i.e., our sample	522	550	134	147	656	697	(1)
2. Number among (1) with one or more subsidiary here	244	263	34	38	278	301	(2)
3. Ratio of (2) to (1)	46.7	47.8	25.4	25.9	42.4	43.2	(3)
4. Number of (2) among 300 largest UK located foreign owned subsidiaries (excluding oil)	140	—	19	—	159	—	(4)
5. Ratio of (3) to (2)	57.3	—	55.9	—	57.1	—	(5)
6. Number of (2) among largest 500 UK companies	40	44	11	13	51	57	(6)
7. Ratio of (6) to (2)	16.4	16.7	32.4	34.2	18.3	18.9	(7)

Source: See pages 4 to 5 above. Figures refer, where possible, to 1967.

5.18 This section, of necessity, presents a great deal of somewhat tedious and hard to digest material. The table above summarises the main results. It is broken down for United States, non-United States, the total, and excluding oil. It should be emphasised that the topic at the moment is not how important is foreign direct investment in the United Kingdom, but how important are larger firms, and firms owned by large firms, in that investment.[2]

[1] The method and sources for these figures is exactly as was described for the United States contribution, drawing now on the *Continental Who Owns Whom.*

[2] For a discussion of the role of giant companies in direct investment generally see Hymer, S. and Rowthorn, R., 'Multinational Corporations and International Oligopoly: The Non-American Challenge', in *The International Corporation*, edited by C. P. Kindleberger, MIT Press, Cambridge, 1970.

There is some reason to regard the table as conservative with respect to the point it is making. For one thing, some of the largest non-American located firms are themselves American owned, reducing the relevant sample. (There are, of course, some large United States located firms owned by non-American firms). Errors will result in overlooking large foreign interests. Foreign influence may be diffuse, i.e., several individual subsidiaries may add up to a large UK interest, and foreign influence may be disguised. And the total asset figures may include some substantial portfolio investment. Nevertheless, the role of bigness emerges clearly. We must now turn to the significance of direct investment in particular United Kingdom industries.

Concentration and foreign direct investment

5.19 We have considered the role of large firms, and firms owned by large firms, in inward direct investment. The next step is to attempt an assessment of the impact, or the significance of, the foreign owned firm in individual sectors. Is this investment more or less evenly distributed across the economy? Does it figure predominantly in particular sectors? And what is its role in the especially concentrated British sectors? In this section we shall try to illuminate these questions, insofar as our data will allow it.

5.20 Basing our information largely on the 1963 Census, and abstracting from those manufacturing industries for which information is not available, we find that foreign owned firms accounted for 6.8 per cent of employment, 9.1 per cent of sales, and 12.6 per cent of capital expenditure. (The industries covered employed 7.9 million workers.) Using the employment criteria to measure proportion of foreign involvement, we have a high of 36.1 per cent in pharmaceutical and toilet preparations and a low of 0.4 per cent in ship-building and marine engineering.[1] A frequency distribution can be drawn as follows:

Table 5.III

Number of industry groupings, out of twenty-three, where foreign proportion is of indicated amounts, on three criteria

Per cent	*Employment*	*Sales*	*Capital expenditure*
0 + 2.0	6	4	3
2.0 + 7.0	6	6	5
7.0 + 15.0	6	5	6
15.0 + 25.0	4	6	4
25.0 + 35.0	0	1	3
35.0 +	1	1	2

The sectors in which, on either sales or employment criteria, over 20 per cent of the activity is foreign are: (capital expenditure for one year can vary too much to use this criteria).

Table 5.IV

	Emp. 000's	*Sales £m.*
Pharmaceutical and toilet preparation	26.8	123.5
Rubber	27.3	107.6
Coke, ovens, mineral oil refining, greases etc	6.0	178.7
Motor vehicles, other vehicles, cycles	11.6	649.4
Scientific instruments and watches	24.8	63.6
Insulated wires and telephone apparatus	34.0	85.4
Total	230.5	1,208.2

[1] Using a much finer breakdown of industries in work described below, we find many industries with no foreign participation.

These sectors account for 3 per cent of the employment and 48 per cent of the sales of the foreign owned component. So it is fair to say that a very substantial proportion of foreign direct investment is in sectors where that component collectively plays a significant role.

5.21 It is interesting to comment on the degree of concentration in these six industry groups. We have figures, again specially provided by the 1963 Census for 1958 and 1963, on the proportion of sales accruing to the top five firms in each of 275 manufacturing sectors. These are at three digit SIC classification or more, i.e. much more detailed than the groupings above. However, broadly speaking, it is clear from the figures that most of the activity of the six broad groups would fall among the top fifth of most concentrated British industry. These are rough indications that where inward investment is larger in proportion, the degree of concentration is greater than average.

5.22 Turning now to this more detailed data on 275 manufacturing sectors, we can examine, in various ways, the degree of association between proportion of foreign activity and concentration, the former measured in proportion of total sales accounted for by foreign owned firms and the latter measured in terms of the proportion of total sales in the sector accounted for by the five largest producers. The foreign participation is broken down in the data for the United States subsidiaries and the total.

5.23 The simplest test of the association between foreigners and concentration is a linear correlation. Table 5.V reports four such results, for all foreign participation and for United States investment alone, and including and excluding those industries with no foreign participation. There are fifty-five of the latter, i.e., non-foreign industries, out of two-hundred and seventy-five. It seemed worthwhile to run additional regressions excluding the zero foreign participation cases, as these will have varying degrees of concentration and in that way obscure any significant relation for the remainder.

Table 5.V

Associations between concentration and foreign participation

	R^2	*t statistic*
1. All industries and all foreign participation	.146	6.84
2. As above, excluding zero participation	.240	8.06
3. All industries, US investment only	.115	5.95
4. As above, excluding zero participation	.214	6.80

We see that on all comparisons there is a highly significant association between the degree of concentration and the proportion of foreign to total sales in the industry. The proportion of explained variance is not high, but the regressions are highly significant. This emerges more clearly looking at all foreign investment than the United States component alone. And excluding the industries with no foreign investment strengthens the results. The important general point is that foreign investment and concentration tend to go together.

5.24 Firm size and concentration are related, given the industrial categories. If the foreign subsidiaries were to be sufficiently large, the presence of one of them in a sector would be sufficient to make that a concentrated sector. However, this is typically not the case. A single large firm will not normally make an industry a concentrated one, which is another way of saying that there are no small industries. Taking 32 cases of high concentration and high United States investment, in only two sectors is a single United States firm responsible for that sector having a heavy American component. (And in one of these sectors there are other foreign firms.) In eight cases there are two Americans, and in over two-thirds of such concentrated sectors there are three or more United States subsidiaries operative. Where a sector is concentrated and has a large foreign component, usually several foreigners, not one, are contributing to that component. And, of course, large domestic firms are adding to the concentration.

5.25 We can get some feel for the clustering of foreign firms through examining a frequency distribution of industries according to numbers of foreign firms. This is given in Table 5.VI. Quite a number of sectors, 55, have no foreign firms, and some have a great many. But most sectors have a few. Roughly two-thirds have between two and ten. Only 5.5 per cent have more than ten foreign firms, and one-fifth of the industries have one, often a very small one. In only ten of the fifty-eight industries with one foreign firm does that firm account for more than five per cent of sales. In no cases does it account for more than forty per cent, and in only two cases more than fifteen per cent. Both of these are highly concentrated industries, 88 and 100 per cent. The characteristic oligopolistic pattern of foreign investment emerges most clearly if we look only at those industries where the foreign proportion of sales exceeds five per cent. Eighty-two per cent of such industries have between two and ten foreign firms. There are five industries with very heavy foreign domination, that is, between seventy and ninety per cent of sales. Three such industries have two foreign firms, one has three and one has four.

Table 5.VI

Frequency distributions of industries according to number of foreign firms

(a) Any level of foreign participation (including zero)

	*More concentrated industries**		*Less concentrated industries*		*All industries*	
Number of foreign firms	*Number of industries*	*Per cent of total*	*Number of industries*	*Per cent of total*	*Number of industries*	*Per cent of total*
0	28	20.3	27	19.7	55	19.9
1	25	18.1	33	24.0	58	21.1
2-3	52	37.7	26	19.0	78	28.4
4-10	30	21.7	39	28.5	69	25.1
11 plus	3	2.2	12	8.8	15	5.5
Total	138	100.0%	137	100.0%	275	100.0%

* Largest five firms domestic and foreign owned account for more than 60.9 per cent of sales.

(b) Foreign sales exceed five per cent of total sales

Number of foreign firms	*Number of industries*	*Per cent of total*
1	10	7.8
2-3	48	37.2
4-10	58	45.0
11 plus	13	10.0
Total	129	100.0%

(c) Foreign sales exceed thirty per cent of total sales

Number of foreign firms	*Number of industries*	*Per cent of total*
1	1	2.9
2-3	16	45.7
4-5	7	20.0
6-8	8	22.9
9 plus	3	8.5
Total	35	100.0%

(d) Foreign sales exceed fifty per cent of total sales

Number of foreign firms	*Number of industries*	*Per cent of total*
1	0	0.0
2	4	33.3
3	3	25.0
4	1	8.3
5	3	25.0
6	0	0.0
7	1	8.3
8 plus	0	0.0
Total	12	100.0%

5.26 When we look at the distribution of industries according to number of foreign firms, taking only those industries with higher than average concentration, we see quite a similar pattern. While there are less with two or three foreign firms, the distribution is much the same. Lest this appear to contradict the finding above that foreignness is associated with concentration, it should be emphasised that foreignness is measured by proportion of sales of foreign firms to total sales, not by number of firms. When we count heads we are as likely to find a few foreign firms in an unconcentrated industry as a concentrated one, but if we know that an industry is unconcentrated, then the odds are roughly five to one that the proportion of foreign sales is less than average in that industry.

5.27 While it is of some value to establish the role of large subsidiaries, and subsidiaries owned by large firms abroad, and to relate these incoming firms to the state of concentration in British industry, this leaves the question of causality untouched. What would concentration in the United Kingdom look like had the inward investing firms not come here? How much of their establishment and growth is by take-over and reduction of the number of meaningful competitors, and how much adds to the competitiveness of industry? To answer these questions involves three difficult problems. Concentration is a problematical index of monopoly power. Imports may keep competition keen in spite of few producers in the country. And, it is not easy to say when a competitor is 'meaningful' .These are intriguing questions which we cannot explore here. However, we can get an interesting glimpse into the inward investment effect on monopoly power, if only a glimpse, by examining changes in concentration.

5.28 A major stumbling block from the point of view of causality is the lack of detailed, that is, industry, figures on foreign penetration for a point of time other than 1963. Some comparison of changes in foreign investment and changes in concentration could be interesting. Failing this, we tried to relate changes in concentration from 1958 to 1963 to the ratio of foreign to total sales in 1963. In principle, this might tell us whether or not those industries which are becoming less concentrated, for example, are those with more or less foreign investment compared to the average. British industry in general became more concentrated over that five year period, so the definition of more or less concentrated could appropriately be related to the average change. We took the absolute difference between the two concentration ratios, which implies that an industry in which the top five firms moved from selling forty-five per cent of the output to selling fifty per cent increased in concentration to the same extent as an industry which moved from seventy-five to eighty per cent.

5.29 Our initial run through on this comparison *appeared* to suggest an interesting result. It looked as if those industries wth smaller foreign proportions were as likely to have risen as to have fallen in concentration, compared to the average, but that those industries with larger foreign proportions were much more likely to have fallen in concentration than to have risen, again, compared to the average change. Subsequent work suggested that this initial finding was illusory. The 1963 Census figures were found to contain substantial errors and were later corrected. (The revised figures are used throughout the Report.) And the initial test was a non-parametric one. With the revised figures, a regression of change in concentration on foreign proportion of sales gives the following result.

$$C_{63} - C_{58} = 3.0 - .02\,F_{63}$$
$$(.03)$$

t statistic $= -.67$ $R^2 = .002$ n $= 216$ (due to lack of certain 1958 concentration ratios).

Clearly we are able to reject the hypothesis that there is a relation between the two variables. Dropping those with no foreign participation, this being in any case less justified than for the previous problems, does not change the picture.

$$C_{63} - C_{58} = 2.3 + .0002\,F_{63}$$
$$(.0295)$$

t statistic $= .01$ $R^2 = .000$ n $= 161$

So again we find no relation between changes in concentration and foreign proportion.

5.30 There is an interesting point, suggested by Professor Ralph Nelson, to be made in this area. A fairly well supported generalization is that rapidly growing industries tend to become, or be, less concentrated. Also, direct foreign investment tends to go into the more rapidly growing industries. This might lead us to expect a negative association between changes in concentration and changes in foreign investment which was not causal. (The above is not a test of this unless foreign proportion in 1963 is positively associated with changes in the proportion up to 1963.) A possible further test which awaits additional data would be to relate changes in concentration to industry growth, imports, and changes in foreign proportions in an attempt to isolate the effect of foreign investment after having taken account of other factors.

5.31 From the above we certainly cannot jump to the conclusion that inward investment does not change competition. It is worth noting that the 1,224 foreign firms making up our sample are owned by 579 companies abroad, 434 in the United States, with many of the foreign interests operating an enterprise in more than one United Kingdom sector. All the data we have examined supports the generalization that foreign investment here is done, to a significant extent, by large firms abroad, their subsidiaries are often large compared to domestic firms, and they tend to appear in the more concentrated sectors. It is now time to ask, so what?

Monopoly power and host country gains from direct investment

5.32 When foreign owned establishments are located in regions of this country where economic activity is depressed and the level of unemployment is high, the gain to the United Kingdom economy can be very great because some factors, particularly labour, are employed which otherwise would be unemployed. Some American investment in Scotland, such as IBM, Joy

Manufacturing and Playtex, all located in Greenock, is of this kind. While it is true that a proper appraisal of foreign direct investment should assume a successful full employment policy with and without the direct investment, the possibility of directing foreign firms to depressed regions, which may prefer them in any case, brings about an exception to the general rule. The kinds of misallocation of resources, and other distortions due to monopoly, fade in importance in depressed regions. The regional aspect of direct investment raises many other issues which we also cannot develop here.[1] Having made note of possible employment effects of foreign direct investment, let us turn to the question of monopoly in the more general setting of full employment.

5.33 The Watkins Report, in a section we referred to above, takes a very strong line on monopoly. It is worth quoting at some length (with references to Canada deleted and *italics* added).

Two key points emerge from this discussion.

> The first is that the nature and extent of the benefits from direct investment depend on the nature of competition in the system and the effects of public policies on the organization of production and distribution. Increased benefits for the . . . public will result to the extent that competition within the . . . economy diffuses the impact of direct investment widely, increasing productivity and decreasing prices. *To the extent that imperfections of competition exist, and are not mitigated, or are even increased, by public policy, the benefits of direct investment will be emasculated.*
>
> (*Report of the Task Force on the Structure of Canadian Industry*, p. 69).

The authors go on to say that too many incoming firms may reduce potential gains from economies of scale, or may be dominant and prevent, presumably desirable, further entry (pp. 69-70). In addition, they make an important point concerning tariff protection of sectors receiving foreign investment.

> If the . . . consumer is to benefit from foreign ownership it is necessary, given the tariff, that direct investment helps the (domestic) industries into which it flows approach world levels of productivity. If it does not assist these industries in approaching world levels of productivity, its effect will tend to be neutral for the . . . consumer, or even negative; the latter possibility can result if the foreign firm, while efficient relative to (domestic) firms, is inefficient by world standards, and diverts (domestic) inputs into relatively inefficient areas of production (p. 71).

Besides the monopoly and efficiency (tariff) point, the 'second' point referred to above has to do with the tax on profits of foreign owned firms.

> The second key point to emerge from the discussion is that the nature and extent of the benefits from direct investment depend on the ability of (host) governments to tax profit accruing to foreigners at an optimal rate (p. 72).

These views on competition, tariffs, and profit tax were expressed in the context of the Canadian economy, and we have no view on them in that setting. But reading them as general statements, we may question the first, and amplify the second and third in the United Kingdom context.

5.34 In the previous section a strong case is established for the importance of giant subsidiaries owned by giant parents in total foreign investment in the United Kingdom. This, in turn, carries a strong implication of monopoly power. If the Watkins Report is right in its first point, that imperfections of competition 'emasculate' the benefits of direct investment, we have good cause to be worried. There are, however, four reasons why the Watkins position may be an overly harsh statement: (1) competition is not perfect in the absence of inward investment; (2) imports, as an alternative to production here, may enjoy some monopoly position; (3) research and development is a real cost and has to be paid for; (4) there is evidence that the cost of monopoly generally is not high, or as high as might be thought. We may briefly amplify these points in turn.

[1] See Chapter Six.

5.35 The first is quite obvious in principle, however intractable it may be empirically. It is no doubt fair to say without presenting additional documentation and drawing on the British experience already discussed, that multi-national firms tend on a world basis to be in industries like automobiles, tyres, petrol, chemicals, computers, detergents, special branded foods, and so on, which are oligopolistic in virtually all industrial countries. The detergent case in the United Kingdom is a classic example of a monopolistic domestic firm in apparently strong competition with another monopolistic foreign owned firm. Though monopolistic, the foreigner here, most people would agree, increases competition here. It may also just be worth mentioning that in a number of our Board of Trade interviews, high officers in foreign owned companies have expressed concern over the viability of some of their British rivals. In our view they correctly appraise their own long-term interests, given the socio-political-economic environment, in not wishing to see them go under, and would be very unlikely to engage in the textbook manoeuvres of holding down prices in the hope of putting on the bite when the field is clear. But the main point is that we should direct attention to whether the incoming firms improve competition over what it would have *been*, not whether they have some monopoly position.

5.36 The position of a foreign large firm is not like that of a large domestic firm. Two things in particular, its financing possibilities, and its power relations in the labour market, are not the same. The ability to shift some, or all, of its operations to another country gives it a threat the domestic firm lacks. Naturally, this is not a threat that can easily or costlessly be made good. But it deserves attention, especially in the light of the frequent observation that the industrial relations of the incoming firm often differ, or attempt to differ, from traditional British practice. Managers, particularly of American foreign owned firms, express the view that they achieve higher productivity and profitability than their British counterparts through more careful labour utilization, rather than through technological advantages or a higher capital input. Of course, this is an explanation flattering to management itself and one probably should be cautious in accepting it without investigation.[1] But it makes the issue of the monopolist exerting pressure in the factor markets, and critically in the labour market, all the more intriguing. While it is the case that the foreign owned firm has a reputation for paying high wages, and in particular cases investigated have been shown to do so, they go for higher quality labour. As purchasers of labour's services they may enjoy monopoly gains, regardless of their hourly rate structures.

5.37 This leads to the second consideration, which turns on direct investment as an alternative to exporting. Like the first point, it suggests a more relevant basis for comparison. A foreign product may be in a monopolistic position whether it is produced abroad and imported, or produced here. If direct investment does not alter the product, it should leave the demand curve for it unaffected. Assuming there are no tariffs, the cost curve for production in the host country presumably would lie below the old cost curve. This would result in a lower price and a larger consumer surplus. So there is a somewhat simple case for the conclusion that direct investment is preferable to importing a monopolistic product on the consumption side. (A tariff can help remove some of the advantage of monopoly from the production point of view, but direct investment across a tariff wall carries with it no presumption of a lower cost curve.) However, there is an analogy to customs union theory here, with a possibility of an adverse production effect and a

[1] See Chapter Four.

favourable consumption effect. Domestic inputs into the foreign owned subsidiary will be subject to some misallocation due to the firm's monopoly power. On balance, the move from importing to production here of a monopolistic product will typically entail two contradictory effects which on balance need not adversely effect welfare even though the proportion of domestic factors engaged in less competitive industry has risen.

5.38 The third mitigating point has to do with the role of product innovation in establishing a monopoly position. After discussing in a general way the welfare problems of private production of knowledge, H G Johnson makes a number of applications to the direct investment case, and also observes the following: 'High measured rates of profit on capital, often taken as an indication of "exploitation", may not in fact be so, since the "excess" profits may represent a return on past investments in creating capital in the form of knowledge which does not appear on the firm's books as an addition to material capital' (Johnson: 1970). No one would say this is the whole story. The question of whether foreign investment in, and advances in, technology are helpful or harmful to this country is a large and difficult one.[1] But insofar as profits of large firms are derived from payments for research, they are not a true cost of monopoly.

5.39 Finally, before going on to the other two topics raised by the Watkins Report, it is relevant to pose the question of the cost of monopoly as a general one. If this cost turns out to be very small, then there is a strong presumption that the monopoly element in direct investment is not such a serious factor. The whole question of whether imperfections in competition matter a great deal or hardly at all has been around so long and discussed so much that one blushes to raise it without having something interesting to add (see Hunter: 1969 for an overview of the literature). However, one must note the ambiguity surrounding the topic, and be careful in condemning direct investment because of its undoubted monopoly element. Attempts to quantify the cost of monopoly, such as those of Harberger and Schwartzman for the United States find very small welfare losses indeed (Harberger: 1954, Schwartzman: 1960 and 1961). So along with legitimate research and development costs, direct investment as an alternative to exporting, and the lack of perfect competition without direct inward investment, we incline to the view that it is easy to over state the welfare loss.

5.40 Let us turn now to the tariff point as raised by the Watkins Report. Numerous studies of direct investment rightly refer to tariffs, some finding in them a major incentive to direct investment. Johnson in the paper quoted, and of course Watkins above, emphasize the importance of traditional international competition in product markets as protection against the abuse of monopoly positions. Any study of concentration is not complete without taking trade into account. One firm may sell all of a given product that is produced in a country, but if imports enter freely there may be no monopoly threat. In their present form our figures do not allow us to relate trade and concentration for the United Kingdom. However, it is possible to gain some impression of the extent of the protection from international competition that the British tariff structure affords some of the foreign companies operating here.

5.41 For this purpose of gauging degrees of inefficiency it is 'effective rates of protection' that are relevant rather than nominal tariff rates. Tariffs raise

[1] See Chapter Three.

the price of the product and afford varying degrees of protection, with a given nominal rate, according to the relative importance of purchased inputs as against value added. The smaller the value added, the greater the effective protection afforded by a given nominal rate. (This must be qualified by taking into account the tariffs on the inputs. A firm where value added is half of price, operating behind a ten per cent tariff wall, but using an input subject to a twenty per cent tariff, is operating at world levels of efficiency, as if neither tariff existed.) Bela Balassa has calculated effective rates of protection for thirty-six British industries (Balassa: 1965). The industrial categories used are the BTN headings (Comparative Tariffs and Trade), and these cannot be matched perfectly with the Standard Industrial Classification in which our foreign investment figures are arranged. However, for twenty-two sectors it is feasible to make a comparison without great fear of statistical mismatching. In this sample there is virtually no relationship between the effective protection afforded by the United Kingdom tariffs and the extent of foreign investment in the sector. In fact there is a slight inverse rank correlation, with a coefficient of — .2, but this is not significant. The lack of a positive relation in this simple correlation indicates only what is well known, namely that many factors besides tariffs bear on the foreign investment decision. In a properly specified multiple regression, a positive tariff relation might well emerge. However, what is important and interesting is the degree of protection we do afford some sectors with large foreign components. Of the twenty-two sectors for which both sets of figures are available, in seven the foreign component is greater than ten per cent, measured in sales. These sectors appear below along with their effective rates of protection.[1]

Table 5.VII

Industry	*Foreign proportion*	*Effective protection*
Automobiles	52.1	41.4
Agricultural machinery	34.2	21.3
Precision instruments	32.5	44.2
Rubber goods	28.1	43.9
Non-ferrous metals	21.3	19.4
Non-electrical machinery	18.2	21.2
Metal casting	10.6	26.9

The average effective protection for the other twenty-nine categories used by Balassa, fifteen of which definitely have less foreign participation and the other fourteen probably so, is marginally lower than for these seven, 29.2 as against 31.2 for this group. This is a highly aggregated listing, and arbitrarily selective due to the vagaries of data availability. But it indicates strongly that many foreign firms (and domestic ones) are encouraged to operate at levels of efficiency which compare adversely with world levels. The point is greatly complicated by the fact that these industries need not be, and in some cases definitely are not, competitive outside the United Kingdom. However, concern with monopoly gains on the part of foreign subsidiaries here should, on the basis of these figures, direct our attention, among other things, to the possibility of an inappropriate British tariff structure.

5.42 Coming to the final point of this section, we may comment on the Watkins proposition that host governments should, '. . . tax profits accruing to foreigners at an optimal rate' (*Foreign Ownership and the Structure of Canadian Industry*, p. 72). This advice raises a number of issues, among them

[1] While acknowledging their existence, we are not examining here the problems involved in calculating effective rates of protection.

the feasibility of a differential profit tax. If the 'optimal' rate for foreign owned firms turned out to be lower than the rate (traditional or optimal) for domestic firms, one might anticipate some grumbling. Such an arrangement would be unacceptable. So a differential rate would have to be the other way around, a higher tax for foreigners. Presumably, where ownership was less than one hundred per cent foreign, this would be pro rated. Immediately several problems suggest themselves: a sense of inequity in contrast to the present legal atmosphere where a foreign subsidiary is treated in every way like a domestic firm; retaliation on the very substantial volume of British investment abroad; a powerful incentive to generate profits in other countries through appropriate intra-firm pricing. The first two points are self evident. A word or two more might be appropriate as to the third.

5.43 All other things being equal, a multi-national firm can vary the profits of its United Kingdom located subsidiary by varying the price of inputs sold to it from other parts of the multi-national network, varying charges for research and development and other services, and varying the price paid for the output of the United Kingdom located unit by parts of the network located outside this country. Of course tax law here forbids artificially lowering profits in this way, and if an item sold crosses an *ad valorem* tariff barrier, customs officials in other countries will object to artificially lowering the export prices charged here. But in complex international manufacturing operations, the enforcement problems are formidable, not to say overwhelming, and certainly costly. The firm's incentive to devote resources to profit manipulation will vary directly with the spread between rates here and elsewhere, restricting the scope for a separate rate for foreign owned firms.

5.44 Two points can be added, the question of what is the optimum rate, and whether a single national rate could be significantly altered in the light of a desired bite on the profits of foreign owned firms. The first is a difficult problem if one assumes no foreign response in terms of volume of direct investment, and much more so if one realistically tries to take account of the response. With foreign investment of the order of ten per cent, and these difficulties of specifying an optimal rate, it certainly does not seem sensible to set or change a single national rate with that object in mind. These considerations, plus the problems mentioned of a differential rate, suggest that the advice to set an optimal rate of profit tax on foreign owned firms is a bit empty. However, it should be emphasized that our work, and that of other investigators, indicates clearly that the tax on foreign profits is a very important source of gain to host countries from inward investment.

The multi-national firm and domestic competitive structure

5.45 To recapitulate, we have attempted to document the role of large firms, and particularly firms owned by large firms, in the phenomena of direct investment in this country. We conclude that bigness and a monopoly element are characteristic of inward investment. The evidence suggests that foreign investment comes mainly from industries which are concentrated and oligopolistic in the home country, and have these same characteristics in this country. We have been unable to relate changes in foreign investment to changes in concentration.

5.46 Next we examined the effect of the monopoly element on the diffusion of benefits to the United Kingdom from inward investment. In contrast to some examinations of this problem which have been done for other countries, we found less reason to be particularly concerned about the loss of benefit to us due to the monopoly factor. Using fairly general *a priori* argument we conclude that the loss is likely to be small.[1]

5.47 Apart from the way the monopoly power of the foreign owned subsidiaries influences the benefit to this economy of their presence here, we may say a few words on the effect of this investment on the competitive structure of this economy generally. Most of what might be said follows from the previously discussed material, hence the brevity of this section.

5.48 With total foreign investment of the order of ten per cent, and the characteristic distribution of investment being as it is, it would be difficult to maintain that there has been a serious distortion of the economy from this source. But what if the investment continues to grow? The very latest trends indicate a tapering off, though we still may ask the question. The most important part of the answer rests on one's view of the reasons for the astounding success of the multi-national firm. Is it due to size begetting size in a process of self-perpetuating power, or is it due to genuine economies of scale. If the latter, these are not the traditional scale returns in combining labour and capital, but rather scale returns to management, marketing, and research and development.

5.49 Particularly the returns to research must be emphasised. In order for the profit maximizing firm to undertake the necessary outlay it must be possible for it to reap the returns to new knowledge. In this sense the scale features represent genuine economic efficiency. It is interesting to note that those foreign owned firms subject to Monopolies Commission and Restrictive Practices Reports, such as Champion Sparking Plug, Kodak, Mullard, Amalgamated Dental and the tyre companies (Goodyear, Firestone, North British Rubber, Michelin and Pirelli) have involved predominantly questions of technology. Nor have the investigations involved outcomes particularly harmful to the firms themselves. This also suggests that while the monopoly question is a serious one, the actual loss due to monopoly power in foreign owned firms is not large.

[1] Chapter Three, on technology, has bearing on these conclusions.

6. The regional aspects of inward investment

Background

6.1 Both a cursory glance at the geographical location of foreign owned firms in the UK and what statistics we have on this topic suggest that the distribution of the firms is not equal across regions. Furthermore, the recent dramatic growth of foreign direct investment (particularly from the USA) in the UK is not distributed regionally proportionately with previously existing investment. It is more prevalent in outlying regions. Scotland, in particular, is an especially noticeable host to recent investment of this kind.

6.2 Employment figures give some picture of the concentration of foreign directed economic activity. Measuring concentration in terms of employment may be rather misleading since foreign investment is, on the whole concentrated in capital intensive, science based industries. We would expect such figures to underestimate the relative importance of the foreign owned firms in a region.

Table 6.I

Per cent of employees in foreign owned firms

Northern	*Yorks & Humber*	*East Midlands*	*East Anglia*	*South East*	*South West*	*Wales*	*West Midlands*	*North Western*	*Scotland*	*Northern England*	*UK*
2.1	2.5	3.3	11.2	12.4	1.2	8.5	4.1	5.6	7.2	4.3	6.8

6.3 The uneven distribution of foreign investment is not surprising for two reasons. Firstly, the foreign investor must obtain permission to engage in business at all in this country. Any conditions, or undertakings may be attached to this permission. Prominent among these has been the location aspect. While it is not the case that a foreign firm is simply told to locate in a certain spot or nowhere, a choice of Development Area locations is often proferred. Through a process of two-way interaction, the final decision often leads to a fairly remote spot. In the course of negotiations, a local champion of a particular area especially in need of new investments is likely to play a part. If he is well connected economically, politically and socially, he may succeed in bringing the new foreign investment to a surprising area (a process of this sort seems to have been instrumental in IBM locating in Greenock, Scotland—see below). So simple regulations, combined with the opportunities for informal pressure which arise in protracted negotiations, can locate the foreign firm outside of the major commercial and industrial centres.

6.4 The second reason why foreign owned firms become established in outlying regions is that they have no particular commitments to, or traditions in, a particular part of the country. Perhaps the foreign firm approaches the location decision for a new establishment with more of an open mind than its domestic counterpart. Economic criteria such as cheaper land with opportunities for expansion, and an ample supply of labour probably receive a heavier weighting for the foreign than the domestic investor. Also our preliminary statistical information enables us to hazard the generalisation that foreign direct investment is more concentrated in light manufacturing and science based industry. These are likely to be instances where location is less predetermined by the necessity of being near particular sources of raw materials or transportation facilities. The latter point follows from the characteristically high ratio of value of product to transport cost in the newer incoming industries. These factors all point towards location away from the more congested industrial areas of the South, especially around London.

6.5 As a consequence of both Governmental policy and the preferences of the inward investing concern, we can expect a disproportionate tendency for the foreigner to locate a new establishment in the more remote regions. If the current policy of regional development is continued as at present, this pattern is likely to become more pronounced over time. One consequence of this is the creation of situations where a single, or several, foreign owned firms play a very important part in the economic life of many communities. It is reasonable to feel that foreign ownership may have special consequences in this type of setting which are not present when a foreign firm is just one amongst many domestic firms in a large economic conurbation. The general issues which are referred to under the headings of autonomy, and foreign domination may be present in a small community and not in a larger economic complex. Later in this chapter we will describe a brief survey we made of such a community.

Economic issues

6.6 Apart from the pure takeover, almost all inward investment will absorb some new domestic factors to complete the investment. These factors may have been previously unemployed, or less effectively employed, or may have been equally effectively employed in domestic employment. In all our efforts to appraise the consequences of inward investment, it is important to bear in mind the elementary point that we must assume an appropriate macro full employment policy. We should not assume that factors engaged in foreign investment in this country, or in the on-going operations of foreign owned firms, would be unemployed in the absence of the foreign investment or if the firm operated at a lower level of activity. However, the one great proviso here comes from the question of local, or regional unemployment. Macro full employment policy cannot ensure local full employment without raising the pressure of demand to a level which may result in an intolerable rate of inflation. Two solutions then are open, bringing work to the workers or encouraging regional mobility. One way of accomplishing the former is to attract or direct foreign capital into the depressed regions.

6.7 The persistence of regional unemployment is well known. In fact Brechling (1967) has concluded from a detailed study of regional unemployment that, on the whole, the contributions by the structural components to the problem of regional unemployment have not become smaller during the period 1952-63. Archibald (1967) has compiled some revealing statistics on the ratio of the unemployment percentages in the regions to the UK percentages at a given time for the period 1951-63:

Table 6.II

Rates of regional unemployment per cent to overall UK unemployment per cent

	South East England	*South West*	*Midland*	*North Midlands*	*East & West Riding*	*North West*	*North*	*Scotland*	*Wales*	*Northern Ireland*
Mean	0.63	0.91	0.69	0.55	0.71	1.15	1.46	1.83	1.59	4.35
Standard dev.	0.91	0.27	0.27	0.20	0.23	0.37	0.51	0.56	0.50	1.46

Furthermore he claims that inspection of the actual time series shows that the means stay for the most part on one side of unity or the other.

6.8 The current and expected volume of foreign direct investment suggest that location regulations of this component of total investment could be a substantial help in achieving a more equitable distribution of unemployment rates. Of course if such a policy were to be actively pursued, as to a considerable extent it already is, we could anticipate an even greater relative importance of foreign owned firms in more remote areas and the problems attendant with a dominant foreign employer in a relatively isolated labour market could grow in importance.

6.9 In the normal case, the contribution of foreign investment to domestic welfare comes about through the additional output generated by our labour force working with more capital. From this we must subtract repatriated profits and payment for services etc. But when investment goes into a depressed area, the entire output less repatriated profits and payment for services, might legitimately be attributed to the foreign investment. Furthermore, this is augmented by local multiplier effects; though Archibald has suggested that these tend to be rather low for depressed regions, with an upper bound of about 1.7.

6.10 Although we might expect the major proportion of new foreign investment in the depressed regions to be in new establishments there is still the possibility of takeovers. The logic of the situation is then somewhat different. The foreign purchase, unless used entirely to support a balance of payments surplus, which means an off-setting operation elsewhere in the economy, will result in more funds available for investment. Of course, this investment need not take place in the region of the takeover, or in another depressed region. But there is some presumption that it is more likely to than investment generally. Furthermore, takeovers more often than not lead to expansion of activity. So even if the replaced domestic investment departs from the region we can expect certain local economic gains.

6.11 One possible problem in the case of the takeover is that foreign firms typically shift to more capital intensive methods and so aggravate rather than reduce local employment. Of course from an overall perspective of economic efficiency the more capital intensive methods will ultimately lead to a greater output per man and are therefore welcome. But this is a long-term consequence and begs the immediate question. The short-run disequilibrium effects are clearly of concern. We might postulate that the answer to a local unemployment problem is the appropriate combination of more investment and more migration but the question remains what combination. The argument for migration is that even though it enforces heavy costs in terms of social overheads, these are mostly obsolete in 'declining areas' anyway and directing firms to anywhere but where they want to go involves some cost to them if they have good reasons to locate elsewhere. But migration of labour need not necessarily be an equilibriating factor. If an unemployed man moves out of the region then it loses his (admittedly low) expenditure and the multiplier effects thereof. Also the loss of regional income may lead to a fall in induced investment. The situation will be aggravated if the Government reduces spending on social services in the region. Migration, in and of itself, is not an unequivocable benefit.

The social issues

6.12 We pointed out earlier that a policy of attracting foreign investors to development regions can have the effect of producing a situation where a foreign firm or firms dominate a community or locality. And just as one feels that a significant proportion of foreign investment at the national level can have social and political repercussions we might expect a high local concentration to have a greater but analogous effect in the locality.

6.13 So far as foreign firms use different techniques from domestic firms, we would expect to see this reflected in changes in the occupational structure and social set up of the host communities. The policies of foreign owned firms with respect to training and promotion etc. could have strong implications for social mobility within the community. A third and related aspect is possible demographic effects, through encouragement of movement of particular skill types into and out of host communities. These effects all follow from investment of any kind, domestic or foreign. However, the scale of foreign investment typically undertaken by those very large organisations lends special potential interest to the impact of the foreign investor.

6.14 Apart from more readily measurable considerations, the role and impact of the foreign firm in the host community may well affect general attitudes. If a foreign owned firm or firms dominate a locality they may become either positive or negative reference points for certain categories of people in the host population. It seems worthwhile to distinguish four categories:

(i) *Business and civic leaders.* General attitudes towards and experience of foreign owned firms are important. But, in particular, changes over time (if any) are interesting. Do they start out hostile and become won over, or change in the opposite way? Or is there no usual pattern, but simply responses to individual situations.

(ii) *Trade union leaders.* Popular 'knowledge' argues to the effect that foreign owned firms, particularly American ones, are likely to disrupt traditional trade union practices. In general it is often suggested that foreign firms are likely to have distinctive personnel policies that carry implications not only for the place of work but for the complete locality.

(iii) *Subsidiary employees.* We have little knowledge of how employees feel about working for a foreign owned concern.

(iv) *Domestic firm employees.* To what extent does a foreign owned firm, with distinctive practices, effect the attitudes and behaviour of employees in domestically owned firms?

6.15 It is customary for business firms to take part in civic affairs, and to support local and national activities in a variety of ways. It is worth studying the role of foreign owned firms in this respect and seeing how they differ in any distinctive manner from their domestic counterparts. In a large city like London it may not matter very much if a particular foreign subsidiary enters into the local life, and the way it does so. But in other areas where the subsidiary provides a substantial proportion of the employment in a community, this could be a very critical consideration. The economy is not just a means of producing and distributing goods and services. It conditions the lives of people who live in it. For those reasons it is important to know the extent to which foreign owned firms differ from domestic firms as social as well as economic entities.

6.16 A further important consideration is the extent to which foreign owned firms attempt to enter or influence the local polity. It is generally held that business has profound influence on local politics. Is this true of foreign owned firms and if so are there any distinctive features?

6.17 In summary, then, if the directing of foreign owned firms to development areas is used as part of regional policy we mght expect high local concentrations of foreign capital. And if this capital is put to use in distinctive ways we might expect significant local economic and social consequences. Whether or not one regards these as local costs or benefits is, in part of course, a matter of individual values.

A study of the impact of inward investment on a local community

6.18 *Method of approach*
Economic research rarely involves field trips and the value of such trips is often doubtful when it does. Nevertheless, a visit to a place characteristic of the phenomena under consideration has played an important part in this aspect of our work. We felt we needed clues, suggestions, indicators of what it was we should be looking for. Certainly one can speculate on these in London, but a first-hand impression seemed worthwhile. The word impression is accurate, as only a short trip of two weeks was contemplated, and this was eventually reduced to one week.

6.19 Discussion at the Board of Trade on choice of area, partly in the Economic Services Unit and partly with other divisions raised a number of issues. Should the foreign firm, or firms, be American or otherwise? It was decided that it, or they, should be as this was a one shot affair, and they would be most representative. Also there is the question of size. Dundee, for example, is host to a number of foreign firms, but seemed too big to yield even an impression on a short visit. Often the foreign firm is located in a new town, but we decided to avoid this on the grounds that a new town in itself contains special aspects that might be hard to separate out. Similarly, we did not want an area where the incoming firm was very new and certain factors might dominate for that reason. More consultation with the Scottish Office confirmed our impression that Greenock, on the mouth of the Clyde would be a good choice.

6.20 In advance it was clear that no one choice would be completely representative. (A feature of our work to which we will be turning, was the importance of different types of circumstances.) There must be a large element of arbitrariness in any choice. Greenock seemed reasonable in advance, and seems a fortunate choice to us now. This report will either confirm or refute that opinion.

6.21 We went with a very open ended programme. There was, however, a general objective—to learn as much as we could about the area that bore on inward investment. We hoped that the visit would be suggestive of ideas germaine to the project, apart from any knowledge of Greenock we gained. And we had a particular pre-disposition in the direction of uncovering drawbacks of foreign ownership, the advantages of new investment in a depressed area being rather obvious.

6.22 To mount this programme, two techniques were used. Clearly, there is an opportunity to observe the physical set up, and we tried to be systematic about this. Published information supplemented what we saw.[1] Secondly, about twenty long, and numerous short, interviews were conducted. When practical, these were tape recorded. An effort was made to cross-check interviews with other opinions. No effort at historical recounting or attribution is made in this report.

6.23 Only three interviews were arranged in advance. These were set up by the Board of Trade in Scotland. Other interviews were generated by snow-ball techniques, and purely under our own initiative. It was explained to the Scottish Office why we were coming, and presumably this information was passed on to the initial three interviewees. At the request of Mr Dry of the Greenock Employment Exchange, we wrote direct to Mr Howard Gibson at IBM who wanted more information. In general people seemed to have little, or no idea, of why we were there, which is probably a good thing. Usually we did not make our objective of finding negative aspects of foreign investment in this setting too explicit, and presented a fairly neutral face. The two members of our project on this particular study were an economist and the sociologist. We feel the interaction of these approaches plays a central part in this phase of work.

Greenock, Gourock and Port Glasgow

6.24 Excellent histories of the area are available, and there is little need to reproduce them here. The basic economic traditions of the area centred on port activities, which declined, however, when river deepening allowed ships to pass to Glasgow. Shipbuilding is prominent, and this industry is subject to difficulty for familiar reasons, though not particularly the establishments here. Water power opened up some textile activity, which is also a troubled industry. Heavy engineering plays a role in the area. Sugar refining is satisfactory, but technological change has continuously reduced employment. Something just under a thousand people leave the district every year. Unemployment stays not far from seven per cent. These are the broad economic facts.

6.25 The drive into Greenock from Glasgow suggests economic separation. By London standards commuting time would not be prohibitive, but apart from the most special circumstances, people from Glasgow would be disinclined to seek work in Greenock. Few people from Greenock seem inclined to work as far away as Glasgow without leaving altogether. We met no one who commuted in either direction, and the data in the Greenock Area Local Employment Survey: 1966 support this subjective impression. There is a clear and sustained break in houses and work places, after leaving

[1] We were fortunate to obtain the results of a survey carried out by IBM among their employees, among much other material.

Glasgow and before arriving at Greenock. However, some observers claim that there is substantial commuting. But the key point remains that this is a local region in which the foreign firm impact could be disturbing.

6.26 Driving to Gourock is another matter, although it is part of the same economic community. There is some open country after one passes Gourock on the way to Largs, but these are residential areas, and have some seaside holiday business. Housing is generally poor and in short supply, which is odd with people moving out of the region. But new building and thorough maintenance are uncommon and that probably explains the shortage. 'Executive' housing is in particularly short supply.

6.27 The Liberal party tends to dominate the Town Council, though there was a Labour interlude five years ago. Our impression is that, loosely put, political and community affairs are not very absorbing to people generally.

6.28 The key population and employment figures, rounded off, are as follows:[1]

Total population	108,000
Population of working age (M. 15–64, F. 15–59)	59%
Insured employees, including unemployed	43,000
Males insured	65%
Unemployment	6–7%

Broadly, unemployment in Scotland tends to be twice the national average, and unemployment in Greenock twice the Scottish average.

6.29 This is, in very brief outline, the area under study. Long-term residents seem to like the area and there is considerable optimism abroad. People brought in, particularly from the South may see it as dead, backward and unsophisticated but our impression of present conditions and future prospects is more favourable than before we came. In spite of emigration and unemployment, there are many indicators that the worst is over. With this background in mind we can turn to the incoming foreign firms.

The question of domination

6.30 There are three American firms in the study area. Playtex produces foundation garments and employs about a thousand workers, mostly women. Mining machinery and air compressors are produced by Joy Manufacturing, who employ about eight hundred men. And IBM employs about seventeen hundred workers, eighty-five per cent men. Together these firms make up roughly eight per cent of the work force. At times it was a source of some disappointment to us to see that we had chosen an area where no United States firm clearly dominated, or even all three, taken as a group. The picture we had in mind, was one where there is clear domination by a single employer. Let us say one where half the people worked for a foreign firm. But the question of domination is a complex one, and by the end of our studies we felt no misgivings about our choice of area on this score. The foreign firms do not, in any immediate statistical sense dominate the district, but as we shall see in a more intangible way, their importance is of greater magnitude than this simple statistic would suggest. It is thus not entirely

[1] Sources: *Greenock Area Local Employment Survey:* 1966 and *First Review of the Development Plan (Draft)*, Corporation of Greenock, 1966 (?).

misleading to speak of a certain dominance exercised by the foreign firms. So our initial criteria for a local study of a medium sized community, relatively isolated, with a significant amount of foreign investment located in more than one firm, are broadly satisfied by the conditions in Greenock.

6.31 Of course the eight per cent refers to direct employment. Naturally there is a lot of contracting out, particularly by IBM—cleaners, transportation service, and a whole range of activities where the Americans regularly pay wages to people not strictly employed by them would raise the proportion, possibly to ten per cent. Depending on what one takes the regional multiplier to be, two is a highish guess, true dependence could be as high as fifteen to twenty per cent. Nevertheless in the Greenock area, the main employers are still the traditional employers. Scott Lithgow, the shipbuilders, employ three thousand. Marine engineering is represented by Hastie and other companies.

Impact of foreign firms on the labour market

6.32 It is normal for incoming firms to require more advanced techniques and a higher degree of skill in the workforce they employ than is common in the traditional existing industry in the host area. This certainly is the case with respect to IBM in Greenock. With respect to Joy and Playtex, there is some tendency to follow the general practice of working people a bit more than average, paying a bit more, and going for the more able labour. As a broad generalisation, it is fair to say that incoming firms recruit from the employed, creaming off the better workers, rather than from the unemployed. The result is a two tier, or possibly three tier, career structure, with people moving into traditional industry, then on to ordinary foreign firms, then to IBM.

6.33 This pattern of recruitment is similar to that observed by R M Jones (1968) at the Ford Motor Company plant at Crumlyn Burroughs near Swansea. He concludes:

> The great majority of employees recruited by Fords were, therefore, taken from the local labour market. Furthermore of the 802 hirings covered by the survey only 83 were recruited from the ranks of the immediately unemployed. The net result of these two factors was that the majority of the Ford labour force was to be recruited from the labour forces of established local employers.

Richard A Lester (1954) reports very similar results for the American economy.

6.34 At first it seemed paradoxical to us that it was generally agreed that (1) IBM required a markedly different skill composition than prevailed in the area, (2) that they employed people from the area, there being relatively little commuting or moving people in permanently and (3) they did not do a great deal in the way of training. How can (1) and (2) be the case and still allow for (3)? First let us discuss the evidence with respect to training at IBM.

6.35 That IBM was not very strong on training was the expressed opinion of other employees in the area, and this opinion was shared by non IBM employers and others, such as the Labour Exchange. There is more in the way of direct evidence. IBM has a policy of a sustained career with the company. Recruits are looked at very carefully with an eye to long-term employment and older people are not taken on. In spite of this policy, they take very few school leavers. Those who are taken are for full-time training in the IBM school, or training establishment. But it is true that in general few school leavers are hired. More hard evidence comes from the company's record on its Industrial Training Board. The IBM levy is substantial, and they get very little back on the grant. Taking all this together, we are convinced that the generalisation that little training is done is fair.

6.36 This brings us to the paradox. How does the company get its work-force? First of all there has been continual change over time in the composition of output. Initially they produced the simplest mechanical parts, which did not call for a drastic change from existing engineering skills in the area. Then they gradually began to move towards electronics, and introduced more and more complex items into the product mix. Though by now some of the most sophisticated machines in the IBM line emerge from Greenock, this does not imply that they are fully understood in the factory. Division of labour is likely to be characteristic of the international corporation. A globally integrated approach to production means that even in very advanced operations, the tasks can be broken down, and the less demanding done where that is relatively more appropriate.

6.37 Another aspect of the highly successful division of labour is that a very limited and specific skill will generally be sufficient for each worker. This s typic ally acquired at IBM in very short training bursts in which the itraining is very specific to the company, and to one task. This is the main reason for lack of qualification for a large grant under the Industrial Training Board Scheme. For example, very little use is made of the local technical school, Watt Memorial College. Though they specialise in marine engineering, there has been a movement towards electronics, mathematics and computer science. However, it appears that such methods as day release or putting people on sustained courses are hardly ever, if at all, utilised. Our guess is that though improvement in Watt College is very much on the cards, at present it may not be very strong in areas of interest to IBM. This could be part of the explanation of why it is little used by IBM. Probably much more important, and fitting in with our other information, is the policy of specific training for one carefully broken down skill or operation. To achieve this type of training the company is well equipped, both with facilities at Greenock and in the rest of the country.

6.38 In economists' terminology, the importance of human capital is very clear at IBM. In their terms people are their greatest asset. But this does not imply high levels of general skills. (Greenock is the strong muscle of the organisation. No research goes on there.) Far more it implies the right sort of person; someone who will fit in with the task required, learn a specific skill relatively easily, a reliable and responsible type of person. So the paradox is not so hard to solve. Training is not all that important. An efficient selection and screening system is. The advantage of hiring people who have acquired their general training elsewhere is partly the saving on this training, and partly the greater knowledge one has of what the worker is like. And the slightly experienced person, in contrast to the school leaver, to some extent selects himself.

6.39 Virtually no use is made by IBM of the Labour Exchange. They hire from other companies, not from the unemployed.Later we will have to touch on the question of the composition of the unemployed workforce. There is much controversy here. But it is universally agreed that they do not constitute the top workers. Certainly from the skill point of view this is clear, and from other points of view it may be the case. For IBM they are not a source of labour their source being the better workers in other local firms.

6.40 We obtained some indirect evidence for the general attitude toward the unemployed from the executives at Playtex. This firm had attempted to expand its labour force by dipping into the unemployment pool but had found the general quality of the labour so low (i.e. absenteeism increased, productivity dropped etc.) that the expansion was dropped. In fact Playtex has since expanded in another town and the Managing Director intimated that despite the high level of unemployment there was no room for another major employer in the district. The entry of such an employer would force up his wage rates and the resulting cost increase would reduce competitiveness. He felt there was a scarcity of 'good labour' in the district and thought this introduced pressures to technological innovation in his firm. We should emphasise that all this is merely an opinion—but the opinion of a man who seemed very sure of himself and fully attuned to the problems of the district. It is interesting to note that Playtex operate a system of strict comparison of productivity etc. with their parent. One wonders, therefore, whether in the practice of setting up very rigorous standards we have a genuine behavioural characteristic attributable to foreign ownership. Would, for instance, a domestically owned firm have been more likely to expand locally in Greenock? Would a domestically owned firm tolerate a less 'efficient' labour force and a lower profit margin? Is it the case that foreign owned firms in taking their parents as reference points set standards which are unlikely to make inroads into pockets of unemployment?

6.41 One might suppose that local employers would be worried about the flow of labour, particularly skilled labour to IBM. However there seemed to be little rancour in the business community. We interviewed numerous employers (Scott Lithgow etc.) who had lost highly skilled manpower to IBM, but they were in no marked sense worried about this—they felt the flow was running at a manageable rate. Though if the rate became much higher difficulties were anticipated. These expressions are in accord with the findings of R M Jones in the previously quoted paper. He notes that of the thirty-five domestic firms who had lost labour only five considered that they had been adversely affected to a significant degree by the Ford recruitment of labour. Furthermore they found little correlation between the degree of hardship experienced and the strength of Ford's drain on the labour force of any particular firm. Jones concludes that the impact upon local firms of the introduction of the Ford plant into the local market was negligible. The disruptive effects of the recruitment operation were both mild and widely diffused. Similar views were expressed by shipbuilding firms in Greenock. However, there was some worry that a new round of training undertaken by them might result in more people going to IBM. This would not be welcomed.

Impact of the foreign firms on the social relations of production

6.42 In a study like the present one an initial methodological difficulty arises; that is to separate out any impact on the community which is a consequence of:

(a) any new investment at all,
(b) new investment based upon particular forms of technology,
(c) the foreign ownership of the new investment.

For example, it became perfectly obvious very early in our study that the IBM Corporation has had, and is having a very substantial impact on the community in a variety of ways. But it is not at all clear whether this impact is a consequence of any one or a combination of (a), (b) and (c) above. In particular, since IBM is based upon a technology that is entirely alien to the Greenock district (i.e. it necessitates a different skill mix to the traditional ones, etc.) it is extremely difficult to separate (b) and (c). In other words, we have no way of being certain whether the impact of IBM is significantly different to what we might expect if a comparable domestically owned firm were located in the district. We could, of course, solve this problem by visiting a comparable community containing such a firm but the likelihood of finding such a situation must be rather remote.

6.43 We feel, however, that the impact IBM is having on Greenock and the surrounding district is very much a 'package deal' comprising the new technology of the computer age and the philosophy of management associated with American firms. There is a natural interplay between the two in the sense that the nature of production tends to break down the established skill distinctions and the management techniques are most appropriate to non-traditional labour relations. The two, as it were, reinforce each other producing a social set-up in the factory that cuts across many of the established work mores of the district. All this is much less true of Playtex and Joy. Although there is evidence of high tempo management technique in both of these, the technical base of production is much more traditional so that the internal social structure of the factories are not qualitatively different from the other domestically owned firms in the district. We take this very notable difference between, on the one hand IBM, and on the other, Playtex and Joy as supportive evidence for the thesis that in the case of IBM we are dealing with a combination of the new technology and distinctive management practices.

6.44 IBM has a world wide policy to avoid unionization. 'We find that we can get along without them'. In some countries there is a legal requirement to have unions, and of course then they go along. But where this is not the case, they resist. At Greenock it is alleged that a vote was taken very early on, with managers and secretaries voting, but we have no confirmation of this. In any case, given the high rate of pay, especially initially, and the conditions and fringe benefits, the problem for an organiser would be formidable. The mix of skills and activities, unfamiliar in this area, adds to the problem. Even the location right out of town, in a pleasant valley, away from all other places of employment, contributes to the separateness and symbolizes the philosophy. Naturally people are allowed to hold cards. In the event of a national stoppage, the company turns a blind eye. 'We understand your problems, and if you want a day off next week, the company has no objections'. We believe that some outside contractors, i.e. cleaners, are organised but this does not affect matters. There is what is called an advisory council, elected from various levels and with a chairman who is in turn elected by the representatives and may be from any level. They meet with management once a month.

6.45 The explicit reason for no unions is that in a modern and rapidly changing industry demarcation is not on. This may be a factor, but clearly the paternalism is a basic factor. An open door policy prevails at all levels, and if a man does not get satisfaction from his boss, he can go to the next level. Wages are negotiated individually between a man and his boss. There is frequent consultation and at least once a year, a general review by each supervisor of those people directly below him. The general welfare of the individual and his effective contribution to the company are very much in mind. Some workers find this style offensive, and leave on that account. Some people talk of a feeling of suspicion, tension and psychological strain. The company doctor said this was no more common at IBM than it is generally. When we raised with the management the persistent comments we had received on tension in this American factory, the reply given was, 'Some call it tension, some call it pace and some call it fulfilment'.

6.46 The attitude of the employees of IBM towards trade unions is of some interest. A survey carried out by IBM showed that 56 per cent of the employees believed that the conditions of employment at IBM would have been *less* good if trade unions had been involved in negotiations in the plant. Only 21 per cent thought they would have been better off and 23 per cent thought it would have made no difference. These figures must be regarded as rather remarkable when we consider that most of the employees come from a region with very strong trade union traditions. Furthermore, the same survey shows that 90 per cent of the employees were either born in the area (75 per cent) or moved there before working for IBM. The very act of conducting an elaborate survey of its employees is indicative of management foresight and attention given to personnel matters.[1]

6.47 The long-term implications for trade unionism in a district dominated by a firm of IBM's nature seem to be rather drastic. As long as such a firm can offer attractive working conditions it seems it will be difficult for the trade unions to gain a foothold. This could ultimately lead to a substantial redistribution of the balance of power in the community at the expense of the unions. Perhaps the unions can adapt, rejecting their institutionalised demarcations which render them inappropriate to the skill demarcations in IBM's production. But if not, it would seem that they are in for a thin time in places dominated by the new technology and American business philosophy. It is not unreasonable to suggest that a community subject to a large amount of American investment may suffer a degree of 'Americanisation' to the extent to which the foreign investment breaks down traditional trade union allegiances and the concomitant cultural and social activities based upon these allegiances.

Social and political impact of the foreign firms

6.48 Clearly this type of employment marks quite a change from traditional industrial relations and economic life in Greenock. At this stage, at least, IBM does not appear to want to proselytise. Indeed, it is rather separatist. It wants to get on with it, without difficulty or interference. Certainly it makes some contribution to the community in an extra-economic way—repairing workers' houses after a hurricane, prizes at schools, this type of thing. 'Does as much as any company,' says the Provost. Given the local standards this does not amount to much. But basically the company stands apart, geographically and in other ways. The numbers directly employed there are large enough to change the community in themselves. Still, we must consider more subtle possibilities, both now and in the future.

6.49 As an example to other employers in providing better conditions and fringe benefits, we found little evidence of any stimulus or impact. The straight

[1] See Chapter Four, part I.

economic impact of competition for skilled and responsible labour is no doubt there. But we could not find, or elicit opinions, that example, either by IBM or the other foreign companies, was important.

6.50 Several times we raised the question with a variety of people in town as to what would be the effect on Greenock if the kind of economic arrangements at IBM were to make up a larger proportion of employment, either through expansion or through similar new firms coming in. Few people expressed concern. Those opposed to America and American firms on principle naturally deplore the 'invasion' and its extension. Only very careful thinkers, even on the trade union side, saw any problem. Most welcomed the competition in the labour market which foreign investment implied. The few saw a possible weakening of the trade union movement, at least in its traditional form.

6.51 We found no evidence at all of political influence in the area. Many people we spoke to had incentive to give us leads, if they had any. And quite knowledgeable people who seemed perfectly open had no instances of political influence to report. One item which did arise of a semi-political nature was housing. Both IBM and their competitors in the labour market felt keenly the shortage of better class housing to attract the top talents. At Scott Lithgow, for example, there was some resentment that IBM could get public money for housing which was demonstrably adding to employment, while they could not, though they needed better housing to hold key workers, and therefore to keep up employment generally.

Conclusions and policy

6.52 Our investigations have led us, perhaps incautiously, to the view that the broad structure of events described here is representative of what is likely to happen and what are the major issues when foreign firms move into relatively isolated areas. Jones' paper describing the Ford Motor Company's impact with its Crumlyn Burrough plant near Swansea gives strikingly similar results to those we report above. Perhaps other case studies should be undertaken, but pending evidence to the contrary, we regard our finding as having some generality.

6.53 In spite of the previous paragraph, our second conclusion is that the impact of foreign firms depends on which foreign firm. In Greenock we saw three, each quite different. If we wish to consider the union question, then certainly legislation is an answer, and probably a very relevant one. While it is true the incoming firm has an incentive not to expand in an area where it is pressing a life style on people who do not want it, they are skilled and diplomatic employers, very able to generate in host country citizens a strong company loyalty in a relatively short time. Most of the cautious and very loyal executives we spoke to had been with their company just a year or two. Interestingly, they also tended to see their company as international, European possibly, rather than American. (Outsiders saw it clearly as American, which did not apply very much to Joy and Playtex.) A way of expressing the pros and cons is as one of expanded choice, in the sense of economic life style, as against a powerful organisation with too much on its side. If one views the United Kingdom life style as having a particular content, rather than choice of content, then the foreign firm is disruptive, particularly in relatively isolated regions. But if one welcomes the expanded choice the foreign owned firm affords, the gains go well beyond the narrowly economic.

6.54 Our third, and most directly relevant conclusion, is that encouragement to incoming firms should not be at the expense of existing firms. The new-comer will compete for the best labour, and will not dip directly into the unemployed. The existing firm may be competitively sound, and may have a good future. Such steps as are possible should be taken to prevent the traditional firm from facing undue disadvantage. Rather than to insist that foreign firms engage in research here, it may be much more to the point to insist that they undertake more training.

6.55 Finally, we conclude that the incoming firm is an effective importer of a way of life. It is not just a matter of capitalism. Important distinctions exist even within this category. (One man's platitude is the next man's revelation.) Many see efficiency, flexibility, the breakdown of distinction between supervisors and men, harder work, and so on, as indicators of where we are going and what we want anyhow. In this case we attach no special significance to foreignness. The broader issues of how people live, or should live, seem to us to be only marginally heightened in the more remote region. The national issue we take up in Chapter Eight.

7. Control of subsidiaries by foreign parent companies

Introduction

7.1 The foreign owned firm differs from the domestic firm in that some or all of its capital comes from abroad, foreigners have a claim on some or all of the profits, and final decision taking authority rests with the parent company. To many observers it is this last aspect of inward investment which is most significant and it is the one we concentrate upon in this chapter. The fact that ultimate authority rests with the parent may, in practice, make no difference to the behaviour of the subsidiary. For one thing, the control may never be exercised. Also, though foreign decisions may be operative, they may be the same ones that would be taken by the subsidiary if it were not foreign owned. But, of course, foreign control may result in different behaviour on the part of the subsidiary, and it is this possibility that seems to cause concern. Furthermore, even if foreign decision making is not operative it is an ever present possibility and, in this sense there is always a *potential* erosion of domestic decision making.

7.2 Several writers suggest that foreign owned firms are less 'loyal' or less inclined to operate in the interests of the host country. These worries are usually not very well specified. However, a possible instance of this is in the area of responsiveness to Government economic policy through persuasion. Informal inducement as opposed to legal compulsion plays a sizeable role in such areas as incomes policy, growth policy and regional planning, and it may be that the foreign owned firm is less responsive to host Government influence than domestic firms. That is, the Government may be involved in *persuasion costs* that it does not incur with domestically owned firms. This is not necessarily the case, of course. Foreigners may be more responsive than domestic firms. It can also be the case that the subsidiary is obliged to follow directives laid down by the parent Government (e.g. embargo on exports to communist countries of goods on the strategic list), which are not in accord with the host Government policy.

7.3 We can usefully separate two aspects of the general problem of autonomy. Firstly, the autonomy of the individual subsidiaries—the extent to which they are, in fact, and potentially controlled by their parents. Secondly, the question of national autonomy—the extent to which a nation state which is host to a 'significant' amount of inward investment may find it difficult to pursue policies, both internal and external, because of the presence at home of foreign economic (and therefore perhaps political) interests. These two problems are clearly related but in a rather complex manner.[1] In this chapter we will consider the first topic and in the next chapter go on to consider the second.

[1] The implicit assumption made by many authors, both friendly and unfriendly to international investment, is that there is a simple correspondence between the degree of foreign ownership of an economy and loss of national autonomy. Such an assumption is, however, over simple for two reasons; firstly, because loss of autonomy may depend on which sections of the economy are in the hands of foreigners and secondly because ownership as such is not necessarily a good indicator of degree of foreign control. We will return to these problems presently.

7.4 This chapter is divided into three parts, which have rather different goals and may be of varying interest to different readers. In Part I we discuss the issue of foreign control in a fairly general way. Much of this discussion has little to do with purely economic issues as such. It is quite taxonomic and raises many more questions than those on which we can bring our data to bear. The goal is to explore what people might mean by the problem of control, whether or not these worries have much intrinsic merit. This part also draws on the foreign control literature.

7.5 Part II sets out the pattern of foreign ownership which we find in our regrettably small sample of foreign owned firms in the United Kingdom. It is largely descriptive, taking up such matters as the proportion of equity owned abroad, the incidence of takeover as against new establishment, the distribution by industry and by source country, size of subsidiary, and so on. Some interrelations between these characteristics are examined.

7.6 In Part III we attempt to relate the degree of control exercised by the parent organization over different areas of decision taking to the nature of the parents and their subsidiaries. In addition an attempt is made to fit some aspects of control together in terms of an over-all pattern of foreign influence. We have emphasized decisions with respect to prices, capital expenditure, and exporting and also the use by the parent, or not, of the technique of target setting. These decision areas are analysed largely on the basis of our postal survey. The influence of the parent organization on production planning and personnel policy is briefly mentioned, drawing here on our interview survey.

7.7 Due to the length of this chapter it may be useful to summarize some of the characteristics of foreign ownership in the United Kingdom and some of the relationships which are suggested by our data. As is well known, new establishments are the most common form of foreign owned enterprise with many fewer takeovers, and joint ventures trailing far behind. One hundred per cent ownership is the most common pattern. This is slightly more characteristic of North American parents as applied to new establishments, but there is no relationship between equity holding and nationality when it comes to takeovers and joint ventures. Nor is there any relationship between equity holding and the type of industry, the age of the subsidiary, and whether or not the parent runs a large international network.

7.8 When it comes to control over the decisions of the subsidiary, size appears to be a critical factor. Size of the parent and size of the parent's network both lead to tighter control over the freedom of the subsidiary to undertake new capital expenditure. Size of the subsidiary leads to financial independence. These relations also apply to exporting policy, except that size of the subsidiary does not appear to be a factor here. Interestingly, only subsidiary size appears to be related to parent organization control over price decisions. The size of the parent, and whether or not it has a large international network of subsidiaries, does seem to influence positively the practice of setting performance targets by the parent organization for the subsidiary. These broad generalizations do not take account of the influence of the subsidiary on the parent organization which is discussed in the text below. There is also some question, particularly with respect to capital expenditure, as to whether absolute amounts or proportions are the more appropriate considerations.

The participant parties

7.9 In its broadest interpretation the problem of autonomy involves six parties: the parent company (i.e. to all intents and purposes its managers and directors); the parent company's equity holders; the government of the country of the parent; the subsidiary (i.e. the subsidiary's managers and directors); any domestic owner of equity in the subsidiary; and the government of the subsidiary's country.[1] The complexity of our problem arises partly from the fact that autonomy and control (i.e. the distribution of exercisable decision making authority between the various parties) is a function of all fifteen relationships between the six parties. Though, clearly, some are of less importance than others; the relative salience of the different relationships will, in general, vary with differing political and economic conditions. It is perhaps worthwhile, therefore, by way of introduction, to take a brief look at their distinctive features.

The parent management/subsidiary management relationship

7.10 Later in this chapter we will concentrate, almost exclusively, on this relationship. Our central concern is the extent to which the parent exerts control over its subsidiaries and ultimately the way in which this control influences its economic behaviour and responsiveness to the social, political and cultural environment in which it finds itself. This involves some conceptualisation of the notion of control and an attempt to 'explain' the varying degrees of control that parents, in practice, do exert. We should note though, that this relationship is essentially two-way in that not only has the parent authority, control, etc. over the subsidiary, but the subsidiary is in a position to 'persuade' the parent. Indeed, the relationship between the two may involve the full range of 'influence relations'—coercion, authority, power, force, persuasion, inducement, suggestion, sanction, right and obligation. While of considerable interest, we have been forced to regard it as being beyond the scope of the present study to disentangle the relative importance of these factors.

The parent/subsidiary relationship has attracted the attention of most of the writers in the field of inward investment (Barlow: 1953; Brash: 1966; Dunning: 1958; Safarian: 1966, etc) but we still appear to have little systematic knowledge. We do know from this literature that there is a marked variation in the degree of control exerted by parent companies—but why this should be so is not explained. In Part III we try to relate variations in control to intuitively plausible explanatory factors.

[1] In certain instances, the picture is complicated even further as when, for instance, the workers in a particular concern take up a position with respect to foreign investment. In the context of inward investment into the UK this factor has not traditionally been an important consideration. The trade unions have not, for example, been particularly responsive at the institutional level to foreign investment, although there are more recent indications of an increased interest. (See Chapter Four.) Perhaps in the future organised labour will become an important element in the implications of foreign control/ownership. There are scattered examples of other groups reacting to inward investment. The research scientists in one British firm effectively vetoed an attempted takeover by a large US corporation. But such occurrences are at present very isolated.

The parent management/parent equity holder relationship

7.11 Ultimately the parent company's management is responsible to the shareholders in the company. The management may, of course, itself have a controlling interest and thus the separation of the two may not occur.[1] But insofar as the management of the parent company is at the behest of the major equity holders so is a subsidiary of that company. However, most authors seem to emphasise the relative freedom of managers in large corporations from direct interference by their shareholders. As long as the equity provides a reasonable flow of income the managers are usually left to their own devices. We can consequently expect little interference in the affairs of a subsidiary by parent shareholders beyond the normal requirements of profitability and may thus discount this relationship as in any way central to our analysis. We may similarly dispense with the relationships between the parent's equity holders and the parent's Government, subsidiary's management, subsidiary's equity holders and subsidiary's Government. Our concern with these relationships will generally be mediated via the parent's management, subsidiary management and subsidiary country Government.

The parent's Government/parent management relationship

7.12 The important question here is the extent to which the parent's Government deems it desirable to regulate, either by legislation or inducement, the behaviour of companies with foreign interests. For example, the February 1965 request by the United States Government for firms to restrict overseas investment later upgraded to mandatory restrictions (1968), may well have affected growth plans of established subsidiaries in this country. In general, an economy subject to a significant amount of inward investment will feel the reverberations of changes in economic and political policy in the source country economy. Most writers have paid little attention to this problem. What are the effects on the British economy of a recession in the United States economy, given the present level of United States investment in Britain? Would the effects be magnified by the presence of inward investment or would they be equally acute in the absence of such investment, as a consequence of the role that the American economy plays in international trade? These specific economic questions fall outside the province of this chapter, but, nevertheless, they indicate the importance of the policies of a parent's Government for the general problem of autonomy.

7.13 Firms with foreign interests do, of course, expect their Governments to maintain political stability in the international system conducive to the conduct of their normal economic functions. And in this context the involvement of 'big business' in the political affairs of countries like the USA is well documented. It would be entirely unrealistic to believe that, in some way, equity holders and the management of international corporations do not act as a more or less concerted interest group within their national polity. There may be significant differences within this group, but experience seems to vindicate the view that international business, particularly in the third world, is an effective political force. In the past decade or so, however, the ease with which the Governments of outward investing nations can dictate the terms of international investment has, perhaps, decreased. The complexity

[1] Despite Burnham and others' attempts to establish the distinction between owners and managers there is a fair amount of empirical evidence that they overlap, especially when viewed as interest groups, to a very considerable degree (Domhoff: 1966).

of the balancing forces in the international system is increasing all the time and as a consequence there seems to be an increased latitude for manoeuvre on behalf of the recipient nations. Governments like that of the United States of America have to be much more circumspect in their reaction to violations of the basic interests of the international corporations (e.g. in Latin and Central America). Considerations of long-term political stability seem to weigh as sufficient inducement to offset short-term economic costs. A balanced view of the present situation would, in our opinion, have to give credence to a certain (and perhaps growing) disparity between Government and international business as interest groups. Clearly here there is a complex and ever changing situation, the ramifications of which go well beyond the scope of our study. But what we would like to resist is the over-simple assertion that Government is always simply an instrument of business interest. The attitude of most United States administrations to monopoly, even across international boundaries, is a case in point. Nevertheless, in some ultimate sense there is a rapport or basic alignment of interest between nationally based international companies and their Governments. However, this picture is even further complicated by the possible development of the genuine international company (see typology, Chapter Eight) with no clear parent in any one country.
One of the most disturbing features of international investment is the increase in the number and size of companies with massive capital assets distributed across many nation states who are increasingly in an ambiguous position *vis-à-vis* nation state Governments. The extent to which companies of these dimensions are in a position to become 'a law unto themselves' must surely be a matter for investigation.

The parent's Government/subsidiary's Government relationship

7.14 This is the political relationship between the two Governments. It is, of course, not static. The economic process of inward investment takes place in the context of the ongoing political relationship between Governments. The degree to which political factors are important in understanding inward investment depends upon the stability of political relationships. Inward investment into the United Kingdom is usually from countries with which we have comparatively stable political relations and thus political factors are of little immediate concern. We have recently seen, however, how the changing political relationship between the French and the United States Governments has altered the rate of inward investment of United States capital and caused difficulties in the French computer industry. There is, though, no *a priori* reason to suppose that changing political relationships necessarily have effects upon these economic relationships or vice versa. But both common sense and what little evidence we have from analytical studies (Barlow: 1953) suggest that a prior condition for a substantial amount of inward investment is a stable political relationship between the two countries involved. Executives see unpredictable political relationships as an effective impediment to inward investment (Barlow: 1953). This concern extends to include the economic policies that the host Government pursues towards subsidiaries of foreign firms (see below).

7.15 While the facts may be very unclear it is still true to say that certain of the misgivings often entertained about inward investment concern the anticipated loss in political autonomy of a nation whose economy is significantly penetrated by foreign capital. This is an extremely complex question about which we have little more than journalistic knowledge. The argument usually runs: the source country's Government can restrict the latitude for political action of the inward invested country's Government by invoking the sanction of disinvestment and all the consequences that would follow. However, the reverse sanction is also at the disposal of the inward invested country, namely that of refusing to allow the capital to remain, and ultimately of confiscation.[1] At present these considerations seem pretty remote from contemporary British experience and fall outside the scope of this chapter, but they will be taken up in Chapter Eight.

7.16 It is important to keep clear two aspects of economic autonomy. Firstly there is what we might term the argument from *pure nationalism* which asserts that any loss or potential loss in decision making autonomy is a bad thing in itself. And secondly, we have the argument from *incurred costs* to the effect that particular economic, political, social or cultural costs are incurred as a consequence of different *decisions* being made by foreigners than those we would ourselves make in the same circumstances. There is much confusion in the popular literature on these two counts. The argument from a purely nationalistic standpoint is almost invariably put forward by opponents to international investment. They quite rightly point out that even though foreign owned subsidiaries may have a very considerable autonomy for decision making, their ultimate sovereignty is, nevertheless, eroded. It may well be that if the flow of income from the subsidiary is regarded as satisfactory, autonomy is granted; but under other conditions the reins of power are inevitably taken up.

7.17 In all of these arguments there is much to be said for specifying the costs more clearly and identifying the relevant determining magnitudes. For instance, *coefficients of dependence* (the ratio of foreign capital to total capital) by industry, sector or even geographical area may be useful.[2] In particular, one may be interested in the growth of foreign operations in certain sectors. These statistics are reported elsewhere in our report. Of course, while autonomy may be greater if foreign firms were domestically owned, this is not the choice open. It is an entirely different matter as to whether or not autonomy is raised by excluding the foreign firm.

The subsidiary's Government/subsidiary management relationship

7.18 This relationship concerns the extent to which foreign owned firms are amenable to host Governmental directive. In the opening paragraphs of this report we pointed out the potential importance of this when economic policy emphasizes persuasion. Opinions seem to be sharply divergent. On the one hand, it is argued that subsidiaries owe a primary loyalty to their parent and this loyalty dominates their behaviour to a degree that can put them into conflict with the host Government. This argument assumes, of course, that Governmental requirements are such that conflicts will arise.[3] Although

[1] We shall see in the next chapter that 'nationalisation' of foreign owned firms is becoming increasingly difficult with the growth of the 'international network'. In enterprises of this sort the individual company is so integrated into the global network that nationalisation or any interference in its affairs becomes extremely difficult.

[2] Often writers emphasize not merely the dependence coefficients but also how *central* the sector is to the economy as a total system. A sector is 'central' if it provides a number of services and goods for other sectors in the economy.

[3] It is imperative to recognise that the question of *power* is only made explicit in conflict situations. The power that a source country has over an inward invested nation may not be at all obvious when their overall interests are in accord. But when they are not, the decisive nature of the inward investment becomes very evident. It is this 'latent' aspect of power relations that makes them so difficult to study. Conflict situations have arisen much more often in the context of foreign investment in the third world.

this line of argument is perhaps overplayed by those opposed to foreign investment there do seem to be grounds for legitimate concern in the context of increased socio-economic and regional planning dictated by goals other than pure economic efficiency as conceived by the individual firm.

7.19 The counter argument suggests that subsidiaries are highly sensitive about their relationship with the host Government and are correspondingly anxious, compared to domestic firms, to conform to requirements. Also, there is always the extra sanction in the hands of host governments. Despite the various studies on foreign investment we seem to have no evidence at our disposal to invalidate one or other of the above arguments. The question we have to ask ourselves is: does the fact that a company is foreign owned make a difference in its response to Governmental requirements, and if so, what difference? We have no reason to suppose that the answer to this question can be embraced by a single generalisation, as the above counter arguments would suggest. The nature of the response to host Government directive will in all probability be a complex issue involving a number of factors.[1] This complexity is not diminished by the fact that a subsidiary can be willing to co-operate with the host Government in one respect but not another. The problem may be posed rather more accurately as follows: does the fact that a company is foreign owned involve the host Government in significantly greater persuasion costs on balance than if a company is domestically owned? The questions of loyalty and persuasion costs only occur when a requirement is made that in some ways runs counter to the perceived interests of the company in question. Foreign ownership might enter the equation in one or both of two ways. First, the foreign subsidiary may involve more potential conflict areas than domestic firms and secondly, foreigners may be more willing to incur costs that arise as a consequence of Governmental interference. As to the first point, we have already seen that foreign owned firms are sometimes subject to constraints, of a political variety, by their parent Governments and, in general, as a consequence of their international links they operate in a more complex economic and political environment. There seems, as yet, to be insufficient evidence to help us make a valid judgement on either point. Experience in the United Kingdom concerning the siting of industry in the development areas, although perhaps only imposing fairly mild costs (if any at all) suggests that foreign owned companies are very ready to co-operate. Though we have no information on intending investors, if any, who were deterred by this policy, in practice, inward investing companies are usually larger and can therefore absorb reasonable costs of this sort rather more easily than the smaller domestic counterparts. Some discussion of these and related matters occurs in Chapters Six and Eight.

7.20 There is a fairly large, and rather speculative literature on how foreign control of subsidiaries may affect their behaviour. Brecher and Reisman (1957) believe that control is of little importance. They argue that two companies, one foreign owned and one not, operating in identical conditions will behave in the same way (assuming appropriate maximising behaviour). But

[1] There is a quite natural tendency for nations to see foreign owned firms as agents of the source country. From a nationalistic standpoint it seems perfectly legitimate to suggest that foreign companies will exhibit a primary loyalty to the managers and equity holders in their home country. Such misgivings are particularly acute when the capital exporting country is as powerful as the USA. However, we have accumulated a certain amount of evidence (see Chapter Eight) that the growth of the international firm, with branches spread throughout the world, leads not to a national loyalty but a company loyalty. But, of course, this may still give rise to legitimate misgivings from a nationalistic standpoint.

Kindleberger (1969, p. 20) on the other hand, argues, that if the two companies are of the same size this might be so, but in general the domestically owned firm would be smaller. The foreigners will

> . . . scan different horizons in space and possibly time and maximise different objective functions. The international corporation may take depreciation allowances out [of the host country] to invest in another source of output, whereas the domestic firm's choice could be between expanding production . . . or not at all.

Of course, we may ask why the domestic firm does not scan these profitable outlets, the answer having as much to do with domestic regulation as with international differences in business practices or in firm size.

7.21 There seems little need to elaborate on the relationship between the subsidiary's equity holders in the host country (if indeed there are any) and the subsidiary management or the subsidiary's Government from the point of view of control. But we may note that one of the reasons often given for full ownership by foreigners is the belief that local participation may in fact make what the company regards as excessive demands on parent company inputs.

The parent management/subsidiary's Government relationship

7.22 This is an interesting and important relationship, and is clearly critical in the period when the direct investment is being initiated. In our study we were unable to do case-work investigation of any actual investment applications in progress and access to historical material was very limited. We do turn to this topic fairly briefly in Chapter Nine. The emphasis in this study is on the ongoing effects of inward direct investment, but even so it would be useful to know how these are effected by the initiating negotiations. It is also the case that as we are looking only at subsidiaries in the United Kingdom, we are in no position to say much about this relationship between the parent management and the United Kingdom Government. The subsidiaries themselves may well know little about it, and in any case it is a highly politically sensitive area. The famous Ford lunch at Downing Street was characteristically uninformative in terms of public knowledge, apart from the fact that it took place.

7.23 Influences involving the opposite parties, i.e., the subsidiary management and the parent company Government are likely to be mediated entirely by the parent company management.[1]

The control of subsidiaries by parent companies

7.24 Most writers on foreign investment have emphasized the distinction between control and formal ownership. For instance, Brash (1966, p. 104) says, '. . . the extent of American ownership of a direct investment enterprise is not always a good reflection of the extent of American control over its behaviour.' He goes on to say, (p. 104) 'American control may be substantially unexercised even in the case of wholly owned American subsidiaries'.

[1] The fact that American nationals serving as executives in foreign subsidiaries are subject to American company law can lead to difficulties. For instance, a Canadian subsidiary of a US company attempted to export goods on the strategic list to Communist countries and was threatened with US law. The unclear legal position of the international company falling as it does between national legal codes is certainly a cause for concern.

Dunning, Safarian and Barlow express similar views. Dunning (1958, p. 106) states, for example, 'There is no common pattern to which the day to day organisation of United States financed firms conforms, nor the degree of supervision exercised by the parent.' And we might add that our results also indicate a wide variation in these respects.

7.25 The degree of control that a parent exerts over its subsidiary can be conveniently conceptualised in terms of the limitations it imposes on the subsidiary in making decisions that effect its overall performance. Complete control is exerted when all such decisions are made by the parent, less than complete control when the subsidiary itself has some latitude for decision making.[1] Formal control is a structural concept concerning the allocation of decision making responsibility between parent and subsidiary and the relative importance of various decisions. A decision is 'important' to the extent that its resolution is a necessary pre-requisite for the resolution of less important decisions. The set of functional decisions facing an organisation may, therefore, be construed as a hierarchical tree (perhaps multi-rooted) where the nodes represent decisions and the lines necessary precedence. So the nearer the 'roots' of the tree a node is, the more important it is. If a parent has in practice an exclusive purchase on the root decisions then it is, in an obvious way, exerting 'complete control'. But this still allows latitude further down the tree. The complexity of the tree gives some indication of the possible extent of this latitude. We will return to these ideas below.

7.26 There are three reasons why the parent organization may want to control the subsidiary; it may be, or believe it is, better at making decisions; the interests of the entire organization may be different from those of the subsidiary; it may have a taste for decision taking. Extensive debate in the management and business administration literature gives support to the idea that there is a problem concerning the allocation of decision making between parent and subsidiary. What we are really after are the conditions, if any, under which optimal behaviour of the aggregate concern (parent and subsidiary) does not entail optimal behaviour of the subsidiary from the host country point of view.[2] If such conditions do exist, we may well expect them to be aggravated if the subsidiary is one of many in an international network, and more integrated decision taking may occur in these cases. Integrated decision taking may still involve significant subsidiary participation.

7.27 The most obvious reason why a parent company exerts control over its subsidiaries is because they are treated as one integrated economic unit, perhaps with an international division of labour taking into consideration various comparative advantages. *In this case it is impossible to leave decision making to the subsidiaries as the decisions reflect upon the overall integrated nature of production and marketing*. This leads us to the hypothesis that the genuine international firm with a network of companies spread over the globe will tend to have a centralised control structure. And since there is a contemporary trend towards the international firm, centralised control may

[1] It is important to distinguish between the actual control and potential control. Clearly even when a subsidiary is in practice given a great deal of latitude for decision making, if it is more than 50 per cent owned by a foreigner, then it is potentially subject to complete control. And such control is always a possibility particularly if the performance of the subsidiary is not up to expectations. It is in this sense that commentators take the foreign owned equity proportion as indicative of the 'power' of the foreign country over the inward investing one.

[2] It should be recognised that such concerns may lead to national policies that, from a global standpoint, are sub-optimal.

well be on the increase. It is, of course, possible that the benefits of integrated production off-set the costs of centralised decision making. Centralised control will go hand in hand with a high degree of information retrieved from subsidiaries, and may also draw on subsidiary judgement.

7.28 On the other hand, it is often suggested that one of the main advantages the inward investing company possesses is high quality managerial knowhow. Hymer (1966) has pointed out that a foreign owned firm must have some advantage over its domestic competitor since there must be at least some remote decision making which will involve costs to the company, and for the firm to remain competitive these must be off-set by some compensating advantage; perhaps the advantage they possess is, in some cases, in part, superior managerial technique. If this is so, and the advantage exceeds any costs incurred because of remoteness, then we might expect the performance of the foreign owned firm to better that which it would achieve if purely domestically owned. In general, the benefits accruing to the parent due to global rationalisation of production and marketing and any utility from decision making *per se*, must be greater than the costs involved due to remote decision making and the remittance of information.

7.29 Over and above the previous arguments supporting the study of the control relationship between parent and subsidiary there is the important question of management morale. If most of the important and challenging decisions are made by the executives of the parent this obviously devalues the occupation of executives in foreign controlled firms. A general reduction in the quality of top executive posts could in principle be a cost of inward investment. A related factor is the placement of foreign nationals in executive posts in subsidiaries. If this is the practice, it quite clearly limits the variety of occupational categories available to United Kingdom nationals. Our work, however, tends to suggest that this possibility is outweighed by expanded opportunities afforded by the multi-national firm which do not, on the whole, base promotion on nationality credentials.

7.30 What we termed the argument from pure nationalism is very close, in spirit, to the last paragraph. One encounters arguments to the effect that it is an undesirable state of affairs for decisions to be made in board rooms overseas rather than within the United Kingdom irrespective of whether the same decisions are made or not. Such arguments can only be construed in terms of a nationalistic 'taste for decision making'. The line of reasoning which values decision making authority *per se* should be sharply distinguished from those which suggest that different economic and social consequences follow from non-national decision making.[1]

7.31 The considerations outlined above suggest two ways of considering each control variable: (1) as a *dependent* 'variable', the variance of which is to be explained by variables characterising the parent, the subsidiary and the relationship between the two and (2) as an *independent* 'variable' to explain variations in the behaviour of subsidiaries, e.g. profitability, amenability to Government direction and inducement, labour relations and so on. In this chapter we describe some empirical results pertinent to the first aspect.

[1] Though the logical grounds for the distinction between the nationalistic and other views of decision making are perfectly clear, it is not in practice easy to make. For, as we have seen, nationalistic concerns about the erosion of decision making may very well be strongly grounded in the anticipation of future conflicting interests. Such concerns seem to have been entirely in order in some third world countries.

Foreign equity and the type of establishment

7.32 It is desirable to have some general idea of the pattern of ownership as revealed by our sample. Amongst other things this provides a rough and ready picture of potential foreign control and of the nature of foreign ownership. Table 7.I gives a breakdown of the proportion of equity ownership for the foreign owned firms in the United Kingdom in our sample.

Table 7.I

Equity pattern of foreign ownership

	% equity owned by foreign parent(s)			
	0–49	50–90	90–99	100
% foreign owned firms (rounded)	11.9	15.2	8.3	64.3

N=420 *Source:* Postal Survey.
(where N denotes the number of fims)

There is a marked variability in the formal ownership pattern, but 100 per cent foreign ownership is by far the most common situation. The table contains, however, examples of new establishments joint ventures and take-overs. The pattern of ownership for takeovers and joint ventures (at time of establishment) is depicted in Table 7.II.

Table 7.II

Equity pattern of foreign ownership for takeovers and joint ventures†

	% equity owned by foreign parent(s)				
	0–49	50–90	90–99	100	
Takeovers (rounded)	4.9	14.7	3.9	76.4	N=102
Joint*Venture (rounded)	52.3	34.1	2.2	11.3	N= 44

Source: Postal Survey.

* Joint Ventures are defined as companies with a foreign parent(s) and a United Kingdom parent(s).

At time of establishment.

7.33 The 11.3 per cent of joint ventures with 100 per cent foreign ownership corresponds to firms that were originally established as joint ventures but were later completely bought out by their foreign parent(s). This provides a certain amount of evidence for the thesis that extent of forcign ownership tends to increase over time, though we have no data pertaining to the possible opposite effect whereby formal ownership becomes less concentrated over time.

7.34 Table 7.III gives the proportions of the different types of totally or partially foreign owned establishments in the United Kingdom, according to our sample.

Table 7.III

Distribution of foreign owned establishment types

% take over	*% joint venture*	*% new establishment*	*% unsatisfactory answer*
24.2	10.4	61.6	3.8

Source: Postal Survey.
N=420.

It indicates that new establishments are by far the most common form of foreign enterprise, there being three times as many as takeovers and six times as many as joint ventures. The time trends for types of establishment are considered below.

7.35 Since there is a marked variability in both the degree of formal ownership and also the type of establishment, it is clearly of interest to know why some firms either establish new concerns or purchase a 100 per cent interest in existing firms, whereas others remain satisfied with joint ownership. There has to our knowledge been no systematic attempt to study this phenomenon. One could guess that technological and distribution inputs could be important. The reasons usually given (Barlow: 1953, p. 145) against establishing full ownership are: (1) smaller capital investment and limitations of risk, (2) fear of discrimination against wholly owned subsidiaries and (3) the belief that local owners bring assets such as local experience, that cannot be readily duplicated by the parent. The reasons against joint ownership seem, on the other hand, to be: (1) expansion may be difficult from retained earnings because of pressure from local shareholders for dividends. It is generally held, for instance, that United States firms are willing to plough back a greater proportion of profits than are British firms. (2) Without all the resources of the parent on which to draw, expenses of the subsidiary for credit and other operating expenses will be higher. (3) Joint ownership leads to problems of valuation of good will and the parent's contribution to management. These pros and cons are precisely those factors one would expect a prospective inward investing firm to evaluate, and a general theory might enable us to explain the observed variability in formal ownership policies.[1]

7.36 Our interview survey gave us some tentative clues. We asked the question: 'What were the reasons for a takeover or a new establishment of the company?' As might be expected, takeovers are favoured when the inward investing company believes that an existing British company has know-how (technical, managerial, knowledge of local markets) that could be to its advantage. It is not so much that potential inward investing firms have a policy of seeking out such British companies, it rather follows as a last option from a desire to expand (overseas because of limitations at home) and also sometimes to diversify. In the absence of suitable British companies the new establishment is generally preferred. There was disagreement about whether a company wishing to invest in the UK would initially search for a suitable takeover. Some firms felt that the policy of the parent was precisely this, others not. Fear of discrimination against wholly owned subsidiaries was never mentioned, nor were capital limitations. In those cases where the interviewee was explicitly pressed on the question of pressure from local shareholders, this was completely disavowed as a problem.[2] The companies interviewed were both takeovers and new establishments.

Foreign equity and nationality of parent

7.37 There are various hints in the literature to the effect that North American parent companies tend to exert a closer control and establish a greater equity holding than parents of other nationalities. This is supposed

[1] It was thought impractical to study these problems in the Postal Survey.

[2] No attempt has been made to treat the data from the interview survey statistically because of the low numbers.

to be a consequence of the greater managerial skill developed in North American companies. They require a high degree of control/ownership to maximise the effectiveness of these skills. Table 7.IV shows the degree of formal ownership against nationality of the parent and gives only very marginal credence to this thesis. Parent companies from the USA and Canada have a greater tendency to hold 100 per cent of the subsidiary's equity than those from other parts of the world. But if one concentrates upon the 50 per cent mark, the picture is not so clear. Approximately 88 per cent of US and 90 per cent of Canadian parents own 50 per cent or more of the equity; parents from the sterling area have a very similar pattern with 87 per cent exerting controlling interests. Swiss parents are the highest with 95 per cent, but of course many 'Swiss' firms are North American by origin. Only parents from the EEC show a significantly lower tendency to own over 50 per cent of the equity. A similar pattern is observed if takeovers are broken out and tabulated separately (Table 7.V). United States takeovers tend to be almost completely of a 100 per cent ownership type; the data for other nationalities is unreliable because of low numbers.

Table 7.IV

Per cent equity owned by parent against nationality of parent*

		Nationality of parent(s)						
		USA	*Canada*	*Latin America*	*EEC*	*EFTA*	*Switzerland*	*Sterling Area*
% equity owned by foreign parent(s)	< 50	11.8	9.5	—	17.0	7.1	4.6	12.5
	50–90	11.1	14.3	—	17.0	35.7	22.7	25.0
	90–99	5.9	4.8	—	17.0	—	22.7	—
	100	70.1	71.4	100	49.1	57.1	50.0	62.5
	(rounded)	100%	100%	100%	100%	100%	100%	100%
	N =	(248)	(21)	(3)	(53)	(14)	(22)	(8)

Source: Postal Survey.

* Table excludes cases with parents of different nationality (i.e. 11).

Table 7.V

Per cent equity owned by parent against nationality of parent for takeovers*

		USA	*Canada*	*Latin America*	*EEC*	*EFTA*	*Switzerland*	*Sterling Area*
% equity owned by foreign parent(s)	< 50	1.3	14.3	—	28.6	—	—	—
	50–90	12.9	28.6	—	—	25.0	33.3	—
	90–99	3.9	—	—	14.3	—	—	—
	100	82.1	57.1	—	57.1	75.0	66.6	—
	(rounded)	100%	100%	—	100%	100%	99.9%	—
	N =	(78)	(7)	(—)	(7)	(4)	(3)	(1)

Source: Postal Survey.

* Table excludes cases with parents of different nationality.

Table 7.VI

Per cent equity owned by foreign parent(s) against industry of subsidiary

		Mineral oil	*Food, drink & tobacco*	*Chemical & allied*	*Metal manufacture*	*Mechanical engineering*	*Electrical engineering*	*Ship B. & motor V. (excl. motor V.)*	*Motor vehicles*	*Textile*	*Paper, print & publishing*	*Rubber*	*Other manufactures*	*Distribution*	*Others*
% equity owned by foreign parent(s)	< 50	—	—	2.2	4.4	1.8	3.5	—	12.5	—	—	—	10.8	2.0	7.3
	50–90	12.5	17.9	14.5	17.3	21.1	24.1	100 (n=1)	12.5	36.4	25.0	57.2	14.2	14.5	16.3
	90–100	87.5	82.1	83.3	78.3	77.1	72.4	—	75.0	63.6	75.0	42.8	75.0	83.5	76.2
	(rounded)	100%	100%	100%	100%	100%	100%	100%	100%	100%	100%	100%	100%	100%	100%

Source: Postal Survey.

Foreign equity and industry of subsidiary

7.38 It is frequently suggested that the greatest ownership/control is exerted in the modern 'science based' industries. Table 7.VI shows, however, little to support this hypothesis. Except for the rubber industry, the pattern of ownership is fairly stable over all industries. Mineral oil, food, chemicals and distribution have the highest proportion of firms with 100 per cent foreign ownership. The chemical industry and mineral oil are 'science based', but neither electrical engineering nor mechanical engineering top the list. It is possible, of course, that our categories are too crude to show up the science based tendency. Electrical and mechanical engineering cover a wide range of activities from fairly traditional to highly modern and technical.

Foreign equity and the nature of the enterprise

7.39 New establishments are usually 100 per cent owned by their foreign parents. Joint ventures and takeovers, however, have a variable amount of their equity owned by foreigners. Table 7.VII shows the distribution of formal ownership for takeovers and joint ventures. It shows that over 43 per cent of joint ventures are more than 60 per cent owned by their foreign parents. So a very significant number of UK parents have only a minority holding in their joint venture.[1] It appears therefore, in present practice, that the joint venture is by no means a guarantee that half or ultimate control will reside in the UK. The table also shows that the vast majority of takeovers involve a very large interest for the foreigner with the 90-100 per cent ownership the most common degree of ownership. In practice, takeovers establish a pattern of foreign ownership only marginally less complete than new establishments.

Table 7.VII

Per cent equity owned by foreign parents against nature of enterprise

	% equity owned by foreign parent(s)								
	< 20	20–29	30–39	40–49	50–59	60–69	70–79	80–89	90–100
Take over N=102	—	—	—	0.9	4.7	2.8	3.7	2.8	84.0
Joint Venture N=44	—	3.3	5.0	6.7	41.6	3.3	5.0	8.3	26.0

Per cent rounded.
Source: Postal Survey.

Foreign equity and the age of the firm

7.40 The phenomena of inward investment into the UK has a lengthy history. Although the spread of international firms largely originating in North America has accelerated in the last decade or so, there are foreign owned firms now in the UK established in the last century. There is some feeling that firms established in recent years are more likely to have a higher proportion of their equity owned by their parent. Table 7.VIII gives the per cent equity presently owned by the parent(s) against year of establishment; the data give very marginal support to the hypothesis of increasing ownership. But it should be interpreted with a certain amount of caution. Firstly, the proportion of equity owned by the parent is the current figure—there could have been changes in this figure over time; though later on we show that

[1] Unfortunately the category 50-59 per cent equity owned has not been broken in our programme into 50 per cent and 51 per cent and above. We might suspect, however, that the major proportion of the 41.6 per cent falling in this category are cases of 50-50 ownership.

equity holding is remarkably stable over time. The second reason for caution is that our response sample contains very few firms established since 1950—the responses are biased in favour of the older established firms.

7.41 For reasons similar to those mentioned earlier it is sometimes suggested that parent firms from the USA are increasing their equity holding to a disproportionate degree. Table 7.IX shows the proportion of equity owned by parents against date of establishment for firms with their major parent in the USA. The pattern is very similar to that in Table 7.VIII, the coefficients of contingency for the two tables being almost identical. Unfortunately the data tell us little about developments in the last couple of decades due again to the low numbers.

7.42 Table 7.X shows the cross-tabulation for the nature of establishment against date of establishment, it gives no evidence for the hypothesis that new establishments are increasing. However, there appears to have been a sharp upswing in joint ventures in the last decade and a corresponding decline in new establishments. But this is likely to be only appearances due to the small number of respondents for the decade.

Table 7.VIII

Per cent equity owned by foreign parent(s) against year of establishment of subsidiary

		Year of establishment									
		before 1879	1880–9	1890–9	1900–09	1910–19	1920–9	1930–9	1940–9	1950–9	1960–9
% equity owned	0–49	—	5.3	4.3	—	4.0	3.3	3.4	—	—	—
by foreign	50–89	25.0	5.3	17.0	14.8	9.0	19.7	18.2	—	50.0	20.0
parent(s)	90–100	75.0	89.4	78.7	85.2	88.0	78.0	78.4	100	50.0	80.0
	(rounded)	100%	100%	100%	100%	100%	100%	100%	100%	100%	100%
	N =	(8)	(15)	(39)	(42)	(18)	(93)	(183)	(1)	(4)	(19)

Source: Postal Survey.

Chi square statistic=85.87 d.f.=18 Contingency coefficient=0.35

Table 7.IX

Per cent equity owned by foreign parent(s) against year of establishment of subsidiary for USA firms only

		Year of establishment									
		before 1879	1880–9	1890–9	1900–09	1910–19	1920–9	1930–9	1940–9	1950–9	1960–9
% equity owned	0–49	—	—	8.5	—	6.3	10.3	14.6	—	—	—
by foreign	50–89	20.0	9.1	20.8	9.7	6.2	6.9	12.3	—	25.0	75.0
parent(s)	90–100	80.0	90.9	70.7	90.3	87.5	82.8	73.1	100	75.0	25.0
	(rounded)	100%	100%	100%	100%	100%	100%	100%	100%	100%	100%
	N =	(5)	(11)	(24)	(31)	(10)	(58)	(130)	(1)	(3)	(8)

Source: Postal Survey.

Chi square statistic=49.41 d.f.=18 Contingency coefficient=0.38.

Table 7.X

Nature of firm against date of establishment

	before 1879	1880–9	1890–9	1900–09	1910–19	1920–9	1930–9	1940–9	1950–9	1960–9
Takeover	12.5	6.7	30.7	23.9	16.7	23.6	35.3	—	—	13.4
Joint venture	—	13.3	2.6	2.3	11.1	9.7	12.0	—	—	40.0
New establishment	87.5	80.0	66.7	73.8	72.2	66.7	52.5	100	100	46.6
(rounded)	100%	100%	100%	100%	100%	100%	100%	100%	100%	100%
N =	(8)	(15)	(39)	(42)	(18)	(93)	(183)	(1)	(2)	(19)

Source: Postal Survey.

Foreign equity and size of the subsidiary

7.43 There is some feeling that larger subsidiaries, since they involve a higher capital risk, tend to be more tightly controlled, and also have a greater proportion of their equity owned by their parents. Table 7.XI shows the percentage of equity owned by the parent(s) against the assets of the subsidiary for both takeovers and joint ventures.

Table 7.XI

(a) Per cent equity owned by parent(s) against assets of the subsidiary for take-overs

		Assets in £ × 10^3					
		1–9	10–99	100–499	500–999	1000–9999	10,000+
% equity	0–49	—	16.7	—	—	4.5	—
owned by	50–89	—	25.0	16.7	13.3	9.1	16.7
foreign	90–100	100	58.3	83.3	86.7	86.4	75.0
parent(s)							
	(rounded)	100%	100%	100%	100%	100%	100%
	N =	(1)	(12)	(36)	(15)	(22)	(12)

Source: Postal Survey.

(b) Per cent equity owned by parent(s) against assets of the subsidiary for joint ventures

		Assets in £ × 10^3					
		1–9	10–99	100–499	500–999	1000–9999	10,000+
% equity	0–49	100	40.0	50.0	—	63.6	66.7
owned by	50–89	—	50.0	33.3	50.0	27.3	33.3
foreign	90–100	—	10.0	16.7	50.0	9.1	—
parent(s)							
	(rounded)	100%	100%	100%	100%	100%	100%
	N =	(1)	(10)	(12)	(4)	(11)	(3)

Source: Postal Survey.

The data give no real overall support for this hypothesis. For takeovers, companies with assets between £10 and 999 x 10^3 exhibit a significant but weak positive relationship between foreign equity holding and assets. For the very large companies, however, this trend seems to be reversed. The data, of course, are very inadequate but we might tentatively conclude that there is a 'non-linear' relationship between the two variables. The data for joint ventures is unreliable because of low numbers, but there is a trend (excluding the first column) in the table in the direction of smaller proportions of foreign ownership with increases in assets. Can any theoretical sense be made of these results? Considering takeovers first, foreign ownership is highest for moderate sized subsidiaries, and the branching off of ownership for very large subsidiaries could perhaps represent risk spreading. A similar line of reasoning could also explain the negative association for joint ventures.

Foreign equity and international network

7.44 In the next chapter we argue that one of the most salient features of international capital movements is the growth of the international network; a company that typically has many subsidiaries dotted throughout the world in different countries. Table 7.XII depicts the equity owned by the parent(s) against the number of countries in which the parent possesses subsidiaries. This is, of course, a rather crude indication of network as we have no information on the size of the subsidiaries or the relationships between them. Nevertheless, network appears to exert no systematic influence on the equity holding by the parent(s). For example the figures for parents with subsidiaries in the UK only are almost identical with those for parents with subsidiaries in twenty or more countries. Very similar results are also obtained for takeovers only (not reported).

Table 7.XII

Per cent equity owned by parent(s) against network

		Number of countries with subsidiaries											
		0*	1	2	3	4	5	6	7	8	9	10+	20+
% equity	0–45	13.2	9.1	29.0	7.1	12.5	21.4	5.8	5.3	8.3	10.0	5.8	13.6
owned by	50–90	22.0	19.2	3.2	7.1	—	21.4	11.7	21.6	—	—	11.6	22.8
foreign	90–100	64.8	72.7	67.8	85.8	87.5	57.2	82.5	72.1	91.7	90.0	82.6	63.6
parent(s)		100%	100%	100%	100%	100%	100%	100%	100%	100%	100%	100%	100%

* i.e. the parent possesses subsidiaries only in the UK.

The stability of foreign equity over time

7.45 Since there appears to be a marked variability in equity holding across foreign firms, one might also expect a variability over time in individual cases. It would be interesting, for instance, to know whether foreign firms that initially purchase only a minority holding in a United Kingdom firm typically tend to 'tighten their grip' by further buying. Results from the interview questionnaire indicate that ownership tends to be very stable. Those companies either buying 100 per cent of the equity of a domestically owned firm or making a new establishment show no tendency to reduce their ownership. (There are few cases of companies 'going public' in the United Kingdom though to a very small extent.) Those companies buying less than 100 per cent of the equity, or engaging in a joint venture, seem, on the whole, to stick, at the initially decided apportionment. Exceptions do arise when the company gets into difficulties where there is a tendency for the foreigner to tighten his grip.

7.46 Respondents on the postal survey were asked to 'Indicate the dates and nature of subsequent [to original investment] principal changes in the composition of ownership'. The overwhelming majority of respondents gave no answer to this question. But because of its wording, perhaps it is not unreasonable to assume that no answer is equivalent to no change. If this assumption is made, we obtain Table 7.XIII.

Table 7.XIII

Stability of ownership

	Takeovers	*Joint ventures*
Increase in % equity owned by parent	9	5
No change	83	37
Decrease in % equity owned by parent	—	2
N =	102	44

Source: Postal Survey.

7.47 These results indicate a marked stability. A close inspection of the cases where there has been a change indicated only two instances of an increase from below to above a 50 per cent holding. Over 90 per cent of the increases were in the range from above 50 per cent towards 100 per cent foreign ownership. There are, in addition, a few cases of new establishments where a small proportion of the equity had been sold to UK parents, this, in effect, changing what was originally a new-establishment into a joint venture.

Pattern of ownership by foreign parents—a summary

7.48 There is a marked variability in equity holding by foreign parents in their UK subsidiaries, though the holding is very stable over time. New establishments are the most common type of concern, followed by takeovers, with joint ventures trailing far behind. North American parents have a slightly greater tendency to take up 100 per cent ownership. There is no relationship between equity holding and type of industry of the subsidiary, date of its establishment, and international network. For takeovers, there is a general increase in proportion of foreign equity holding associated with size (assets) of the subsidiary, except for the very largest companies. Joint ventures, on the other hand, exhibit a negative relationship between the assets and foreign equity holding. Various attempts were made to use different categorisations and multiple regressions were carried out using a variety of integer scoring techniques for the categorised variables—but to no avail. We must conclude, therefore, that in terms of the variables studied in this report, there are no systematic reasons for the variability in equity holding. On the positive side, we do seem to have repeated some of the more widely believed findings concerning the pattern of foreign ownership. This lends some support to the usefulness of our sample for further generalization.

III: The pattern of foreign control

The control literature

7.49 The equity holding by a parent or parents is not necessarily indicative of the degree of control exerted, Dunning (1958, p. 107) distinguishes three types of subsidiary classified according to their 'degree of autonomy'.

Type (a) 'The United Kingdom branch tends to be simply a duplicate mouthpiece of the Parent company, having little autonomy or freedom of its own. There exists regular remittal of reports, a large degree of interchange of executives and technical staff and detailed supervision of production effort. Reference to the Parent is made on all matters of finance, changes in production, profit margins, etc.'

Type (b) Usually only partially owned. 'A high degree of controlled autonomy' is the way Dunning characterises this type. Responsibility for decision making is delegated and 'advice' rather than 'orders' are given. Major decisions are made by the parent but many less important ones by the subsidiary.

Type (c) In this case the parent appears to exert little or no control on administration. There is little channelling of information and exchange of personnel.

Dunning found from his survey of United States owned companies in the United Kingdom that 32.7 per cent are of type (a), 39.3 per cent of type (b), and the remaining 28 per cent of type (c). However, apart from the extremely vague definitions of the three types, Dunning admits that the distribution of companies across them is such that many appear to fall in between. This suggests that his categorisation is too crude and some more discerning distribution is called for.

7.50 Brash (1966) in a study of foreign investment in Australia, seems to have been equally unsuccessful in studying the nature of the control relationship. 'There appears to be no infallible standard by which control can be measured.' He further notes, '. . . the actual supervision of the branch subsidiary and degree of autonomy which it is allowed will depend upon the overall relationship which exists between the two organisations . . . e.g. the date of establishment, extent of financial interest, environmental factors, etc.'

7.51 Brash (1966, p. 105) uses a variety of indicators to study this relation:

(i) *The nationality composition of the subsidiary's board:* He found that 'almost without exception that United States subsidiaries and Anglo-American concerns have United States citizens on the Board of Directors.' But he also states, 'it was perfectly clear that the board of many American subsidiaries are purely nominal entities in existence to comply with Australian company law.' It would appear, therefore, that this indicator is not at all suitable for studying the control relationship.

(ii) *The nationality of executives:* This, again, is not a good indicator. Foreign personnel may be placed in a subsidiary either because they can be relied upon to report back and seek advice from the parent or because they can be relied upon to take the initiative. Brash also points out that many Americans become 'Australian in attitude'. Data on the nationality of executives are useful, however, in the context of the management morale question mentioned in our opening paragraphs.

(iii) *The existence of a department in the parent's organisational structure specifically for supervising foreign operations:* This seems on the face of it a pretty fair indicator. However, many parents exert complete control without possessing such a department. Controlling departments of this sort seem to be most likely in companies with a number of foreign subsidiaries.

(iv) *Level of supervision:* Brash studied the frequency of reporting back and the extent to which invoices, etc. had to be remitted to the parent. Such measures seem, however, to be of little value in reflecting the overall control. Indeed, it appears that a high degree of supervision does not necessarily imply tight control although the reverse does seem to be the case.

7.52 Most writers on this topic have canvassed subjective opinions about degree of control. Dunning, (1958, p. 107) for example, included the following item in his questionnaire—'Do you consider that the administration, operation and overall management techniques adopted by your British plant are (a) strongly, (b) partially, or (c) negligibly controlled by your American associate?' There are obvious objections to such questions. They not only assume comparability of different respondents' frames of reference, but also the veracity of the replies on a subject where one naturally feels there is a likelihood of distortion. This seems to be a particularly important consideration. Indeed, in the small sample we interviewed, there was a very slight *negative* correlation between subjective estimate of control in interviews and objective financial control (defined below) as reported in the Postal Survey! We therefore placed little reliance on questions of this sort and where possible searched for objective factors. *In passim* it is perhaps worth noting that this negative correlation is in all likelihood the result of a degree of status insecurity on the part of executives in subsidiaries.

7.53 The amount of control, as indicated in Part I, is not as easy to measure as might be expected at first sight. It was suggested above that we can conceptualise control in terms of the permitted latitude for decision making. *Subsidiary decisions are those that can be taken by the subsidiary without consulting the parent.* This will, from one point of view, underestimate the role of the subsidiary in the overall process of decision making, for many decisions will normally be the result of joint consultation between parent and subsidiary, a process undoubtedly involving persuasion by the subsidiary's executives. In fact, one of the most striking features of our study (interview survey) is the degree to which respondents emphasised the importance of their senior executives being able to argue their case forcibly and persuade the parent's executives of the cogency of their argument.

7.54 Additional problems in studying the control relationship involve the distinction between the *actual control* exerted at any particular time and the *potential control*. Furthermore our surveys, being cross-sectional necessarily elicit information at one point in time. But the allocation of actual decision making responsibility may well fluctuate over time or exhibit some systematic time trend. Since, however, we elicited information from firms which have been in the United Kingdom for varying amounts of time, we can in principle locate any systematic time trend in exerted control in a subsidiary's life cycle. This will not, however, capture any overall trend. For example, the rapidly growing literature on the international corporation emphasises the contemporary trend toward this type of administrative structure with a concomitant increase in centralisation of decision making.

Decision making areas

7.55 In the main, investigators have been concerned with the *overall* latitude for subsidiaries to make decisions. It appeared from our pilot survey, however, that it is probably advisable to distinguish between five basic *decision making areas* which may vary independently of one another in the sense that a subsidiary may have a large amount of decision making discretion in one area and not in another. The following areas seem to be the most important:

(i) Financial decisions (particularly capital expansion).
(ii) Exporting policy decisions.
(iii) Pricing policy.
(iv) Production planning (including changes in production process and products).
(v) Personnel policy decisions.

We will consider the first three of these decision making areas in turn and attempt two things. Firstly, to 'measure' each area and then to explain the variation of each in terms of some of the variables characterising the subsidiary, the parent and the relationship between the two. In addition, a study will be made of 'target setting' by parents.

7.56 Table 7.XIV shows the intercorrelations of some of the control variables. Personnel policy and production planning decisions are not included as these areas of control were only studied by the interview survey.

Table 7.XIV

Intercorrelations of decision making areas*

(a) Goodman and Kruzkal Gamma

	1	2	3	4
1. Expenditure control	—	0.50	0.17	0.14
2. Exporting behaviour	—	—	0.16	0.18
3. Price determination	—	—	—	0.09
4. Setting targets	—	—	—	—

Source: Postal Survey.

* The measurement of the decision making areas is described below. The correlations are computed so that they come out as positive.

(b) Spearman's R

	1	2	3	4
1. Expenditure control	—	0.46	0.14	0.10
2. Exporting behaviour	—	—	0.15	0.14
3. Price determination	—	—	—	0.15
4. Setting targets	—	—	—	—

Source: Postal Survey.

7.57 The different measures of association give only marginally different results. Except for the correlation between expenditure and exporting control, they are quite low. This supports the tactic of considering several dimensions of control, rather than one general index. But the crudity of our measurement techniques and limitations of cross-sectional survey data should be borne in mind. In the rest of this chapter we make an attempt to explain these interrelations, but a word or two concerning the very tentative nature of this undertaking must first be given. Our work can be viewed at two levels. Firstly we have presented a series of data showing the relationship (or lack of relationship) between the decision area variables and variables like the size of the parent, the size of the subsidiary, the equity holding of the parent, and so on. These are straightforward two-variable contingency tables and have intrinsic interest in their own right as many of them dispel or confirm received views about relationships of this sort. For example, we have shown that the nationality of the foreign parent is not a significant feature in the control of operations of subsidiaries. Secondly, we have attempted the much more ambitious task of erecting some tentative models to explain the pattern of control. We would, however, like these to be taken as suggestive rather than in any way definitive. To our knowledge there has been no previous systematic research in this area and there is a lack of applicable theory. Our work is of rather an inductive and exploratory nature, and nobody is more aware of its weakness than the authors. In this work we have placed little emphasis on tests of significance or numerical values of measures of association. Where the expression 'significant association' is used, it implies an association significant at the 95 per cent level. And unless otherwise stated, the tables where the categories have been collapsed (due to small numbers) associations have been shown to be reasonably invariant to the type of categorisation. By 'reasonably' invariant we mean they do not change sign or disappear. But because of the crudity of our measures we have made no attempt in the sections on 'causal' models to operate with the values of measures of association. Rather we have remained content to specify 'significant' positive and negative associations between variables, again underlining the tentative nature of the enterprise.

Control of financial decisions

7.58 When a subsidiary is established as either a takeover, joint venture or new establishment it involves financial transactions and the corresponding decisions on behalf of the parent. Some parents carry on as they start off and retain a very strong purchase on financial decisions, others do not—permitting their subsidiaries to raise capital for expansion and conduct their general financial affairs with little or no interference. Our interview survey indicated that even those subsidiaries who are rigidly controlled are usually permitted a certain degree of consultation. In the postal survey, however, we wanted to construct an objective measure as we felt opinions would be unreliable.

7.59 The most obvious way of measuring this decision area is to take the maximum monetary value of decisions left to the complete discretion of the subsidiary. In the postal survey we asked the following question: 'What is the maximum capital expenditure which can be undertaken without reference to your parent company?'[1] Although we initially included this question with some trepidation, the responses were surprisingly good and are used as a basis for our analysis of financial control. As indicated in the introduction, there is some question as to whether the amount of financial discretion should be analysed in terms of the absolute amount of capital expenditure the subsidiary can undertake without reference to the parent, or in terms of the ratio of this number to, say, the assets of the subsidiary, or possibly, of the parent. The ratio of amount of discretion to turnover is another possibility. In all the work reported below the absolute amount is used. We did also run most of the relations in the ratio form, taking capital expenditure over subsidiary assets as the dependent variable. In no case did any significant relationship emerge where the ratio form was employed. We will see below that there is some evidence that subsidiary size is associated with discretion, and parent size is associated with tighter control.[2] But relative, or proportionate, discretion is uncorrelated with any of the variables we have considered.

Maximum capital expenditure and size of the subsidiary

7.60 Table 7.XV shows maximum capital expenditure against assets of the subsidiary.

Table 7.XV

Maximum capital expenditure against assets of the subsidiary

		Assets of subsidiary £ × 10^3					
		1–9	10–99	100–499	500–999	1000–9999	10,000+
	0–2	80	40	47.1	40.9	34.9	25.0
	2–4	—	4.0	7.0	15.9	7.8	—
	4–6	—	4.2	10.6	6.8	12.2	7.1
Maximum	6–8	—	—	1.0	—	1.1	3.6
capital	8–10	—	—	1.0	2.3	1.1	—
expenditure	10–12	—	2.9	3.8	2.3	6.7	14.3
£ × 10^3	12–14	—	—	—	—	1.1	—
	15–19	—	—	1.0	2.3	—	—
	20+	—	40.7	19.2	20.5	26.6	42.8
	No answer	20	54.3	8.6	9.1	8.9	7.1
		100%	100%	100%	100%	100%	100%

Source: Postal Survey.

[1] Due to an oversight in the design of our questionnaire we didn't specify any time constraint in connection with this question. However, most respondents seemed able to answer the question. Telephone follow up clarified in many cases whether the reply referred to total expenditure per year or per item.

[2] No attempt has been made to operate with the values of correlation coefficients because of the crudity of our data and measurement techniques. The results must rather be construed as tentative quantitative/qualitative analysis.

As might be expected there is a general trend in this table whereby the larger the assets of the subsidiary the larger the maximum capital expenditure without reference to the parent. The value of Spearman's Rank correlation coefficient is 0.4 (excluding the cases giving no answer). Very similar results were obtained from the cross-tabulation of maximum capital expenditure against sales (7.XVI). Furthermore, the results are almost identical if the companies are broken down into takeovers, new establishments and joint ventures.

Table 7.XVI

Maximum capital expenditure against sales of the subsidiary

		Sales of Subsidiary £ × 10³						
		1–9	10–99	100–499	500–999	1000–4999	5000–9999	10,000+
Maximum capital expenditure £ × 10³	0–2	—	60.0	39.7	58.3	35.8	38.1	21.9
	2–4	—	—	5.1	8.3	11.0	4.8	4.9
	4–6	—	—	7.7	12.5	10.1	—	9.8
	6–8	—	—	—	—	0.9	—	4.9
	8–10	—	—	—	—	2.8	—	—
	10–12	—	—	2.6	—	4.6	14.3	12.2
	12–14	—	—	—	2.1	0.9	—	—
	15–19	—	—	—	2.1	0.9	—	—
	20+	—	24.0	20.5	16.7	24.8	28.6	41.5
	No answer	—	16.0	24.3	—	8.3	14.3	4.9
		100%	100%	100%	100%	100%	100%	100%

Source: Postal Survey.

7.61 These results are summarized in Table 7.XVII which gives the rank correlations between the size of the subsidiary (assets) and the expenditure limit for the three categories of firms.

Table 7.XVII

Rank correlations between assets of subsidiaries and expenditure limit for takeovers, new establishments and joint ventures

	*Coefficient**
Take overs	0.37
New establishment	0.39
Joint ventures	0.42

Source: Postal Survey.

* Spearman's coefficient; other coefficients give almost identical results.

Maximum capital expenditure and nature of the enterprise

7.62 Table 7.XVIII shows the maximum capital expenditure of the subsidiary against the nature of the enterprise—takeover, joint venture or new establishment.

Table 7.XVIII

Maximum capital expenditure against nature of enterprise

		Take-over	*Joint venture*	*New establishment*
Maximum capital expenditure £ × 10³	0–2	40.2	38.5	41.5
	2–4	6.2	3.9	8.1
	4–8	8.3	11.5	8.1
	6–8	1.0	—	0.9
	8–10	2.1	—	0.4
	10–12	6.2	—	4.6
	12–14	—	—	6.8
	14–19	1.0	—	—
	20+	23.7	34.6	22.8
	No answer	11.3	11.5	12.7
		100%	100%	100%

Source: Postal Survey.

It appears that the nature of the enterprise exerts no marked influence on maximum capital expenditure. The distributions of maximum capital enterprise are very similar indeed for takeovers and new establishments.

Maximum capital expenditure and per cent equity owned by the foreign parents

7.63 Other things being equal, one might reasonably expect parents with the greatest equity holding to control capital expenditure most tightly. Table 7.XIX depicts for takeovers and joint ventures, maximum capital expenditure against equity holding by foreign parents. It demonstrates very clearly that as the percentage foreign equity increases maximum capital expenditure decreases (i.e. financial control increases). For joint ventures these findings are entirely in accord with our findings on the relationship between the size of the subsidiary and foreign equity holding (Table 7.XI). There is a negative association between the size of the subsidiary and foreign equity holding and a positive association between size of subsidiary and maximum capital expenditure. We could thus predict a negative association between equity holding and capital expenditure—the size of the subsidiary being the common 'causal' antecedent variable as in Fig. I.

Figure I

A partial model of financial control of joint ventures*

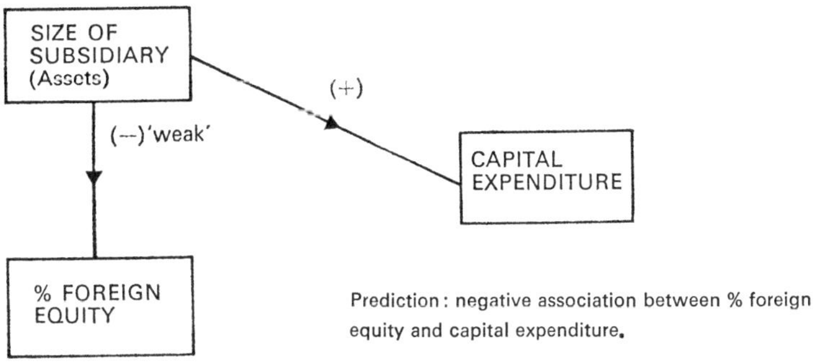

* The direction of the 'causal link' between size of subsidiary and per cent foreign equity should not be taken too seriously. The reverse is clearly theoretically possible; the size of the subsidiary is an intervening variable. This does not alter the argument about the sign of the associations.

In accord with our general strategy, we have not attempted to operate with values of measures of association, but the association between per cent foreign equity and capital expenditure is fairly strong (7.XIX (a)) which leads us to suggest a direct 'causal' between these two variables also.

Table 7.XIX (a)

Maximum capital expenditure against per cent equity owned by foreign parents for joint ventures

		% equity owned by foreign parents†		
		< 50	50–90	90+
Maximum	0–8	3.3	32.5	45.2
capital	8–12	43.7	45.3	30.2
expenditure	12–20	53.0	22.2	26.6
£ × 10³	20+	—	—	—
		100%	100%	100%

Source: Postal Survey

† Some categories have been collapsed because of low numbers.

7.64 Turning now to takeovers, Table 7.XIX(b) still shows a negative (but very weak) association between foreign equity holding and maximum capital expenditure. We have already established a positive association between the size (assets) of takeovers and maximum capital expenditure and a weak 'non-linear' relationship between the size and per cent foreign equity holding (Table 7.XI). Thus, for 'small' subsidiaries, i.e. below 999 $\times$ 10^3 assets, there should be a positive association between foreign equity holding and maximum capital expenditure. In fact, it is negative demonstrating an intervening direct negative association between these variables. This leads us to postulate the simple model depicted in Fig. II.

Table 7.XIX(b)

Maximum capital expenditure against per cent equity owned by foreign parents for takeovers

		% equity owned by foreign parents		
		< 50	50–90	90+
Maximum	0–8	12.5	25.6	30.3
capital	8–12	39.0	23.2	26.4
expenditure	12–20	18.6	28.1	24.5
£ $\times$ 10^3	20+	30.0	23.1	19.8
		100%	100%	100%

Source: Postal Survey.

Figure II

A partial model of financial control of takeovers

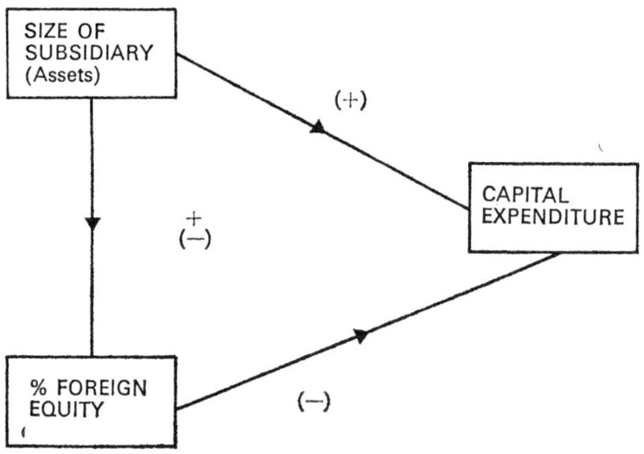

Table 7.XX

Maximum capital expenditure against equity held by foreign parent for takeovers and joint ventures

		% equity owned by foreign parents			
		>50	50–90	90–99	100
	0–2	14.3	27.3	29.4	46.3
	2–4	—	6.8	14.7	7.0
	4–6	9.5	11.3	2.9	8.2
Maximum	6–8	—	—	—	1.1
capital	8–10	—	—	—	1.1
expenditure	10–12	—	2.3	5.8	5.2
£ $\times$ 10^3	12–14	—	—	—	0.7
	14–19	—	—	2.9	0.3
	20+	42.8	38.6	32.5	19.3
	No answer	33.3	13.6	11.7	10.7
		100%	100%	100%	100%

Source: Postal Survey.

Maximum capital expenditure and the number of countries where parent has subsidiaries (networks)

7.65 Table 7.XXI shows a definite tendency for the parents with subsidiaries in many countries to permit lower capital expenditures than those with a few (1-4). That is, financial control increases with increase in 'size' of the network. This is in accord with our theoretical preconceptions where we suggest international networks tend to exert a tighter control over their subsidiaries.

Table 7.XXI

Maximum capital expenditure against number of subsidiaries

		Number of countries with subsidiaries			
		1–4	5–10	10–20	20+
	0–2	22.2	53.3	—	40.0
	2–4	11.1	13.3	—	7.5
	4–6	—	6.3	—	8.7
Maximum	6–8	—	—	—	2.5
capital	8–10	—	—	—	1.3
expenditure	10–12	—	6.3	—	8.7
$£ \times 10^3$	12–14	—	—	—	—
	14–19	—	—	—	—
	20+	44.4	20.0	—	26.3
	No answer	22.2	—	—	—
		100%	100%	100%	100%

Source: Postal Survey.

Maximum capital expenditurc and size of major parent

7.66 Unfortunately we only had a very crude measure of the size of the parent. It was thought impractical to ask subsidiaries about the size of their parents as our pilot survey had indicated difficulties in obtaining such information. We therefore resorted to a dichotomous measure, namely whether or not the major foreign parent of the subsidiary is listed in *Fortune's* top 500 US firms or top 200 non-US firms. The insensitivity of this measure must be borne in mind in the analysis that follows. Table 7.XXII indicates a negative association between the size of parents and capital expenditure. In other words, the larger the parent the more tightly it controls its subsidiary in respect to financial matters.

Table 7.XXII

Maximum capital expenditure and size of parent

		'Small' not in 500/200*	*'Large' in* 500/200
	0–2	39.1	44.2
	2–4	6.3	9.3
	4–6	5.8	11.6
Maximum	6–8	—	2.3
capital	8–10	0.9	0.8
expenditure	10–12	3.2	7.8
$£ \times 10^3$	12–14	0.5	0.8
	15–19	0.5	0.8
	20+	28.7	16.3
	No answer	15.3	6.2
		100%	100%

* Parent listed in *Fortune* as in top 500 US firms and 200 non-US firms.

A model of financial control (maximum capital expenditure)

7.67 In the preceding few paragraphs we have found that:

(i) There is a positive association between the size of the subsidiary (assets or sales) and its expenditure limit.

(ii) There is a negative association between the size of the major foreign parent and the expenditure limit of a subsidiary.

(iii) There is a negative association between the size of the 'network' of the parent and the expenditure limit of a subsidiary.

(iv) For takeovers and joint ventures there is a negative association between the percentage equity owned by the foreign parent and the expenditure limit of a subsidiary.

Table 7.XXIII shows, in addition, a strong positive association between the size of the foreign parent and the size of 'network'.

Table 7.XXIII

Size of foreign parent and size of network*

		Number of countries with subsidiaries		
		1–4	5–10	10+
	500/200	19.5	62.3	80.1
Size of parent	Not in 500/200	58.3	37.7	20.0
	No answer	22.2	—	—
		100%	100%	100%

Source: Postal Survey.

* Association remains with different categorisation of network variable.

There is only a very slight positive but insignificant association between the size of parent and size of subsidiary as Table 7.XXIV indicates. This remains true if joint ventures, takeovers and new establishments are considered separately.

Table 7.XXIV

Size of foreign parent against size of subsidiary (assets)

		Assets of subsidiary £ × 10^3				
		10–99	100–499	500–999	1000–9999	10,000+
	500/200	43.4	61.3	37.7	45.8	60.2
Size of	Not in 500/200	32.3	30.1	43.2	45.3	32.7
parent	No answer	24.3	8.6	9.1	8.9	7.1
		100%	100%	100%	100%	100%

Source: Postal Survey.

There is, however, a positive association between the size of the parent and the proportion of equity owned by the parent as Table 7.XXV(a) indicates.

Table 7.XXV(a)

Size of foreign parent against proportion of equity owned (joint ventures and takeovers)†

		% equity owned by foreign parents		
		0–49	50–89	90–100
Size of parent	500/200	—	65.0	77.3
	Not in 500/200	100	35.0	22.7
		100%	100%	100%

Source: Postal Survey.

† Categories collapsed for convenience.

Surprisingly there appears to be no association between the 'size of the subsidiary' and network (table 7.XXV(b)).

Table 7.XXV(b)

Size of subsidiary against network*

		Number of countries with subsidiaries		
		1–4	5–10	10+
Assets of	1–500	21.4	32.0	20.4
subsidiary	500–9999	37.2	36.2	43.2
£ × 10^3	10,000	41.4	31.7	36.4
		100%	100%	100%

Source: Postal Survey.

* Categories collapsed for convenience—slight association located with two categorisations of network (1-4), and 10+.

These results invite the tentative 'causal' model, depicted in Fig. III, to account for the variation in expenditure limit of subsidiaries. The tentative nature of the model must be emphasised—in particular the associations between the variables are often extremely low. But we feel there is perhaps a grain of truth in the model and more accurate measurement techniques possible with a larger sample could perhaps bring further insight and elaboration.

Figure III

Tentative models for the financial control of subsidiaries by the parents

(a) Takeovers*

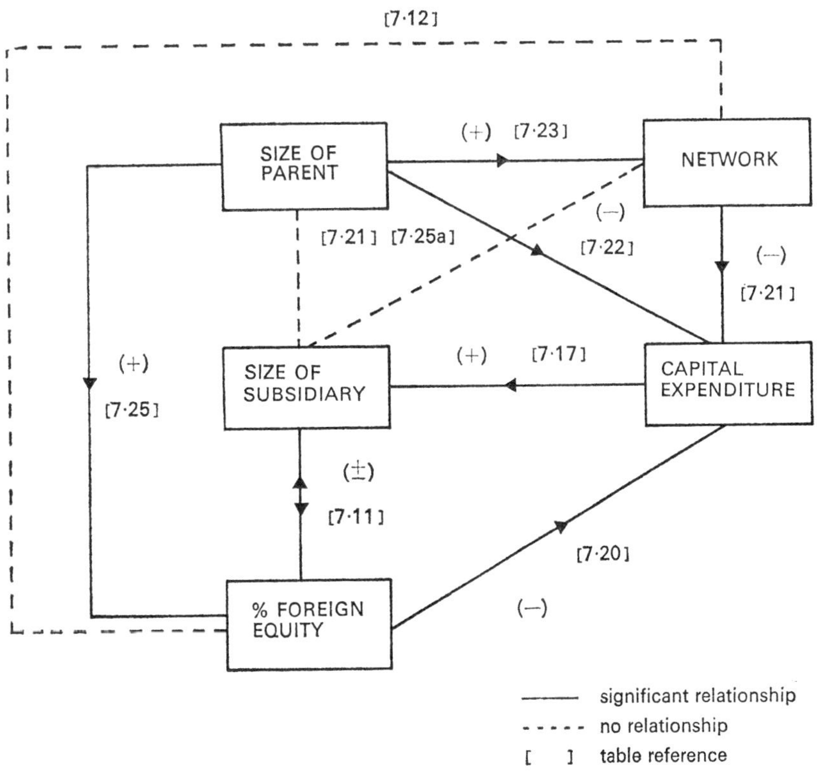

Figure III
(continued)
(b) Joint ventures

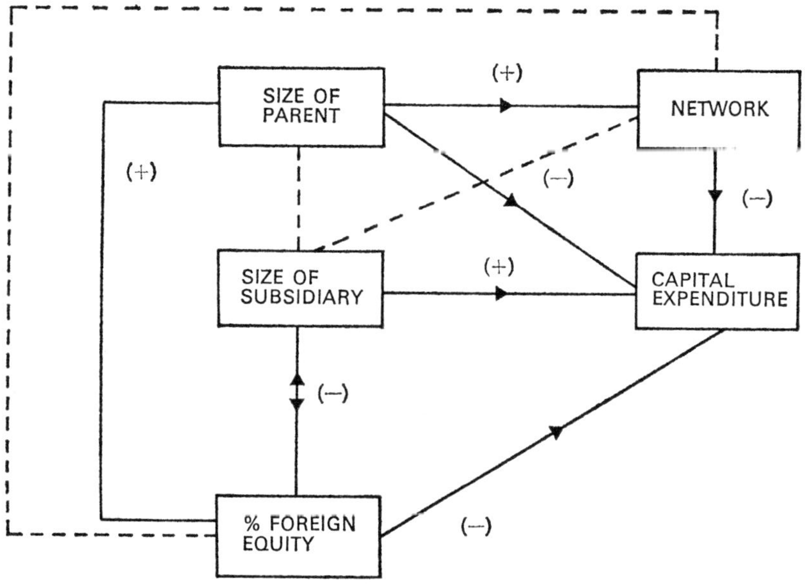

7.68 An interpretation of the model would run somewhat as follows: large parents tend to exert a tighter control on subsidiaries than smaller ones, they also tend to have an international network of subsidiaries which leads to integrated operations which in turn lead to tighter financial control. There is no relationship between the size of the parent and the size of the subsidiary, but the larger the subsidiary, the greater the pressure from its executives for financial freedom and thus the higher the expenditure limit. Large parents tend to aim at a higher proportion of the equity of subsidiaries (joint ventures/ takeovers) and the higher this proportion the greater the financial control. A key prediction of the model is:

(a) The association between size of parent and capital expenditure limit should not disappear when network and equity holding of parent are held constant. The model predicts a direct effect of size of parent on expenditure limit as well as indirect effects via network and equity holding.

7.69 This prediction has been tested and the association remains for different categories of the control variables. There is, however, evidence of 'inter-action effects'. For example, the association between size of parent and expenditure limit depends on the size of network. (Space limitations preclude us from presenting these results in full.) Clearly we have only scratched the surface of a very complex problem, and further research with much more discerning measurement instruments could perhaps reveal the causal connections more clearly.

Financial control and the interview survey

7.70 In addition to the above quasi-quantitative analysis we also pursued the question of financial control in the interview survey. The following questions were asked and in most cases very detailed replies were given:

1. What is the nature of the financial control (if any) that your parent company exerts over you?
   (Note: We are interested here in the general level of 'interference' in financial matters, e.g. capital expenditure, distribution of profits, repatriation of profits, etc. We would like to know whether the relationship between parent and subsidiary in these matters is characterised, for example, by command or mutual agreement.)
2. Does the parent company set targets (for example, with respect to rate of return on capital, sales, etc.) and if so, what is their general nature?
3. Have there been any major changes in the past in the role of the parent company with respect to financial matters, and if so, why?

7.71 In general, the degree of financial control may perhaps best be characterised by 'supervision', with big differences between firms. Some firms are very highly controlled where 'all financial decisions of any significance are made by the parent' whereas others are negligibly controlled. Ninety per cent of the firms described themselves as subject to "some control". Detailed reporting back to the parent is in general, highly developed, varying from monthly to yearly. Targets are quite characteristic on return on capital, and profit margins are frequently set, but these seem, on the whole, to be by consultation even for wholly owned subsidiaries. The general conclusion of our interview survey must be that overall financial control is not tight. Furthermore, the control exercised seems to show a very marked stability over time; no subsidiaries reported marked changes in financial arrangements. The exception, as might be expected, occurs in the early stages of a takeover or a new establishment. Initial control is characteristically very close but tends to be relaxed 'as confidence of the parent increases'. Companies did agree that financial control is a function of performance. 'If the company is doing okay then they let us alone, but if not they are over here like hell.' As our interview sample included many highly successful firms, our results may be biased in the direction of understating the extent of control.

7.72 The major exception to the above conclusion is in connection with repatriation of profits. Even the companies subject to minimal overall financial control often have their rate of repatriation of profit dictated to them, or under much closer scrutiny than the rest of their activities. There is a certain amount of evidence that this form of control has been increased recently, which may be related to uncertainties about sterling. A rather surprising feature concerning financial control is that it is characteristic for parent companies to set upper limits on capital expenditure *per item* not per period of time. Many companies pointed out that this enabled them to circumscribe the limit by breaking down the expenditure. Finally, due to the nature of the responses, we have not made any attempt to quantify the results, in respect to financial control, from the interview survey. But qualitatively we gain the impression that multi-national companies have a much more 'organised' approach to financing. Control is perhaps the wrong word for there is much consultation, but latitude for financial manoeuvre independently of the parent appears to be less for these companies compared with the bi-national firm (see typology of firms in Chapter Eight).

Control of exporting policy decisions

7.73 We noted in the opening paragraphs of this chapter that a certain amount of concern has been expressed about limitations of various kinds on exports of subsidiaries imposed by parent companies. Subsidiaries were therefore asked—'In what way does your parent company influence your exporting behaviour, other than in its capacity as a buyer?' On the basis of a careful post-coding the distribution of responses was as follows:

Table 7.XXVI

Control of exports

	Parent restricts geographically	*Parent co-ordinates or controls*	*Parent helps but sets no limits*	*No interference*	*Not applicable**
%	21.9	9.2	13.5	36.7	18.6

N=420.

Source: Postal Survey.

* The not-applicable category includes those that gave no answer. The statistics suggest therefore, a three-way break between some interference, no interference, and not applicable.

The most surprising feature is the amount of geographical restriction imposed. Some of this may be accounted for by restrictions in relation to Communist countries by the US Government. But Table 7.XXVIII indicates that United States parents are not particularly prone to impose geographical restrictions compared with other nationalities. It is difficult to evade the conclusion, therefore, that geographical restrictions on exporting are not atypical. Unfortunately we have no details from the postal survey, but one would suspect that a significant amount of this is due to restrictions on exporting to the country of the parent. This was borne out in the interviews.

Control of exports and size of the subsidiary

7.74 Table 7.XXVII shows the control of exporting behaviour of subsidiaries against the assets of the subsidiary:

Table 7.XXVII

Control of exports against assets of the subsidiary

	Assets £ × 10³					
	1–9	10–99	100–499	500–999	1000–9999	10,000+
Parent restricts geographically	20.0	15.7	25.0	31.8	20.0	17.9
Parent co-ordinates	—	7.1	7.7	4.5	14.4	17.9
Parent helps but sets no limits	—	14.3	11.5	11.3	15.6	17.9
No influence	60.0	11.2	41.4	38.5	39.9	41.8
No answer	20.0	21.4	13.4	13.6	10.0	3.6
	100%	100%	100%	100%	100%	100%

Source: Postal Survey.

The data lend no support to the idea that the larger subsidiaries are more likely to be 'controlled' in respect of their export policy. Very similar results were obtained for other criteria of size of the subsidiary—sales and employment (not presented). So in contrast to financial decisions, there is no systematic relation between the size of a subsidiary and control of exports. (This contrast may not stand up if capital expenditure latitude is treated in proportional rather than absolute terms.)

Control of exports and nationality of parent

7.75 Table 7.XXVIII seems to demonstrate that the nationality of the foreign parent has no marked effect on exporting policies. There is certainly no evidence that North American parents are more likely to control exporting behaviour.

Table 7.XXVIII

Control of exports against country of parent

	*Nationality of parent**						
	USA	*Canada*	*Latin America*	*EEC*	*EFTA*	*Switzerland*	*Sterling area*
Restricts geographically	20.9	20.0	33.3	31.1	15.4	27.8	—
Co-ordinates	8.7	5.0	—	8.9	15.4	22.2	—
Helps, sets no limits	16.4	10.0	—	6.6	—	5.6	14.3
No influence	42.3	30.0	33.3	37.2	53.7	38.9	57.1
No answer	11.5	35.0	33.3	15.6	15.4	5.6	28.6
	100%	100%	100%	100%	100%	100%	100%

Source: Postal Survey.

* Excludes cases with more than one major parent of differing nationality.

Control of exports and nature of enterprise

7.76 Table 7.XXIX shows exporting behaviour against the nature of the subsidiary. It indicates that takeovers have the highest proportion with no parental influence and the least proportion with geographical restriction. Joint ventures and new establishments appear to be subject to more restrictions on their exporting behaviour. Takeovers presumably have an established pattern of exporting behaviour which the parent prefers, on the whole, not to disturb. Exceptions occur where the purpose of the takeover is to insure a source of supply of components for parent company activity.

Table 7.XXIX

Control of exports against nature of enterprise

		Nature of enterprise		
		Take-over	*Joint-venture*	*New establishment*
Control of exports	Restricts geographically	14.4	34.6	23.3
	Co-ordinates	5.1	15.4	9.8
	Helps, sets no limits	21.6	—	12.3
	No influence	48.3	30.7	38.6
	No answer	10.3	19.2	14.0
		100%	100%	100%

Source: Postal Survey.

Control of exports and equity holding by foreign parent(s)

7.77 Table 7.XXX indicates no systematic relationship between control of exports and equity holding by foreign parents. Once again this contrasts with control of financial decisions.

Table 7.XXX

Control of exports and equity holding by parent (Joint ventures and takeovers)

		% equity owned by parent			
		< 50	50–90	90–99	100
Control of exports	Restricts geographically	33.3	18.2	41.8	19.3
	Co-ordinates	9.5	9.1	8.8	9.3
	Helps, sets no limits	—	6.8	8.8	16.3
	No influence	42.8	49.9	35.3	41.0
	No answer	14.3	15.9	5.9	14.1
		100%	100%	100%	100%

Source: Postal Survey.

Control of exports and number of countries with subsidiaries of parent (network)

7.78 Table 7.XXXI depicts a general increase in control of exporting with the size of the network. There is an increase in proportions of 'co-ordination', 'geographical restriction' with increase in size of the network, and a decrease in proportions with no control in the same direction. This finding is entirely in accord with our theoretical ideas that members of international networks tend to be more tightly controlled.

Table 7.XXXI

Control of exports and number of subsidiaries of parent

		Number of countries with subsidiaries		
		0–5	5–10	10+
Control of exports	Restricts geographically	15.4	22.2	35.5
	Co-ordinates	15.4	—	19.1
	Helps, sets no limits	7.6	11.1	10.0
	No influence	46.1	22.2	16.7
	No answer	15.4	22.2	8.8
		100%	100%	100%

Source: Postal Survey.

Control of exports and size of the foreign parent

7.79 Table 7.XXXII seems to indicate no systematic relationship between the size of the foreign parent and control of exporting policy.

Table 7.XXXII

Control of exports and size of parent

		Small Parent not in 200/500*	*Large Parent in* 200/500
Control of of exports	Restricts geographically	23.8	20.1
	Co-ordinates	7.2	12.4
	Helps, sets no limits	11.6	18.6
	No influence	33.9	36.9
	No answer	13.9	11.6
		100%	100%

Source: Postal Survey

* 200/500 means in the *Fortune* list of the 500 biggest US firms and 200 non-US firms.

This finding is theoretically interesting, for we have already established a positive association between the size of network and control of exports and between size of network and size of parent. We would expect (in the absence of a direct influence of size of parent on control of exports) a positive association between these two variables. The fact that one is not observed is, perhaps, indicative of a compensating direct negative association between size of parent and control of exports. The association of these two variables for fixed values of the size of the network does indicate very small negative associations. But we do not have sufficient faith in the measurement techniques to place heavy reliance on this result. As stated before, these findings generally should be regarded as suggestive rather than definitive.

Exporting control and the interview survey

7.80 The degree of control over exporting policy was also pursued in the interview survey. The most salient feature of the replies to the same question as on the postal survey were:

(a) Most subsidiaries are restricted from marketing in the country of the parent, but not all. Examples of competition between parent and subsidiary do occur.
(b) Subsidiaries of United States companies are (by law) not permitted to trade with Communist China, the USSR, and Eastern Europe. This technically only applies to goods on the strategic list but many companies impose a voluntary ban. Restriction is enforced with respect to Cuba and North Vietnam. However, some subsidiaries do trade with Communist countries.
(c) Only a few parents impose a strict policy of international market sharing, but it is usual, nevertheless, for there to be consultation about markets. Product diversity is obviously relevant; subsidiaries with unique product lines are less likely to be restricted.
(d) The larger firms (especially those with an international network) tend to have 'a centralised exporting and trading policy', whereby the parent in consultation with the subsidiaries adopts an integrated trading policy.
(e) Some parents allow subsidiaries to compete with them in the international market but perhaps not the very large ones (point d).
(f) Subsidiaries normally trade through other subsidiaries of the parent, where they exist, in the foreign markets.
(g) There is almost universal agreement that the international network of companies provided by the international firm is helpful in terms of knowledge of markets, etc.

Tentative model of export control

7.81 The data and analysis presented in the previous paragraphs suggest a 'causal influence' model along the lines depicted in Fig. IV. It must once again be emphasised that this model is highly tentative. The relatively high association between financial control and export control (Table 7.XIV) is explicable in terms of the variable network as a common 'causal' antecedent. Fig. V depicts a partial model consonant with this and the findings on financial control presented in the previous section.

Figure IV

A tentative model for control of exporting policy of subsidiaries

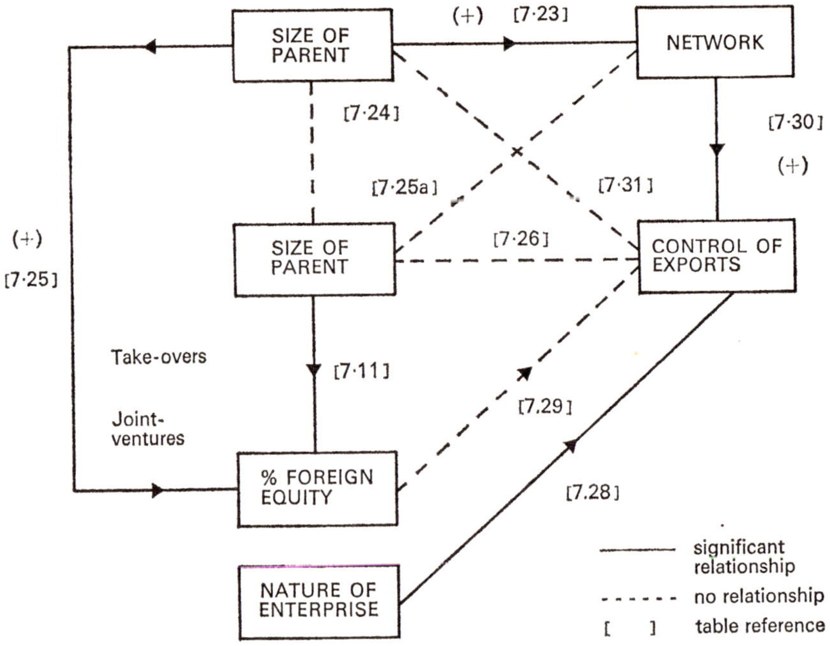

Figure V

A tentative model of control of exporting policy and financial decisions

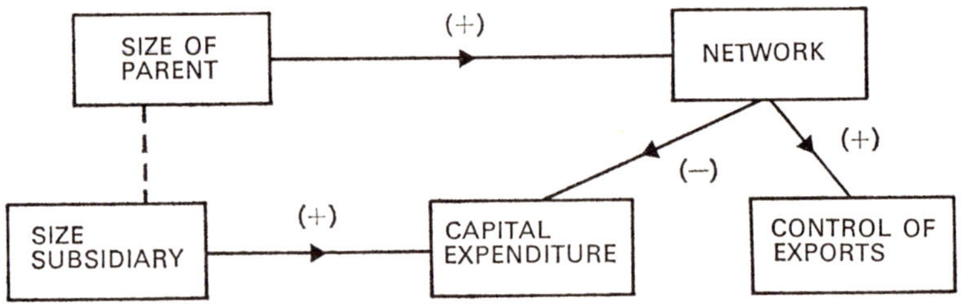

Confirmation of this model can be found in Table 7.XXXIII where the co-variation of capital expenditure and control of exports is present for parents with 'small' and 'large' networks indicating little or no association.

Table 7.XXXIII

Control of exports against capital expenditure for small and large networks*

		'Small' Network 0–10 £ × 10³					*'Large' Network* 10+ £ × 10³				
		0–5	6–10	11–15	16–20	20+	0–5	6–10	11–15	16–20	20+
Control of exports	Co-ordinates or restricts	42.0	—	68.5	45.4	57.0	28.2	54.0	23.4	68.5	40.0
	Helps, sets no limits	58.0	100	31.5	54.6	43.0	71.8	48.0	76.6	31.5	60.0
		100%	100%	100%	100%	100%	100%	100%	100%	100%	100%

Source: Postal Survey.

* Excludes cases of no answer; if control of exports is trichotomised by separating 'Helps, sets no limits' and 'none' there is still no relationship.

Control of pricing policy decisions

7.82 On the basis of the postal survey the following distribution was obtained in response to the question—'Describe briefly the procedure with respect to the determination of your product prices, indicating the role of the parent company.' Over two-thirds of subsidiaries are free to set the prices of their products independently of their parent(s). There is, thus, far less interference by parents in this respect than for exporting policy. These results may be due to the fact that pricing policy is something that may involve quick decisions and detailed knowledge of local markets.

Table 7.XXXIV

Control of pricing policy

	Prices set in consultation with parent	*Prices controlled by parent*	*Prices set independently of parent*	*Not applicable*	*No answer and other*
%	10.3	7.6	70.0	4.6	4.6

N=420.

Source: Postal Survey.

Price determination and size of the subsidiary

7.83 Table 7.XXXV depicts a fairly general, but small, increase in control of prices with the size of the subsidiary. This should be contrasted with financial control (a decrease) and exporting policy (no relationship). The results are, however, by no means clear cut. Though there is a steady increase in 'consultation with parent' and decrease in 'independent of parent' (excluding the very small subsidiaries) with size of the subsidiary, the category 'direct control' decreases in this direction. But direct control in any case accounts for a relatively small number of respondents.

Table 7.XXXV

Influence on price determination against assets of subsidiary

		Assets of subsidiary £ × 10³					
		1–9	10–99	100–499	500–900	1000–9999	10,000+
Control of price	No answer/not applicable	40.0	7.1	8.4	9.0	5.5	10.6
	Consultation with parent	—	5.7	11.1	9.0	12.2	17.8
	Direct control by parent	—	11.4	8.6	4.5	6.7	3.6
	Independent of parent	60.0	74.3	71.2	75.0	67.8	67.8
	Export prices controlled by parent domestic consultation	—	—	—	—	1.2	—
	Export prices controlled by domestic independent	—	1.4	—	2.3	6.7	—
		100%	100%	100%	100%	100%	100%

Source: Postal Survey.

7.84 A similar result turns up when sales are used instead of assets as a measure of subsidiary size. In Table 7.XXXVI again 'consultation' seems to increase and 'direct control' decreases with the size (sales) of the subsidiary.

Table 7.XXXVI

Influence on price determination against sales of subsidiary

		Sales of subsidiary £ × 10³						
		1–9	10–99	100–499	500–999	1000–4999	5000–9999	10,000+
Control of price	No answer/not applicable	—	20.0	6.4	—	4.2	4.8	9.8
	Consultation with parent	—	4.0	6.4	12.5	8.3	19.0	19.5
	Direct control by parent	—	20.0	10.3	8.3	1.8	14.3	4.9
	Independent of parent	—	52.0	76.9	75.0	80.7	52.3	63.4
	Export prices controlled by parent domestic consultation	—	—	—	—	0.9	—	—
	Export prices controlled by parent domestic independent	—	4.0	—	4.2	3.7	9.5	2.5
			100%	100%	100%	100%	100%	100%

Source: Postal Survey.

Price determination and nationality of parent

7.85 From the contents of Table 7.XXXVII it appears that the nationality of the major parent exerts no marked influence on the pattern of price control.

Table 7.XXXVII

Influence on price determination against nationality of major parent

		Nationality of parent						
		USA	*Canada*	*Latin America*	*EEC*	*EFTA*	*Switzer-land*	*Sterling area*
Control of price	No answer/not applicable	9.1	—	—	11.1	—	—	28.6
	Consultation with parent	10.3	25.0	—	6.7	7.7	11.1	—
	Direct control by parent	7.6	16.0	33.3	4.4	7.7	—	14.3
	Independent of parent	68.7	50.0	66.7	77.8	88.6	88.9	67.1
	Export prices controlled by parent domestic consultation	0.4	—	—	—	—	—	—
	Export prices controlled by parent domestic independent	3.8	—	—	—	—	—	—
		100%	100%	100%	100%	100%	100%	100%

Source: Postal Survey.

Price determination and nature of the enterprise

7.86 From Table 7.XXXVI it appears that joint ventures and takeovers are somewhat freer in matters of price determination than new establishments. This finding is, of course, not surprising. Takeovers will generally have an established policy of price determination and joint ventures will perhaps have executives from the domestic parent with experience in such matters.

Table 7.XXXVIII

Influence on price determination against nature of enterprise

		Take-over	*Joint venture*	*New establishment*
Control of price	No answer/not applicable	6.1	3.6	5.5
	Consultation with parent	8.3	7.7	11.8
	Direct control by parent	6.2	—	9.3
	Independent of parent	78.3	76.9	65.3
	Export prices controlled by parent domestic consultation	—	—	0.4
	Export prices controlled by parent domestic independent	1.0	3.8	3.4
		100%	100%	100%

Source: Postal Survey.

Price determination on per cent equity owned by foreign parents (takeovers and joint ventures)

7.87 Table 7.XXXIX indicates that for parents with a controlling interest (i.e. more than 50 per cent) there is an increase in control of price determination with larger equity proportions. The results for equity holding below 50 per cent (not shown) do not, however, conform to this pattern.

Table 7.XXXIX

Influence on price determination against equity owned by parent(s) (takeovers and joint ventures)

		< 50%	50–90%	90–99%	100%
Control of price	No answer/not applicable	9.4	9.2	5.8	4.8
	Consultation with parent	9.5	2.3	5.8	12.2
	Direct control by parent	—	—	5.8	9.6
	Independent of parent	76.2	86.4	82.4	65.6
	Export prices controlled by parent domestic consultation	—	—	—	0.4
	Export prices controlled by parent domestic independent	4.8	2.3	—	2.9
		100%	100%	100%	100%

Source: Postal Survey.

Price determination and the number of countries in which the parent has subsidiaries (network)

7.88 Table 7.XL does not indicate any clear cut pattern for the relationship between price determination and network. If consultation with parent and direct control by parent are classified together, there is an increase in control with size of the network, but the category of those subsidiaries independent of their parents does not show a steady decline. This is a surprising result and may involve some less than frank answers, particularly due to the delicate question of transfer pricing.

Table 7.XL

Influence on price determination against network

	No. of countries with subsidiaries		
	0–4	5–9	10+
No answer/not applicable	12.2	7.6	10.0
Consultation with parent	4.2	7.7	15.0
Direct control by parent	12.5	7.7	8.7
Independent of parent	66.7	76.9	61.2
Export prices controlled by parent domestic consultation	—	—	—
Export prices controlled by parent domestic independent	—	—	5.0
	100%	100%	100%

Source: Postal Survey.

Price determination and size of the parent

7.89 Table 7.XLI seems to hint at some relationship between the size of the parent and influence on price determination. The bigger firms consult slightly more and have slightly fewer independent subsidiaries but direct control also goes down. All these changes are minute.

Table 7.XLI

Influence on price determination and size of parent

		not 500/200	500/200
Control of prices	No answer/not applicable	7.9	9.2
	Consultation with parent	9.8	12.4
	Direct control by parent	8.9	6.2
	Independent of parent	70.8	67.4
	Export prices controlled by parent domestic consultation	—	0.7
	Export prices controlled by parent domestic independent	2.2	3.8
		100%	100%

Source: Postal Survey.

A tentative model of price determination

7.90 On the basis of the previously presented data and analysis the model depicted in Fig. VI is tentatively suggested. The major theoretical point of note is that the size of the parent does not result in more influence on price determination either directly or via a 'network'. The correlation of 0.14 between expenditure control and control of prices (Table 7.XIV) we could assume is due to a spurious variable, per cent foreign equity (c.f. Fig. IV). The data are too crude to make any meaningful tests of this hypothesis.

Figure VI

A tentative model for price determination

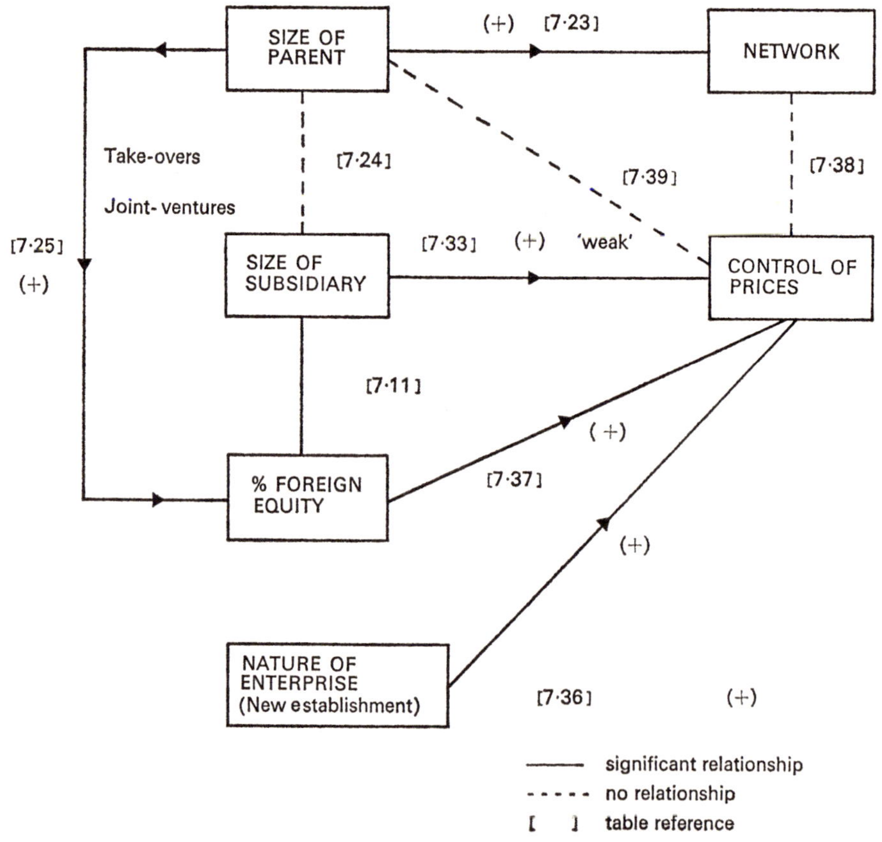

The setting of targets

7.91 The literature on international investment suggests that one way in which parents exert supervision and control over their subsidiaries is by setting targets. We, therefore asked the question—'Does the parent company set targets for you (for example, with respect to rate of return on capital, sales, etc.), and if so, please indicate their general nature.' The following table gives the distribution of replies. Nearly two-thirds of foreign owned companies in our sample are not subject to target setting.

Table 7.XLII

Setting targets

	No answer	*Target set by parent*	*Targets in consultation with parent*	*Yes/other*	*No target set*
%	4.8	20.8	7.6	2.7	64.3

Source: Postal Survey.

Setting of targets and the size of the subsidiary

7.92 Table 7.XLIII seems to indicate no systematic relationship between 'setting of targets' and 'assets of the subsidiary'. Similar results were obtained for 'sales' and 'employment', the other major indices of size.

Table 7.XLIII

Setting of targets against assets of the subsidiary

		Sub assets £ × 10^3					
		1–9	10–99	100–499	500–999	1000–9999	10,000+
Setting of targets	No answer	—	7.1	4.8	2.3	3.3	3.5
	Targets set by parent	—	15.7	16.3	29.5	22.2	21.4
	Targets set in consultation with parents	20.0	5.7	5.7	6.8	7.8	21.4
	No targets set	60.0	71.4	67.7	59.1	64.4	53.6
	Other	20.0	—	5.7	2.3	2.2	—
		100%	100%	100%	100%	100%	100%

Source: Postal Survey.

Setting of targets and nationality of parent

7.93 Table 7.XLIV gives no evidence to suggest that the nationality of the parent has any effect on target setting.

Table 7.XLIV

Setting of targets against nationality of parent

		USA	*Canada*	*Latin America*	*EEC*	*EFTA*	*Switzerland*	*Sterling area*
Setting of targets	No answer	4.6	10.0	—	2.2	—	—	14.3
	Targets set by parents	22.6	35.0	33.3	11.1	15.4	16.6	—
	Targets set in consultation with parents	8.4	—	56.6	2.2	7.6	11.1	—
	No targets set	61.1	55.0	—	84.4	76.9	72.2	71.4
	Other	3.4	—	—	—	—	—	14.3
		100%	100%	100%	100%	100%	100%	100%

Source: Postal Survey.

Setting of targets and nature of enterprise

7.94 From table 7.XLV it appears that there is very little relationship between setting of targets and nature of the enterprise.

Table 7.XLV

Setting of targets against nature of enterprise

		Take-over	*Joint venture*	*New establishment*
Setting	No answer	2.0	7.6	4.2
of	Targets set by parent	21.6	23.1	19.9
targets	Targets set in consultation with parent	9.3	3.8	7.6
	No targets set	59.8	65.3	66.9
	Other	7.2	—	1.3
		100%	100%	100%

Source: Postal Survey.

Setting of targets and parents equity holding

7.95 Although the setting of targets seems to increase fairly regularly with equity holding of the parent, the data for 'no target set' shows an irregular decline matched, of course, by the irregularity in 'Targets set'. These, and other, rather inconclusive results with respect to equity holding are probably due to the very uneven spread across the equity proportions.

Table 7.XLVI

Setting of targets against per cent equity owned by parent—joint ventures and takeovers

		% Equity owned by parent(s)			
		< 50%	50–90%	90–99%	100%
Setting	No answer	9.5	4.5	5.8	3.7
of	Targets set by parent	4.7	13.6	8.8	24.8
targets	Targets set in consultation with parent	—	6.8	—	9.3
	No targets set	85.7	75.0	85.3	58.5
	Other	—	—	—	3.7
		100%	100%	100%	100%

Source: Postal Survey.

Setting of targets and the number of countries in which the parent has a subsidiary (network)

7.96 Table 7.XLVII indicates a clear increase in setting of targets with the size of the international network. This is entirely in accord with our theoretical preconceptions.

Table 7.XLVII

Setting of targets against network

		Number of countries with subsidiaries		
		0–4	5–9	10+
Setting	No answer	5.1	—	11.1
of	Targets set by parent	15.3	27.3	33.3
targets	Targets set in consultation with parent	8.4	9.1	—
	No targets set	69.4	63.6	44.1
	Other	1.6	—	11.1
		100%	100%	100%

Source: Postal Survey.

Setting of targets and size of parent

7.97 Table 7.XLVIII shows for our sample that 'large' parents are much more likely to set targets for their subsidiaries than 'small' ones. It appears, therefore, that both the size of network and size of parent exert a positive influence on setting of targets. The association between size of parent and targets was studied for fixed values of size of network; where for small values of network (0-4 and 5-9) the association disappeared, and for large networks a positive association remained. These results would indicate that for low size networks, the parent size does not influence target setting directly (i.e. network is an intervening variable).

Table 7.XLVIII

Setting of targets against 500/200

		'Small' *not in* 500/200	*'Large'* *in* 500/200
Setting	No answer	4.9	3.8
of	Targets set by parent	17.9	27.2
targets	Targets set in consultation with parent	5.8	11.7
	No targets set	69.9	51.9
	Other	1.4	5.4
		100%	100%

Source: Postal Survey.

A tentative theory of target setting

7.98 On the basis of the data and analysis presented in the previous sections the model depicted in Fig. VII is suggested. It is, of course, highly tentative and analytically incomplete.

Figure VII

A tentative model of target setting

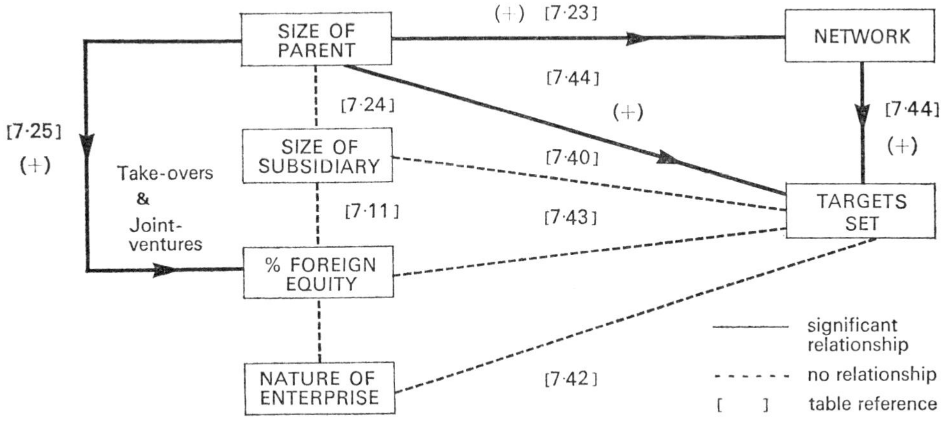

Summary control model

7.99 This investigation suggests very complex relations determining of control exerted by foreign parents, and differing behaviour across different dimensions of control. The strongest result is that the large 'international network' type of company is much more likely to impose a higher degree of financial control, to monitor exports more, and to use explicit target setting. A summary of our isolated findings is given at the beginning of this chapter and in so far as we have erected a plausible model to account for the diversity of exercised control they are synthesised in Fig. VIII. What we have not explored is the degree to which the control over one dimension is a complement to or a substitute for control on another dimension.

Figure VIII
The control of subsidiaries by foreign parents

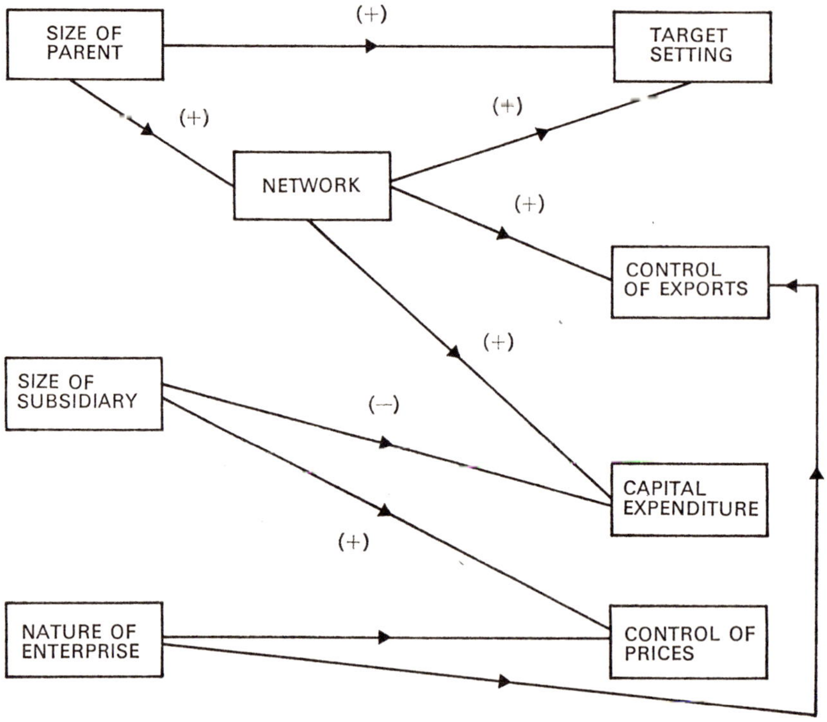

Production planning decision and control

7.100 It was not thought appropriate to pursue this question on the postal survey so our results in this decision area are confined to the interview survey. A very general question was utilised—'What is the role of the parent with respect to production planning?' Again, there is a marked variation in policy. Some subsidiary companies have little or no authority to introduce new products or change production processes, and others have almost complete freedom. It is clear, however, that with the larger international companies there is a tendency towards 'integrated production' and in these cases, centralised control is the rule. Those companies with a different product line to that of their parents are generally much less strongly controlled by their parents.

Control of personnel policy decisions

7.101 This question was pursued in the interview survey where the respondents were asked what the parents' policy was concerning appointments, and how, in general, personnel problems are handled. As might be expected, without exception, the topmost appointments in the subsidiaries are the prerogative of the parent. The managing directors and senior executives are appointed by the parent company but quite often guidance is sought from the subsidiary. There is, however, a great deal of autonomy over less senior appointments. Approval almost invariably has to be obtained but this is usually a formality. The senior executives of the subsidiary show much initiative in this respect. The local Board of Directors is usually appointed by the parent but it is characteristic for the subsidiary's advice to be sought.

8. Inward investment and national sovereignty

Introduction

8.1 Both the advocates and opponents of the international corporation seem to agree that in some way inward investment restricts the national autonomy, or sovereignty of the recipient nation. It is not altogether clear what is meant by this, but broadly speaking the implication is that a nation state subject to a 'significant' amount of inward investment finds it more difficult to pursue independent policies, both internal and external, without special recourse to foreign economic (and perhaps political) interests.[1] Of course it is possible that even if this is true there may be no manifest tension; if the perceived interests of the nation state and the foreign economic and political forces are identical, then the problem of sovereignty will not become an issue. But it would, no doubt, be argued by the opponents of inward investment that there is still the ever present potentiality of tension and consequent reduction in sovereignty. Furthermore, so it is argued, these *sovereignty costs* to the nation are sufficiently large to off-set any possible benefits. The advocates, on the other hand, fall into two groups; those for whom the sovereignty costs are minimal and do not off-set the benefits, and those who see the reduction in national sovereignty as a desirable feature anyway—usually as a consequence of some supposed supra-national benefits.

8.2 Considerations of national sovereignty fall within that complex of problems lying at the interface of politics and economics and as such generate heated debate. But even a very sober report (the 'Watkins' Report) on foreign investment in Canada emphasized the point that:

> Foreign direct investment is not an economic phenomenon alone. It is also a political phenomenon. Foreign control means the potential shift outside the country of the locus of some types of decision-making. (*Foreign Ownership and the Structure of Canadian Industry:* 1968, p. 27).

We have shown in the previous chapter that the actual shift at the firm level is perhaps not as marked as some have supposed. Nevertheless the argument is clear; economic control/ownership by foreigners has political consequences and the report goes on to suggest that one of the very real costs of inward investment is loss of national autonomy in terms of imposed restrictions on the nation state in pursuing and implementing 'independent' policies.[2] But that report, like most other investigations dealing with this problem, does not explore the topic in any systematic way. Although the issue of sovereignty seems to warrant a prefatory paragraph or so, it becomes completely submerged in the subsequent 'purely' economic arguments and thus

[1] By special recourse we mean something over and beyond that which is involved with domestically owned companies.

[2] The Watkins Report, and it is typical in this respect, seems to assume that tight control of subsidiaries (i.e. parental decision-making) implies loss of sovereignty at the national level. The implicit hypothesis then seems to be that highly controlled subsidiaries are less amenable to host government directives and persuasion. This may, however, not be the case and we shall have occasion to examine this hypothesis more closely later.

effectively excluded from the overall cost-benefit analysis. It is, of course, not difficult to see why this is so—the conceptual and operational problems of tying down the notions of sovereignty and autonomy are clearly immense. The chances of 'measuring' the loss of national sovereignty in a meaningful way so that it can be slotted into an overall cost-benefit analysis are, to say the least, remote. And ultimately the question of loss of national sovereignty must be a matter of judgement. But judgements can be more or less informed and so this chapter attempts to facilitate reasonably informed judgement in an area where prejudice and special pleading are the rule rather than the exception.

8.3 The view that loss of sovereignty is necessarily a cost contains an embedded value judgement which it is worthwhile making explicit. Even if loss of national sovereignty can actually be established, placing it on the cost side of any cost-benefit analysis tends to imply it is always a 'bad' thing.[1] Looking at the other side of the coin, loss of sovereignty by a host country may be a gain in sovereignty to somebody else—possibly the international corporation or the parent government. This need not be a zero-sum phenomenon, but the point is that from a rather different perspective this gain may be viewed as desirable. The problem is, who or what is the beneficiary of the surrendered sovereignty? Some authors have argued that the spread of the international firm is likely to be a major force breaking down traditional nation-state boundaries which, it is implied, will lead to 'international integration' and perhaps a supra-national authority with certain sovereign powers. For example, the Chairman of the Board of the United States Steel Corporation is on record as saying:

> The multinational corporation may ultimately prove to be the most productive economic development of the twentieth-century for bringing the people of nations together for peaceful purposes to their mutual advantage and . . . it can thus provide the cohesion which can do more to bind nations together than any other development yet found by man in his pursuit of peace.

Most of us would, I think, recognise this statement as a case of special pleading, but it is characteristic of a contemporary ideological trend, propagated by the international corporation, which tries to emphasise the global integrative functions of the international capitalist system. This ideology is, in some ways, an international parallel to the nineteenth century British experience of Economic Liberalism, which attempted to resist the encroachment of the State into the affairs of the business enterprise. Now the plea is similarly for a world market unfettered by political constraints in which the international corporation can operate freely and, it is argued, in so doing maximise human welfare. We will return to these ideas later in the chapter. But the point we are making is that in automatically placing any loss in national autonomy as a cost, one is taking a narrowly nationalistic standpoint. From a different standpoint we may wish to construe the loss as a benefit to the inward investing nation or company. And from yet a third standpoint, we may interpret it in the light of ideas surrounding the notion of a world or supra-national community. But it is by no means self-evident, as the above quotation implies, that trans-national investment by the international corporation as we are seeing it today is a socially and politically cohesive (benefit) force in a projected world community.

[1] Any cost-benefit analysis normally involves some basic value judgements and the implicit if not explicit assumption behind our report concerns UK interests. However, the special feature of sovereignty costs is that it is possible to take a restrictive nationalistic viewpoint on other purely economic considerations but at the same time a non-nationalistic stance on sovereignty.

Conceptual and theoretical issues

8.4 The sovereignty of the host government is called into question in so far as it is unable to alter the behaviour of the subsidiary or to the extent that it incurs excess costs in so doing.[1] The issue of national sovereignty involves three major behavioural entities; the host government (HG), the parent government (PG), and the international corporation (IC). It is as a consequence of the interaction of these entities, as they implement and pursue their various objectives that the problems of national jurisdiction and sovereignty emerge. Since the IC, in general, operates in a shadowy region between national legal jurisdictions where the lines of legal responsibility and obligation are not always clear, informal pressures and inducements often play a very significant role and, as a consequence, the basic loyalties of the IC become a key issue.

8.5 For our purposes we will view a nation state as comprising (a) a 'responsive' government and (b) a population which has the expectation that the government will act in such a way as to secure a continuing flow of goods and services both private and collective. By 'responsive government' we mean one that attempts to retain power by endeavouring to satisfy the wants of the population.[2] This it does by providing: (i) an environment in which private wants can be satisfied normally by maintaining the institutional and legal framework in which a market economy can successfully operate, though there is no reason to exclude state ownership in domestic market economies nor even a state monopoly system of production; and (ii) the support of various agencies providing collective consumption 'goods'. These will be produced at the expense of forgone opportunities for 'private' consumption by the imposition of taxes and/or restrictions on the disposition of real and monetary resources. We are thus overemphasising the utilitarian aspect of governmental power at the expense of the coercive and normative aspects. It is not that we believe governmental power is solely utilitarian, but for the purposes of our present analysis this aspect takes on prime analytical importance. Normative and coercive considerations will be raised in context where appropriate.

8.6 Although later in the chapter we will draw some detailed distinctions between different types of ICs, for the moment we will view them in classical terms as rationalising enterprises, operating in at least two countries. Typically, they will be large (compared with domestic competitors), have a distinct superiority in technical and managerial skills which is usually more than adequate to off-set the friction costs of operating at a distance across cultural and national boundaries. The IC will, furthermore, usually be the source of continuing technical innovation leading to new products and processes over which it will often have a near monopoly purchase. In this respect the subsidiaries of an IC will operate in an imperfect market and the issues of monopolistic and oligopolistic decision-making and profit taking are relevant. Its organisational structure will be characteristically 'organic' adapting to continuous expectations of innovation and decentralised to the extent that the marginal gains it reaps from local flexibility are off-set by the marginal losses due to a reduction in global and centralised control and planning.

[1] A national government may incur costs in coercing, persuading or inducing domestically owned companies. So the correct concept here is the *excess* costs it incurs as a consequence of foreign ownership of ICs.

[2] We are thus not necessarily excluding totalitarian government. Though one might argue that extreme totalitarian regimes retain power primarily through coercive means.

8.7 We now return to our central problem of national sovereignty. A nation state is sovereign or autonomous in so far as it can, in an unconstrained manner, make and implement its own decisions concerning its goals and its means towards those goals. Thus, the sovereignty of a nation state is infringed to the extent that its main decision-making institutions are subject to extra-national constraint. We will assume that the national government is the ultimate source of decision-making and construe the sovereignty costs to the nation state in terms of constraints on its behaviour.[1] The problem then facing a host government is that the subsidiary of an IC may, either as a consequence of its own vantage or at the behest of its parent government, pursue objectives inimical to those of the host government. The host government may then be involved in significant *persuasion costs* or even in extreme cases find itself faced with a situation where its sovereignty is completely ineffective. There is also a *potential* aspect to the concept of sovereignty; even though the goals of all three parties might well, at some instant, be mutually compatible there will nevertheless be a constraint upon possible alternative policies (goals or means) that any party can adopt without incurring persuasion costs. In other words, a host government wishing to maximise possible future opportunities will experience sovereignty costs in this respect also.

8.8 A further complication concerns the relative importance of goals. If we have the power to set some objectives but not others, then clearly we regard it as a greater infringement of our sovereignty if we lose those we regard as the more important rather than the less important. There is normally some sort of natural hierarchy of importance of objectives for functioning system in the sense that less important objectives (decisions) depend upon more important ones having been made. That is, it is a necessary prerequisite of certain decisions that others have already been resolved. We may thus view the objective hierarchy as a multi-rooted decision tree, and if we lose autonomy over or are constrained in decisions near the roots of this tree, then we would regard this as an important restriction in sovereignty, whereas those lower down would represent less of a sacrifice. Governments try to maintain a strong purchase on basic goals like national defence but are perhaps willing to forgo what they regard as less strategic objectives.[2]

8.9 There are four typical situations where different aspects of national sovereignty are thrown into relief. Firstly where the IC (and its subsidiary) pursue normal 'rational' economic objectives (profit maximising) whereas the host government seeks to maximise a function containing non-economic goals like national ownership or control of the domestic economy. Secondly, where the IC, usually acting under constraints from its parent government, seeks to maximise goals other than purely economic ones whilst the host government is a 'pure economic' maximiser, concerned with gross domestic product and related issues. Thirdly, where both the IC and the host government pursue some non-economic goals which are, at least in part, incompatible. Fourthly, where both parties pursue economic goals but where there is conflict over the distribution of the profit. We will now examine the sovereignty costs inherent in each of these typical situations.

[1] In one sense the subsidiaries of the ICs are decision-making institutions within the national boundary and so national sovereignty is infringed in so far as their decision-making is located overseas (In this sense domestic firms also infringe sovereignty.) But what we are really after is the extent to which government finds it difficult to regulate, in accordance with its objectives, the subsidiaries.

[2] It is impossible within the scale of this chapter to pursue these issues any more deeply. But we should note that it is not necessarily the case that what we perceive as important goals are so perceived by somebody else.

IC and host government in pursuit of economic objectives

8.10 It is generally held that the IC, pursuing normal economic objectives, increases the national product of the recipient nation. This does not, of course, prejudice the argument that some alternative arrangement may be more beneficial. But we will operate with the view that characteristically the inward investing corporation brings about an increased domestic consumption of goods and services. Conflict arises, however, since unlike a nationally owned company, where profits will eventually contribute to the nation's net product, profits of the IC do not, except in so far as they are taxed.
The first question is: are there any additional costs involved in raising tax from a company merely because it is a subsidiary in an IC?

8.11 It is well known that the IC can, by a process of internal costing and accounting, attempt to realize its profits in a country where the tax burden is relatively light. Although national governments usually have legislation to prevent this (the UK being no exception) the degree of effectiveness is questionable. The problems of monitoring the *internal* transactions and assessing the local value added are clearly immense. This is especially true of an IC with a marked international division of labour, where separate components of a product are manufactured in different subsidiaries. Such operations may well be distributed across a large number of countries and the intra-company transactions become correspondingly complex. And since it is this sort of IC which is very much on the rise, we might expect that the *monitoring costs* to host governments will increase accordingly in the coming years. Such costs do of course arise with ones 'own' ICs as well. A government like that of the UK whose jurisdiction is over an economy that is both an exporter and importer of direct investment capital is faced with monitoring costs on both counts. Our impression is that governments in the economically developed countries have to a large degree ignored the possible tax 'evasion' of the ICs, remaining content with the off-setting flow of other benefits. It is difficult to estimate the extent to which tax evasion of this sort is carried on and equally difficult to estimate what the monitoring costs might be if the problem were taken more seriously. But evidence from our interview survey suggests that manipulated generation of profits is by no means exceptional and we can anticipate a growth of the phenomena in the forthcoming years. Although, at the moment, the proportions of this problem do not warrant viewing it as a major contemporary issue, some projected macro statistics might nevertheless help to place it as a burgeoning issue. The IC is one of the fastest growing and pervasive economic institutions in the world today and the economy of modern capitalism is rapidly outgrowing the traditional confines of the nation state. The resources available to giant international companies in calculating and single-mindedly pursuing their relative advantage, in a world populated with nation states each running different tax rates, are immense. And one cannot help feeling that we are on the threshold of a very real problem. Unless something effective is done on an international scale to limit the powers of the IC with respect to the accounting practices of its internal transactions, the monitoring costs to host governments are likely to rise quite drastically in the coming decades. This argument is particularly poignant for the less-developed countries. A very significant proportion of the governmental budget may well have to be allocated to scrutinising the activities of the inward investing IC. The combination of small weak nation states with a scarcity of resources and know-how, and consequently little bargaining power, with large powerful ICs with very sophisticated back-up resources has often been remarked upon. And the future in this respect gives no cause for comfort (at least from a nationalistic standpoint)—the ICs are growing at a faster rate than most underdeveloped countries and the possibilities of one weak nation being played off against another is increasing rather than decreasing. Clearly the imposition by *one* host nation of a higher tax rate to off-set the monitoring costs is no answer; this would merely aggravate the problem. But in this restrictive context at least, there does appear to be a strong argument for international agreement on a common tax rate, thus removing the IC's incentive to manipulate its cross-costing. The host government is necessarily involved in understanding and evaluating the investment opportunities of the IC. It has to scan horizons in space and time which are not traditionally its concern. A country like Canada, for instance, with over fifty per cent of its economy in foreign hands, cannot make domestic decisions about the economy without surveying the other national markets within which most of its companies operate. It is difficult to see how a country subject to a significant amount of foreign investment can avoid the costs of establishing and running a department specifically designed for these purposes.

8.12 The standard response to an increase in monopoly by inward investment is to stimulate domestic competitors. But this can lead to a reduction in sovereignty also for it can put a host government in a position where it must seek rationalisation of competitors across its own national boundaries. If the domestic economy is of such a size that only one firm can benefit from inherent economies of scale the 'domestic' competitiveness can only be induced by encouraging merger or extension into other domestic markets. This, in many ways, seems to be the dynamic behind the UK's moves towards the Common Market.[1] It quite naturally raises the question of sovereignty costs accruing to a government with its own ICs. There are two important situations: firstly where the host-government like the IC pursues economic objectives and secondly, where it tries to impose its own national will on subsidiaries in pursuit of 'non-economic' objectives.

8.13 Considering the first situation, as we noted above, monitoring costs arise with a country's own ICs just as with foreign ones. The exception to this argument might be where companies of domestic origin show a greater 'loyalty' to the parent state. The supposition being that firms which have originated, say in the UK, and subsequently expanded overseas will still see themselves as essentially British and be more hospitable to persuasion and inducement from the British Government. But of course, the more genuinely international a company becomes, the less likelihood there is that one can rely on this sort of sentiment. We will examine the concept of national loyalty in the empirical section of this chapter.

8.14 The most obvious form of sovereignty costs will arise where the foreign host government seeks to impose 'non-economic' objectives on the subsidiary company. This, however, is merely the other side of the story we examine in a later section of the chapter and we leave a full consideration until then. The important observation in the present context is that a national government, like that of the UK, can become a double loser in the national sovereignty stakes; inward investment imposes its characteristic pattern of costs but in addition 'necessitates' the creation of 'domestically' based competitors which can only prosper across the national boundary; thus once again reducing national sovereignty. Of course many observers might construe the latter dynamic as a benefit leading towards supra-nationalism.

[1] This was written prior to UK entry into the Common Market.

If the competition for US based ICs forces the UK into Europe then they would argue that the possibilities of European political union are accordingly enhanced. If the political institutions of an integrated Europe can be effectively forged this must necessarily imply a reduction in sovereignty to the UK, but hopefully the corresponding gain would go not to the giant ICs but to a European supra-national authority, an authority with the will and power to monitor the activities of the IC. If this does *not* happen then one can envisage the sovereignty accruing to the ICs themselves—a sovereignty that will permit them to play off one national government against another and to operate beyond a non-existent international code of conduct.

8.15 In conclusion then, it appears that even when the IC and the host government are in pursuit of normal 'rational' economic objectives conflict can arise and national sovereignty costs become involved. A government both as host and parent to the IC does face additional monitoring and decision costs over and above those it faces where the economy is entirely domestically owned and controlled. We now turn to the situation where the host government is in pursuit of non-economic objectives.

IC in pursuit of economic objectives, host government in pursuit of non-economic objectives

8.16 If a host government chooses to pursue goals other than purely economic ones the issue of sovereignty can arise in a most dramatic way. For instance, governments have at one time or another seen it as their concern to keep ownership and control of some basic or strategic industries in the hands of nationals or to control the pattern and rate of investment (in pursuit of other than purely economic objectives) or even to nationalise parts of the economy. The question we have to ask is: does the fact that the companies are owned and ultimately controlled by foreigners, who for the moment are presumed to be rational economic agents, involve the host government in sovereignty costs when it tries to maximise a welfare function containing some non-economic objectives. Does it find it more difficult (or even impossible) to maintain non-economic goals and, also, are the effective options open to a host government reduced by the presence of ICs within the boundaries of its political jurisdiction? If it could be shown that the IC increases the domestic consumption of goods and services, then any justification for interference in its affairs would be because the same increase could be generated by alternative means at less cost, e.g. by licensing agreements or the like. However, what we want to establish here is that a national government can, whilst still operating in an entirely rational manner, seek to impose constraints on the IC in order to pursue certain non-economic objectives.[1]

8.17 There are two classes of non-economic objective which may be *rationally* pursued by a responsive government. Firstly, *objectives of an intrinsically nationalistic character*, like the domestic ownership and control or even nationalisation of all or certain key sections of the economy. Secondly, objectives which although not intrinsically nationalistic, do involve governments in *persuasion or inducement costs* of one sort or another when they seek to impose their will upon economic maximising private companies. These costs may be aggravated or alleviated by foreign ownership.

[1] Following Breton and Johnson (see bibliography on p. 206).

8.18 With objectives of an intrinsically nationalistic character the host government clearly comes into very direct conflict with the aims of the IC. If a country establishes a policy of national ownership of all or part of the economy[1] and so effectively *excludes* the IC then this raises the question of what it has to forgo in preserving this sort of exclusive sovereignty. But any realistic assessment of these costs would necessarily involve a consideration of 'alternatives' to the IC which may carry some (or all) of its benefits without its costs.[2] For example stimulating national facsimiles of potential IC subsidiaries; borrowing money abroad; hiring managerial know-how and purchasing the appropriate technology; or obtaining the product through international trade, which under a wide range of circumstances is a substitute for direct investment.

8.19 However, the situation facing many countries, including the UK, is one where the foreign IC is well established, contributing significantly to domestic consumption. One might ask how difficult is it to move from this situation? The most extreme case is that of outright nationalisation. Although some of the less-developed countries have succeeded in nationalising foreign operations these tend to have been in primary producing industries where the industry concerned has been relatively isolated and exposed. At the other extreme, it is difficult to believe that Canada (with 55 per cent of its productive capacity in foreign hands) could suddenly turn around and pursue a policy of nationalisation or indeed any policy enforcing much constraint on the activities of foreign companies within its boundaries. We can surely say that the national sovereignty of Canada has been eroded in that a whole range of political objectives open to a fully sovereign state are effectively denied it. The fact that very few Canadian citizens and even less of its politicians advocate radical policies of this sort is beside the point. Even if they wished to pursue such policies they would not have the effective sovereignty to do so. In a very real sense the fate and destiny of Canada is tied to that of the IC.

8.20 Turning to a less clear-cut case, the UK: could a democratically elected 'socialist' government implement a policy of nationalisation? And if so, at what cost? If the likelihood of nationalisation were mooted then disinvestment would in all probability be the response. The host country can attempt to acquire the foreign subsidiary, *but the important point is that in 'taking over' a subsidiary of an IC one is not necessarily purchasing a viable economic entity*. Firstly because, with the emergence of the genuine IC with a marked international division of labour, a nationally based subsidiary may well be producing only integral components of a final product which is assembled elsewhere. What is the use of nationalising an axle factory if there are no suitable vehicles to put them in! Secondly, because the very life-blood of the modern IC is a continuous flow of technical innovation from its RD establishment and a characteristic feature of most ICs is the location of its major RD effort in its country of origin. This may be changing slowly with the emergence of a genuine global orientation where comparative overheads will dictate the location, but our results seem to indicate a notable nationalism in this respect. Stimulating our own nationally based RD effort is a possibility. This could then be married to the nationalised industry, but this would, in all likelihood, be very difficult unless there was a strong indigenous research tradition already established. This then raises the general issue of techno-

[1] This might be national ownership or equity ownership in national hands.

[2] On a different pattern and type of costs and benefits.

logical dependence to which we will return again later; but for the moment suffice to say that by *reducing effective options open to a host government, technological dependence does lead to a reduction in national sovereignty.*

8.21 Similar arguments apply to other policies of an intrinsically nationalistic character; for instance, in the previous chapter we introduced the idea of a taste for decision-making where it was pointed out that one implication of the IC may be that 'top jobs' naturally become the proclivity of foreigners and a government may rationally pursue a policy of retaining certain high prestige occupational roles for nationals. This must (given our present assumption of an economically rational IC) impinge upon the efficiency of the subsidiary. For under this assumption, the nationals would be naturally employed and if any governmental directives are necessitated this must imply a sub-optimal economic performance. A nationalistic policy will cause tension and may even deter further investment or in extreme cases lead to disinvestment.

8.22 It is perhaps worth noting *in passim* the probable distribution of costs and benefits in pursuing a nationalistic policy of this sort. The costs (in terms of forgone opportunities for private consumption of goods and services) will fall upon the members of the national population who would naturally do the consuming, whereas the benefits (in terms of 'consumption' of high prestige occupational roles) will accrue to a particular stratum of society. Unless the potential consumers and this stratum are identical there will be an overall redistributive effect.[1] The realities of inward investment seem to imply the costs will fall upon the consuming public at large (either directly or indirectly) and the benefits will go to a select section of the upper-middle class. So the mal-distribution of the real product (i.e. private goods and services plus occupational prestige) is aggravated. This could, of course, be off-set by a counter distributive tax. Alternatively one could argue that the population at large enjoys (gains utility) from the nationalistic policy in a purely symbolic sense—we control our own resources, etc.—or even in terms of a perceived opportunity for social mobility into high prestige jobs. But in general it seems that too little attention has been paid to the redistributive effect on the national product—in the broad sense that we are using it—in pursuit of nationalistic objectives.

8.23 Apart from setting objectives of an intrinsically nationalistic nature all governments in the modern world expect to exert an influence over the bread and butter issues of the domestic economy. They are concerned with regional policy, level of aggregate demand, stimulation of exports and so on. Legal compulsion, financial inducement and informal persuasion may all play a part in this, but the common denominator is that for reasons of 'national' interest companies are constrained to operate in ways in which they would not if left to their own devices. Who should bear the cost of pursuing objectives of this sort—the government collectively or the company—is a common cause of issue even with domestically owned firms. But the question naturally arises as to whether the presence in the domestic economy of foreign owned ICs makes things more difficult for the host government and in so doing in a broad sense reduces national sovereignty. As before, this could happen in one of two ways, either by ruling out entirely certain objectives normally open to the host government or by increasing the costs of implementing them. If the host government is willing to run a policy of persuasion and fully compensate companies for the costs that their policies impose then there seems no reason to suppose that ICs are any differently

[1] See Breton for a Canadian example (see bibliography on p. 206).

placed from domestic companies. The only difficulty that might arise would be where the extent of compensation is a matter of debate and the *bargaining power* of the company becomes an important variable. In a process of distributive bargaining the extra[1] bargaining over power of the IC may then be a crucial matter; likewise if the government tries to run a policy of forcible legal constraint. Then not only will the possibility or otherwise of enforcing constraint depend on the extra bargaining power of the IC, but also on the extent to which the government can call upon any sentiments of national loyalty within the company

8.24 The extra bargaining power of a foreign IC is a function of:

(i) *Size and resources*—in general ICs are already large and growing with vast resources of know-how and bargaining skills. Most pay more for their top executives than governments. Traditionally, concern has been expressed about the resources of the IC only in relation to the governments of less-developed countries but present trends would perhaps warrant concern in relation to advanced countries also.

(ii) *Overall role in the domestic economy*—if the host economy is highly dependent on the contribution of the foreign IC then this clearly increases its bargaining power. We have already remarked on technological dependence and if the IC is a supplier of other firms the 'centrality' of the foreigner in the economy also enhances its bargaining power. Monopoly power will also be a consideration here—can the host economy be stimulated to provide an alternative to a recalcitrant IC?

(iii) *Alternative investment opportunities*—in so far as the IC has the opportunity to increase production elsewhere then its bargaining power is correspondingly enhanced.

(iv) *Degree of penetration of the economy*—the problem here is the possibility of ICs forming a concerted interest group within the host nation. This may happen on the basis of common interest of all ICs, or if numbers permit, on the basis of national loyalty to the parent nation. And ultimately, of course, a nationality grouping may be able to rely on the sanctions of the parent government.

(v) *Absence of local loyalty constraints*—for matters of persuasion national loyalty may be a key factor. It is reasonable to assume foreign ICs will exhibit less loyalty to the host nation than domestic firms. There is also some presumption that ICs with a global strategy (the genuine international firm) will be entirely bereft of national loyalties.

8.25 Although the record of ICs in the UK is, at present, very good in respect to policies like regional development—the role of 'good corporate citizen' is often emphasised—the future may well give cause for anxiety. In all the above aspects the bargaining power of the IC is increasing. In the UK economy, for instance, the ICs are growing in size, their centrality is also increasing especially in respect to technology, the proportion of the economy in foreign hands is growing and finally we are observing the emergence of the genuine IC with a global orientation. *The persuasion costs accruing to governments are likely to increase in the future with a corresponding reduction in national sovereignty. In certain cases the costs may become so high as to effectively preclude certain national objectives.* It is impossible to quantify these aspects of inward investment but they are no less important for that; and an assessment of the advantages of inward investment to the economy must involve sound judgement of sovereignty costs of this sort.

[1] By extra we mean over and beyond domestically owned companies.

IC in pursuit of non-economic objectives, host government in pursuit of economic objectives

8.26 Since issues of this sort have been raised repeatedly in other chapters we need not dwell on them in any detail here. It is well known that the US government, for instance, imposes legal constraints on the foreign operations of companies incorporated in the US. Export control acts, balance of payment regulations and anti-trust laws, give the US authorities some purchase on the activities of its companies overseas. Most governments, probably to protect their own sovereignty, have regulations of this general nature.

8.27 Stated abstractly, one of the national sovereignty worries of a recipient nation is that the IC will act as an agent of the source country. Thus a US owned company operating in the UK may operate in the sectional interests of the US government, equity holders in the US, managers or even the US military. Interference by foreign governments through the agency of its companies overseas is well documented, particularly in the relatively weak, less-developed nations. Foreign investment often flows from powerful countries to less powerful countries and it would be idle to pretend that investment across national boundaries does not take place against a significant backcloth of international power politics.

Technological dependence and cultural variety

8.28 International corporations are over represented in industries based upon high-technology and we have had repeated cause, in both this and the previous chapter, to point to the possibility of a host nation becoming dependent on the technology of foreigners. If ICs tend to locate their RD effort on their country of origin and the on-going production is dependent on a continual input of technical innovations then a host country becomes correspondingly dependent on the foreigner. We have examined the economics of technological transfer inherent in inward investment in Chapter Three. Here we want to draw out some of the sovereignty implications for a nation state with a very significant proportion of its sources of RD in foreign hands. All the issues we referred to above are clearly implicated. ICs with a monopoly or near monopoly purchase on a flow of a particular style of technology are in a correspondingly strong bargaining position. But in addition concern must be expressed about the international distribution of externalities. Stephen Hymer has popularised a vision of the future where the majority of the world production capacity is in the hands of a few hundred ICs who for historical reasons will have originated predominantly in the US and to a lesser extent in Europe. He envisages the world divided into regions; firstly where the IC has its central controlling research and high prestige organisations engendering strong cultural and social externalities leading to a rich cultural life characteristic of contemporary capital cities; secondly a vast hinterland relatively speaking culturally and socially deprived. In other words a picture, multiplied on an international scale, of most advanced capitalist countries. Related to this is the fact that the ICs are becoming the major producers of new ideas and in a sense dictate the nature of the technical infrastructure of modern society.[1] Many under-developed countries have remarked on the unsuitability of 'western technology' for their needs and it is difficult

[1] The suggestion is that this phenomenon is on the increase. One does not have to be a technological determinist to entertain the proposition that the technology of a society influences the style of life in a very fundamental way.

to evade the conclusion that if the growth of the IC continues unabated, in its present form, this will severely curtail the *cultural diversity* in the world. It is often said that Europe is going the way of North America and North America the way of California. Perhaps if the IC is given free reign then there will be a global capitulation to the 'American way of life'. In this context the penetration of American business into advertising, marketing and consumer goods industries is worthy of mention. If any utility at all is placed upon cultural diversity then the IC must be seen (on present practice) as a threat. A world wanting to resist uniformity in its cultural patterns must search for technical progress and economic growth which responds to local tradition, preserving that which is good, destroying that which is not. A host government pursuing a policy of encouragement of indigenous cultural traits may well find itself in open conflict with the IC.

Types of international corporations

8.29 In the previous sections no attempt has been made to differentiate between different styles of IC. However, we have repeatedly emphasised the growth of the IC with a 'genuine international orientation' and in this context we have found it useful to operate empirically with the typology set out in Table 8.I. It is self-explanatory and use will be made of it in the next section.

Some suggestive empirical results[1]

8.30 The theoretical considerations outlined in the earlier sections of this chapter emphasised the emergency of the supra-national corporation (Table 8.I) as a contemporary phenomenon with a characteristic pattern of sovereignty costs. On the basis of these considerations we entertained the following interrelated hypotheses:

H.1 *The greater the international division of labour of an IC the more centralised its control structure.*

By international division of labour we mean—the distribution of manufacture of components of a product across a number of subsidiaries usually taking into consideration various comparative advantages.

H.2 *The more centralised the control structure of an IC the greater the global orientation of its subsidiary* (i.e. its chief executives).

By global orientation we mean an attitude on behalf of the subsidiary's decision-makers which emphasises a global strategy and thinking towards manufacture, marketing, and so on.

H.3 *The greater the global orientation of a subsidiary the less amenable it is to host government directives* (i.e. the less is its loyalty to local political interest).

H.4 *The less amenable a subsidiary (an IC) is to host government directive the greater the persuasion costs.*

[1] We would emphasise that these results are based on interviews with only sixteen ICs selected to range over the types of IC in Table 8.I. There is no pretence of statistical significance.

The following hypotheses may then be deduced from those four hypotheses:

H.5 *The greater the international division of labour of an IC the greater the global orientation of its subsidiaries.*

H.6 *The greater the international division of labour of an IC the less amenable it is to host government directives.*

H.7 *The greater the international division of labour the greater the persuasion costs.*

H.8 *The more centralised the control structure of an IC the less amenable it is to government directive.*

H.9 *The more centralised the control structure of an IC the greater the persuasion costs.*

Table 8.I

Name	*Typical equity ownership pattern*	*Control*	*Typical flow of profits*	*Typical financing*	*Loyalty of subsidiaries*
Domestic firm with non-controlling	Foreign interest less than 'controlling' (often < 50%)	Domestic	Proportion to foreign interest	Domestic with possibility of foreigh input	Domestic: ethnocentric
Joint venture with foreign associate	50/50 or agreed proportion	Often domestic (advantages of locality)	Proportion to foreign interest—normally fixed in proportion to equity holding	Joint	Domestic: ethnocentric
Bi-national; Parent (foreign) and subsidiary	Parent normally < 50% tendency to 100%	Parent has potential control but variation in exercise (see previous chapter)	Repatriation to Parent, but much variation negotiation	1. Domestic profits 2. Domestic money market 3. Inflow from Parent	Conflict: varying loyalty (little known see below)
Multi-national; Parent with subsidiaries in a number of countries	Parent, normally 50% in all subsidiaries, tending to 100%	Parent tends to control but each subsidiary has some autonomy. Little overall integration	Repatriation to Parent	1. Domestic profits 2. Domestic Money Market 3. Inflow from Parent	Conflict but probably more to parent than for Bi-national? Polycentric
Centralised multi-national	Parent, normally 50% strong tendency to 100%	Strong overall control by Parent: tending to integrated operations	Repatriation to Parent or other subsidiaries for financing expansion etc	Cross financing—global orientation developing	Loyalty to Parent develops?
Supra-national Corporation	As for centralised multi-national	Independent control centre. Parent seen as 1 among a series of concerns. Controls centre not necessarily in country of Parent, integrated operations	International	Cross financing	Less to parent nationality?
Trans-national Corporation	Complex cross-national ownership. *No Clear Parent*	Independent Control Centre	International	Cross financing	Tendencies to supra-national orientation

8.31 From our typology in Table 8.I and H.6 we further deduce:

The amenability to host government directive has the following ranking—

bi-national, multi-national, centralised multi-national, supra-national

In the context of this ranking we asked two questions:

(1) What is the attitude of the company to the United Kingdom Governmental requirements?

and

(2) Where does the loyalty of the company (i.e. the subsidiary) lie—mainly with the UK or with the parent's nation state?

8.32 These are quite evidently very naive questions and it is difficult to obtain truthful answers, though on the basis of extensive probing we felt that our results were reasonably reliable. Although quite naturally none of the companies admitted to any 'disloyalty' to the UK it was possible on the basis of a post-coding of the responses to establish a variation in this respect. At one extreme we have subsidiaries who characteristically say they regard themselves as UK companies, no problems of loyalty ever arise, and if they did UK interests would come first. Responses of this sort came from bi-national and multi-national firms (N=12); typical responses were as follows:

> This company is exactly like all other UK companies in its attitude to government. We sometimes find politicians irksome but we always fall into line—sometimes we argue—but the fact that we are foreign makes no difference at all.

and

> We are entirely loyal to the UK. We think of ourselves as a British company and there is no question of loyalties lying elsewhere. Indeed we have a positive policy approach to government. Our parent exerts no pressure, they expect us to play the game with national politics.

At the other extreme the characteristic response was, 'We recognise that we are a foreign owned concern and must ultimately feel our responsibilities in that direction.' In other words, there was an explicit admission of external interests. These responses (without exception) came from what we have termed centralised multi-national (N=5) and supra-national (N=1) companies. The responses to the two questions from the latter were:

> You will appreciate that we find ourselves subject to governmental requirements from *home* [note the respondent was a UK citizen] and here. This can make things awkward but we are, of course, entirely loyal to the government *over here*—you must remember that we operate in nearly every country in the non-Communist world and have to learn how to handle politicians as part of the job these days . . . First and foremost we are an international trading company benefiting the consumer on an international scale and that is where our duty lies.

We may certainly interpret these results as supportive of our central hypotheses though clearly much more research needs to be carried out.

8.33 A key test of our hypotheses turned on companies' attitudes to the wage pause introduced by the Labour administration. Four of the centralised multi-national firms said they 'tried to comply but failed' whereas eight of the twelve bi-national and multi-national firms said they complied.

8.34 Kindleberger has suggested that a good way of distinguishing between what he terms the national firm with foreign operators, the multi-national firm and the international firm is their attitude to foreign exchange risks and equalisation of profit. The national firm will not hold foreign currency (i.e. currency of host nation); the multi-national firm will 'as a matter of policy', i.e. a 'good citizen policy'. The international firm, however, takes a global view on the stability of currencies. We found it impossible to test these ideas as most companies we interviewed were extremely reluctant to discuss their foreign exchange position or policy. Though some of the larger firms admitted restricting sterling reserves before devaluation. In connection with equalisation of profit, Kindleberger suggests that national firms with foreign operations will require 'a higher return on foreign capital than at home' whereas the multi-national firm 'takes on a life of its own' with its 'own rate of profit'. The international firm will however 'equalise at the margin everywhere in the world, subject to discount on risk'. Again we found it impossible to obtain direct answers to questions of this sort, though we did detect a global attitude to profits on the part of network firms.

Pressure groups

8.35 Most subsidiaries of United States parents have 'connections' with the American Chamber of Commerce, but there seems to be no indication that it is utilised in a concerted way as a pressure group. It is normally regarded as an information source. We did find evidence for informal contacts between large American firms. NCR, Heinz, Kodak, General Motors and a few others have an informal 'dinner party' grouping where 'common problems' are discussed. It is carefully selected so that competitors are not members (e.g. Ford is excluded). For what it is worth, the existence of any such grouping was denied by some of the members. American owned firms resisted the notion that they, in any sense, form a connected pressure group in United Kingdom politics. 'Those differences of interest through competition are often more than their common interests.'

8.36 Isolated examples of political discrimination do occur. For instance, Canadian Breweries (Great Britain) Ltd., told us: 'After 1964 [General Election] investment stopped—we were told that the Canadian Board declined to invest any further money while the United Kingdom had a Labour Government.'

Summary

8.37 We have included a chapter on sovereignty more because we feel it belongs on the agenda of an appraisal of inward investment than because we feel either the conceptual framework or the limited evidence presented does justice to the topic. Part of the problem lies in the fact that the greatest fears from the point of view of possible loss of sovereignty in the United Kingdom due to inward investment have to do with expected future expansion of multi-national activity rather than with past experience. The major conclusion which emerges is that existing institutional arrangements in the United Kingdom are not adequate for properly monitoring the activities of foreign owned firms. It would be wise to concentrate on this rather than emphasising government to government co-operation which could be difficult to achieve, and itself involve a loss of sovereignty.

9. United Kingdom regulation of inward investment

Introduction

9.1 It is useful for the purposes of the present study to have a summary statement of the regulations surrounding foreign direct investment in this country. This chapter will first discuss the legislation in this area, and will then go on to consider the criteria on which this legislation is based and how it is applied.

9.2 A foreign company wishing to make a direct investment in this country may have to obtain permission to export capital from its own financial authorities, will certainly have to obtain permission, under the Exchange Control Act, 1947, to import capital into this country, and will then have to conform to the English law relating to the establishment of new companies or the purchase of existing companies.

9.3 The first and last stages in this legal process can be briefly dealt with. Until quite recently, for the large majority of foreign companies, no encumbrances existed on the export of capital. In the USA, Canada, Switzerland, France and Germany, no regulations concerning the export of capital existed. The Netherlands, on the other hand, had, and still has, roughly similar requirements to the United Kingdom; exchange control regulations compel Dutch firms to seek permission to export capital, and the general criterion applied is that the investment should be of long-term benefit to the Dutch economy. An important recent development has however been the restraint on foreign investment imposed on US firms by the US Government. This restricts the amount of investment which may be financed in the UK by outflow of funds from the US to 60 per cent of its 1966 level. Though this is not a permanent restriction, its duration is uncertain since its termination presumably depends on an improvement in the US balance of payments.

9.4 With regard to the last step, in setting up a company, or taking over an existing one, the foreign investor is subject to exactly the same requirements as a British company. He can choose the status of a public or private company, the latter choice implying that he must publish annually a balance sheet and profit and loss account. Finally, in its continuing operations, the foreign owned company is treated from the legal standpoint exactly as a British company, except for the Exchange Control regulations now to be discussed.

9.5 The Exchange Control Act, (subsequently referred to as 'the Act') is the only British legislation which specifically affects foreign investors: in all other matters their subsidiaries are treated as British firms. The provisions of the Act affect inward investors in two ways: in the initial establishment of a subsidiary; and in the subsequent control of the subsidiary's financial affairs. It will therefore be useful to discuss the Act under these two separate heads.

Initial investment

9.6 The Act prohibits, except with the permission of the Treasury, virtually all financial transactions between residents of the United Kingdom and residents outside the Scheduled Territories ('non-residents') and also transactions involving non-residents which take place in the UK. Thus, broadly speaking, except where the permission of the Treasury is given:

(a) Section 1 and 2 prohibit persons in or resident in the UK, other than an authorized dealer, from buying, borrowing, selling, lending or holding foreign currency.

(b) Sections 5(c) and 6(i) prohibit persons in or resident in the UK from placing sums to the credit of non-residents.

(c) Section 8 prohibits the issue of securities to non-residents where the securities are to be issued or registered.

(d) Section 9 prohibits the transfer of securities to or from non-residents.

(e) Section 30(2) prohibits any act whereby a body corporate which is directly or indirectly controlled by UK residents ceases to be so controlled, but this does not apply to dealings in the ordinary course of business on a stock exchange. Though this exception in principle permits control to be gained through the purchase of shares on the stock market, it is generally believed that this would be such a slow and expensive way of gaining control of a company that it is thought unlikely to represent a serious loophole. There are also safeguards against this happening embodied in the technical exchange control permissions given to professional dealers in securities.

9.7 The import of capital in order to set up a new firm or take over an existing company requires specific permission from the Treasury, and this permission, if given, may, or may not, be subject to conditions. It is unnecessary to determine precisely which Sections of the Act may catch a given transaction. It is sufficient to establish that permission is required under one Section, while, if permission is given, for a particular transaction, it is given for all purposes of the Act.

Foreign exchange criteria

The criteria on which the decision to permit inward investment depends are clearly of crucial importance. We can distinguish two sets of criteria: those concerned with the effect of the investment on foreign exchange reserves; and those relating to the broader implications of inward investment.

9.8 These criteria were as follows up to April 1972:

(a) the investment must make an 'appropriate' contribution to the reserves. What is 'appropriate' depends on the degree of control being taken by the foreign company. Where, for example, the foreign company will take 100 per cent of the voting shares of the subsidiary, i.e. it has 100 per cent control, then it may be expected to finance the fixed assets of the subsidiary also by 100 per cent. In other words, the amount of foreign currency brought in to finance the fixed assets of the company must be proportionate to the interest of the foreign company in the subsidiary. A major exception to this is where the subsidiary's activities 'promise special advantage' to the United

Kingdom economy, e.g. the subsidiary would be in an assisted area. In this case, the foreign company is permitted to raise finance in this country for a new project up to an amount equal, for the first three years, of up to 50 per cent of the fixed assets attributable to its stake in the subsidiary, e.g. where the foreign company owned 100 per cent of the equity it could raise fixed interest loans in this country of up to 50 per cent of the total value of the equity. This example is more likely to apply to a new establishment than to a take-over.

(b) The purchase price must be a 'fair consideration' for the assets acquired by the foreign company. That is, the purchase price must reflect the market value of the assets, including the capitalised value of patents, research results, etc.

(c) Any further finance for fixed assets required by the company shall also be provided by capital imports by an amount proportionate to the foreign stake, except where concessions have been made (see (a) above), although once the fixed assets are appropriately financed, the subsidiary may in most cases have free access to sterling borrowing for working capital purposes.

9.9 In the 1972 Budget it was announced that subsidiaries in the UK of companies directly owned by residents of EEC countries, Denmark and Norway, and which were not indirectly owned by residents of other non-sterling area countries, might in general now borrow sterling in the UK without limit for direct (but not portfolio) investment in any part of the United Kingdom. All foreign owned UK companies would now normally be allowed to borrow sterling in the UK without limit for new direct investments in the assisted areas and Northern Ireland. The intention of the concession for companies owned by EEC residents was to bring UK arrangements into conformity with EEC directives on capital movements.

9.10 The rationale of these criteria is clearly a *quid pro quo* argument. In return for the given degree of loss of control, and also of rights to future dividends, we should at least receive some sort of benefit in the form of an addition to foreign exchange reserves.

9.11 These criteria are not laid down in legislation. They are, however, made known from time to time, and the merchant banks, who will in general advise a foreign company wishing to invest in this country, have full knowledge of them.

General criteria of desirability

9.12 Successive UK Governments have reserved the right to examine on their merits economically important foreign take-overs, but have refrained from publishing any hard and fast criteria of acceptability. In practice, the outcome of all important cases has been approval of the investment, subject in a few cases to undertakings about future intentions (see 9.18-19 below).

Procedure

9.13 The foreign company wishing to invest in this country will first of all contact a bank, or legal adviser, who will then inform it of the exchange control regulations and corresponding exchange control criteria. The company will then have to decide on a financial structure which conforms to these criteria, and apply to the Bank of England for permission under the Act to invest, or alternatively, decide not to invest at all. In this way, knowledge of the criteria helps to 'screen' investment proposals, and helps to make the procedure as rapid as it is.

9.14 The Bank of England has delegated authority to settle, without reference to the Treasury or other Department, cases where the amount is less than £500,000, except cases involving special considerations of national interest (it also has authority in respect of transfers of funds of existing companies, for which see below, para. 9.21).

9.15 All cases outside the Bank's delegated authority are considered by the Treasury in consultation with DTI and other Departments where appropriate (e.g. because they sponsor the industry in question). The Treasury attempts to deal expeditiously with the applications, and in straightforward cases gives approval within a week.

9.16 Finally, any application which involves a merger within the ambit of the Monopolies and Mergers Act, 1965, may be referred by the Mergers Panel of the Department of Trade and Industry to the Monopolies Commission. This occurs where the firm resulting after the merger would supply more than one-third of the total amount of the relevant commodity or where the value of the assets taken over exceed £5 million. Exchange control consent is generally not given until the monopoly aspect has been cleared and any requirements of the City Panel on Take-overs and Mergers have been met.

Experience in regulation of inward investment

9.17 In no case of any importance, where the applicant has been prepared to meet the conditions about finance, has permission for any genuine manufacturing or service investment been refused, and in general refusals of permission have been extremely rare. This is partly because in the large majority of cases, which are relatively straightforward, knowledge of the financial criteria by banks and others ensures that investment proposals which do not comply with them are not made. In the case of proposals affecting so called important industries, applications have been approved after the companies concerned have given undertakings about their future intentions. The Government has been prepared to waive these subsequently where national interests were no longer believed to be at stake.

9.18 The undertakings which have been requested by the former Ministry of Technology tend to relate not only to matters concerning the general conduct of the company in its relation with the Government, labour, shareholders, and public, but also to quite specific considerations. For example:

- (i) In the Rootes-Chrysler case, Chrysler undertook to:
  - (a) Maintain a majority of British directors on the Rootes Board.
  - (b) Confirm the plan of expansion covering development work at various factories and especially at Linwood.
  - (c) Achieve a progressive increase in exports, making its full international organisation available for this purpose, the test of

fulfilment of this undertaking being that the export percentage of Rootes products should be at least as high as the average for the British motor industry.

(d) Nominate a British Rootes director to each of the Boards of Simca (French Chrysler) and Chrysler International.

(e) Leave 15 per cent of the entire equity in the hands of shareholders other than Chrysler.

(ii) In the Pye-Philips case, Philips undertook to:

(a) maintain a majority of British directors on the Board of Pye;

(b) ensure that any re-organisation would not involve a diminution in volume of production in the UK, or exports from the UK;

(c) ensure that all contractual arrangements for exchange or granting of technical information and patent licences will only be entered into on such conditions as would be considered fair and reasonable commercially.

9.19 There are no sanctions which can be applied against breach of these undertakings and no systematic procedure has been laid down whereby policies of the companies will be reviewed to see that the undertakings are being kept. The Government thus relies on the good faith and social responsibility of the companies concerned; but this reliance has been justified by experience, nor would it be in the best interest of these firms to get at odds with the Government or public opinion in this country.

Repatriation of profits and continuing investment

9.20 The above discussion was concerned with the legislation, procedure, and criteria surrounding an act of initial inward investment. In the case of subsequent import or export of capital, in the form of further investment or repatriation of earnings, the position is more straightforward. The repatriation of profits by way of dividends or capital distributions requires specific consent. However, in the case of dividends, continuing authority for subsequent remittances is often delegated to the UK company's bankers. Permission for subsequent imports of capital to finance an existing business has to be sought each time, but for obvious reasons there is no difficulty in obtaining this permission.

Conclusions

9.21 The Exchange Control Act and the surrounding criteria obviously reflect the official attitude to inward investment. This is one of qualified welcome. The speed of the procedure, the reluctance to interfere with profit repatriation, the absence of rejections, and the lack of hard-and-fast general criteria of desirability all point to the desire to encourage inward investment. On the other hand, the criteria relating to the finance of the investment represent a determination not to lose one of its major advantages, namely the initial gain to foreign exchange reserves. The practice of securing undertakings in important take-over cases has not developed into an accepted policy for countering possible ill-effects from inward investment, nor is it clear that in its absence the companies concerned would have acted differently in any important respects. It is not clear to what extent these ill-effects can be shown to result from inward investment, either in principle or in fact. It is also not clear that if they exist, the procedure of requesting undertakings from firms concerned is likely to constitute a long-term preventative.

9.22 Given the implied attitude to inward investment, the Act and its surrounding procedure are satisfactory. The criteria are not contained in legislation and so they are flexible; yet they are based on legal powers, because without permission under the Act direct inward investment (other than new investment from the Sterling Area) is illegal. Finally, the procedure and publicised criteria are straightforward and unexacting, and so not likely to deter a serious investor, although in principle the authorities could impose stringent conditions. Post-war practice in dealing with inward investment applications has at times gone beyond what the analysis in the present study would hold to be in the national interest, and in other respects has not gone far enough. In particular, the criteria with regards to implications for British technology appear to be based on poor economic reasoning, and also insufficient attention has been given to redressing the balance of power between organized labour and foreign management.

10. Statistics of direct inward investment

I: General introduction

10.1 At several points in this report we make reference to statistics of direct inward investment, and draw inference based on them. The purpose of this final chapter is to collect the statistical material for convenience of reference and for their inherent interest. Broadly, the data may be divided into three categories: published and unpublished data from official British sources; United States published data; and the statistical material generated by our postal survey. While some reference is made to the last source in other chapters, it has not been possible to present a complete picture of this material in the report. The present chapter is therefore restricted to the first two sources with most attention given to the British data. The United States data are dealt with separately at the end of this chapter and while obviously collected from a different viewpoint, and employing some differences in definition compared to British practices, they have the advantage of providing longer time series than are available from our sources. They also make possible some check on accuracy, and interesting exercises in comparability. Some comment on these two points may be found in Chapter One.

10.2 The British official data are summarised under several headings which have been chosen because of their economic interest and care has to be taken when comparing data derived from different sources. Experts in direct investment figures, and economic statisticians generally, will be aware of the problems of collection, presentation, and interpretation involved in an array of this kind. We have included a brief introductory discussion for each section setting out the main considerations.

10.3 Direct investment, as distinct from portfolio investment, is concerned with the control of an enterprise. In principle this is a complex concept but in practice certain conventions are employed. Only investment by companies is taken into account. The following types of enterprise are distinguished in which foreign investment takes place (United Kingdom definitions):

(a) *subsidiaries*, being incorporated in the United Kingdom, and, broadly speaking, being more than 50 per cent owned overseas;

(b) *branches*, being permanent establishments not incorporated in the United Kingdom and being necessarily 100 per cent owned overseas;

(c) *associates*, being companies less than 50 per cent owned overseas.

These enterprises are usually referred to collectively as *affiliates*. A further point of definitional importance is the treatment of *undistributed profits*. The United Kingdom authorities follow the IMF recommendation in including undistributed profits as a debit item in the current account and as a credit in the capital account. This, however, is not universal practice and in particular it is not followed by the United States authorities.

10.4 The principal British data are collected by the Department of Trade and Industry by means of:

(a) an annual inquiry for inward investment flows, earnings and other related flow items (excluding oil and insurance);

(b) a periodic inquiry (1962, 1965 and 1968) for the stock of inward investment with intervening years estimated from the flow data of (a) (excluding oil, banking and insurance);

(c) the 1963 Census of Production for employment, sales and capital expenditure (subsidiaries in manufacturing industry only).

Details definitions of these items will be found in the DTI's Business Monitors (*M4 Overseas Transactions*) and the *Report on the Census of Production 1963* (summary tables). Estimates of the stock of inward investment in the oil industry have been taken from the CSO's United Kingdom Balance of Payments yearbooks.

10.5 It is important to distinguish between stocks and flows of direct investment. Where possible the flow data has been averaged over a number of years in order to remove some of the erratic fluctuations in the data for individual years.

II: World direct investment flows

10.6 In order to place the direct investment flows into the United Kingdom in perspective the direct investment inflows and outflows of the leading countries and major areas are shown in Table 10.I. As the size of the asymmetry and the notes indicate the figures are very approximate. Nevertheless, there can be no doubt of the dominant position of the United States as a supplier of direct investment capital, although the peak was reached around the middle sixties. The United Kingdom is easily the next largest source. However, the outflows from the EEC and Japan have been growing more rapidly than those from the USA and the United Kingdom. Direct investment inflows are more evenly spread amongst countries than are the outflows. As with trade, it is noteworthy that most of the direct investment flow is between industrial countries.

Table 10.I

Net direct investment flows: averages 1960-63, 1964-67, and 1968

US$ m.

	1960–1963		1964–1967		1968	
	Outflows	*Inflows*	*Outflows*	*Inflows*	*Outflows*	*Inflows*
United States[1]	—2,980	300	—4,683	465	—3,220	660
Canada	— 92	468	— 83	535	— 208	550
North America	—3,072	768	—4,766	1,000	—3,418	1,210
Japan[1]	— 93	56	— 92	58	— 220	76
Belgium/ Luxemburg	— 41(e)	61(e)	— 31(e)	178(e)	— 50(e)	150(e)
France[1]	— 62	198	— 198	323	— 340	200
Germany[1]	— 203	183	— 253	725	— 390	380
Italy	— 164	331	— 163	353	— 210	200
Netherlands	— 107	44	— 158	66	— 240	25
EEC	— 577(e)	817(e)	— 803(e)	1,645(e)	—1,230(e)	955(e)
EFTA (excluding UK)[3]	— 79(e)	146(e)	— 163	190	— 190(e)	200(e)
Other Western Europe	— 6	110	— 15	189	— 12	204
United Kingdom[1 2]	— 645	463	— 787	505	— 984	638
Total industrial	—4,472(e)	2,360(e)	—6,623(e)	3,587(e)	—6,054(e)	3,303(e)
Developed primary producers	—	271	—	456	—	489
Developing primary producers[4]	—	583	—	1,039	—	1,100
Total non-industrial	—	854	—	1,495	—	1,589
Grand total	—4,472(e)	3,214(e)	—6,623(e)	5,082(e)	—6,054(e)	4,892(e)
Asymmetry	—1,258		—1,541		—1,162	

Source: International Monetary Fund *Balance of Payments Yearbook* and Country Publications.

[1] Including re-invested earnings.

[2] Transactions of oil and insurance companies are excluded.

[3] Figures for Portugal and Switzerland not available.

[4] Not complete.

(e)—Estimated.

III: Direct inward investment flows and the balance of payments of the United Kingdom

A. Overall importance

10.7 The principal items relating to inward and outward direct investment flows which appear in the balance of payments account are shown in Table 10.IV. Both inward and outward investment have grown strongly although the latter has always been the more important. The growth in the earnings on direct investment has been even more marked and the payments to the United Kingdom are about twice the payments overseas from the United Kingdom. The royalty and service payments to and from the United Kingdom between related concerns have almost exactly balanced each other.

10.8 Table 10.V shows the direct investment flows in the context of the investment account of the balance of payments where an attempt has been made to distinguish the long-term capital items. The direct investment flows are clearly of great significance in the investment account and unlike the other items shown the net direct investment outflow has continued to grow strongly since devaluation.

10.9 The transformation of the balance of payments since devaluation is shown most clearly in the current account (Table 10.VI). The deteriorating trend which characterised the sixties has given way to a substantial surplus. The invisible balance has contributed a good deal to this turn round in which the rise in net income from direct investment has played its part.

B. Composition

10.10 The investment can take the form of acquiring new or existing share and loan capital, additions to working capital including changes in trade credit extended, and the investors share of the profits retained by the enterprise.[1] Because of the rather special legal position of branches all capital transactions between them and the parents are classified as a single item. These items are shown in Table 10.VII. Unremitted profits of subsidiaries and associates accounted for more than half of the net investment over the years.

10.11 Direct investment generates outflows in the current account of the balance of payments in the form of profits, interest charges, and payments for various services rendered by the parent companies to the affiliates or vice versa (Table 10.VIII). As noted earlier undistributed profits are included in net earnings. If the current account is considered in isolation there are advantages for some purposes in excluding undistributed profits since they constitute a potential rather than an actual drain on the current account. Table 10.VIII shows they constitute on average a little under half of net earnings.

10.12 Service charges are partly for general management and administrative services provided by the parent and part for technological information and know-how. The separate distinguishing of payments in respect of royalties etc. in 1964 appears to have led to the inclusion in some returns of transactions of this kind previously omitted, and the totals for the earlier years may be something like £5m. too low in this respect.[2]

10.13 Net royalty payments abroad by inward investment firms have been rising strongly. However, in the case of related companies, royalty payments may not be an adequate reflection of the value of the information received since the parent companies of fully owned subsidiaries and branches may not bother to charge for all the information provided. Conversely it is possible that in order to reduce profit remittances inflated prices may be charged for the information. In both these cases the profits of affiliates will reflect the transfer of information.

[1] It is clear from the above classification that net investment cannot be equated with capital expenditure. Apart from anything else, depreciation provisions, which are not included in the direct investment figures, are a major source of capital expenditure funds.

[2] 'Overseas Investment', *Board of Trade Journal*, 30 June 1967 p. x.

C. Effects on visible trade

10.14 In addition to the current account flows already discussed resulting from inward investment there will be other less easily measurable effects on the balance of payments. Foreign investment may lead to the substitution of internally produced goods for previously imported goods or perhaps in the case of highly integrated international firms to the substitution of imports for goods previously bought from other United Kingdom firms. On the export side, if foreign owned firms are more efficient than United Kingdom firms, then an increase in foreign ownership may lead to a better export performance. Besides the conceptual difficulties involved in assessing these effects, there is the problem of data: there are no figures on the imports of foreign owned firms and only a few relating to exports.

10.15 Table 10.II shows the exports of subsidiaries and branches of overseas firms in 1966, broken down by the industry of the enterprise and compared with the exports of all United Kingdom enterprises.

Table 10.II

Analysis of exporting firms by industry, 1966*

Analysis of returns received — £ million

Industry group		*Food, drink & tobacco*	*Chemical & allied trades*	*Metal manfr.*	*Mechanical engineering*	*Elec. engineering*	*Vehicles*	*Other manfg. activities*	*Distribution*	*Other activities*	*Total all industries*
All enterprises		213	439	284	551	376	865	642	324	87	3,771
Subsidiaries and branches of overseas companies	TOTAL	41	89	73	193	74	344	81	58	47	1,000
	of which related exports	17	42	25	66	35	239	21	27	29	501

Source: Board of Trade Journal, 16 August 1968.
* Excluding oil companies and public corporations.

However, the figure given in the table for the exports of all United Kingdom enterprises is only some 75 per cent of exports as reported for the balance of payments. This is because small exporting firms, which are collectively important, were not included in the survey from which the information was obtained. The exports of all foreign owned subsidiaries and branches constituted 27 per cent of the exports of all firms as given in the table and 19 per cent of the balance of payments export figures,[1] about half of these exports were to the overseas parent company. The net assets of foreign owned manufacturing affiliates[2] by comparison accounted for roughly 12 per cent of the net assets of all manufacturing companies in the United Kingdom.[3] Even allowing for the approximations involved in the figures there seems to be a significant difference between the share of foreign owned firms in exports and in industry generally.

10.16 One explanation of this is that many foreign owned companies are large, and large companies export proportionately more than small companies (Table 10.III).

[1] Including oil companies the proporation rises to just over 20 per cent.

[2] Including the overseas investors share in the net assets of associates.

[3] See section on on value of assets for the derivation of this estimate. Manufacturing industry was chosen because there are few foreign affiliates in the construction, distribution, etc. sectors.

Table 10.III

Importance of large exporters, 1966

£ million

Size of exports recorded	*Large**	*Medium†*	*Small‡ §*	*Total*
All enterprises	2,580	1,120	71	3,771
Subsidiaries and branches of overseas companies	705	282	13	1,000

Source: Board of Trade Journal, 16 August 1968.

* £5,000,001 and over.

† £200,001 to £5,000,000.

‡ £200,000 and below.

§ Figures are probably incomplete.

The largest one hundred and thirty-four exporting companies (thirty-four of which are foreign owned) had exports valued at £2,580 m. in 1966, which was about half of our total exports of £5,122 m. (balance of payments basis). This still leaves unanswered, however, why foreign owned companies are relatively large.

10.17 Chapter Two contains a more complete theoretical discussion of the balance of payments issues. The above remarks are intended to draw attention to some features of the data themselves.

Table 10.IV

Direct investment flows and income from direct investment in the UK balance of payments: averages 1960-63, 1964-67, 1968 70

£ million

		1960–63	1964–67	1968–70
I	DIRECT INVESTMENT FLOW			
	Into the UK (Inward)*	+165	+181	+303
	Out of the UK (Outward)†	—230	—282	—481
	Balance	— 65	—101	—178
II	EARNINGS ON DIRECT INVESTMENT			
	In the UK (Outflow)†	—142	—215	—326
	By the UK (Inflow)*	+278	+409	+640
	Balance	+136	+195	+314
III	NET ROYALTY AND SERVICE PAYMENTS ON DIRECT INVESTMENT			
	In the UK (Outflow)	— 30	— 46	— 80(e)
	By the UK (Inflow)	+ 30	+ 46	+ 66(e)
	Balance	—	—	— 14(e)
IV	TOTAL INCOME FROM DIRECT INVESTMENT (II + III)			
	In the UK(Outflow)	—172	—260	—406(e)
	By the UK (Inflow)	+308	+455	+706(e)
	Balance	+136	+195	+300(e)

Source: Department of Trade and Industry, *Business Monitor* (*M4 Overseas Transactions*), and CSO *United Kingdom Balance of Payments.*

* Excluding oil and insurance.

† Excluding oil, and before 1963, insurance.

(e) Estimated.

Table 10.V

Direct investment flows and the investment account of the balance of payments: averages 1960-63, 1964-67, 1968-70

£ million

	1960–63	1964–67	1968–70
Direct investment flows			
Inward*	+165	+181	+303
Outward†	—230	—282	—481
Direct investment (net)	— 65	—101	—178
Other private investment (net)‡	+ 32	— 29	+131
Official long-term capital (net)	— 89	— 85	— 95
Balance of long-term capital	—122	—215	—142
Current balance	— 1	—161	+244
Balance of current and long-term capital transactions	—123	—376	+102

Source: CSO *United Kingdom Balance of Payments.*

* Excluding oil and insurance.

† Excluding oil, and before 1963, insurance.

‡ Including oil.

Table 10.VI

Direct investment and the current account of the balance of payments: averages 1960-63, 1964-67, 1968-70

£ million

	1960–63	1964–67	1968–70
Total income from direct investment			
Outflow	—172	—260	—406(e)
Inflow	+308	+455	+706(e)
Net income from direct investment	+136	+195	+300(e)
Other invisibles (net)	+ 48	— 10	+204(e
Net invisible balance	+184	+185	+504
Visible balance	—185	—345	—260
Current balance	— 1	—161	+244

Source: CSO *United Kingdom Balance of Payments.*

(e) Estimated.

Table 10.VII

Direct net inward investment flows by component*: averages 1960-63, 1964-67, 1968-70

£ million

	1960–63	1964–67	1968–70
Investment in branches†	2	6	17
Net acquisition of share and loan capital	76	63	107
Change in inter-company accounts	25	16	22
Total of above	102	84	145
Unremitted profits of subsidiaries‡ §	63	97	158
TOTAL INWARD INVESTMENT	165	181	303

Source: Department of Trade and Industry, *Business Monitor* (M4 *Overseas Transactions*).

* Excluding oil and insurance.

† Changes in indebtedness of branch to parent company.

‡ Including associated companies.

§ Share in profits, after tax and depreciation, less dividends.

Table 10.VIII

Total income from direct inward investment by component*: averages 1960-63, 1964-67, 1968-70

£ million

	1960–63	1964–67	1968–70
Profits of branches	9	15	34
Remitted profits of subsidiaries†	67	97	124
Interest paid	3	6	9
Total remitted profits	79	118	168
Unremitted profits of subsidiaries†‡	63	97	158
Total net earnings	142	215	326
Royalties	} 30	28	52(e)
Net service payments		17	28(e)
TOTAL INCOME	172	260	406(e)

Source: Department of Trade and Industry, *Business Monitor* (*M4 Overseas Transactions*).
* Excluding oil and insurance.
† Including associated companies.
‡ Share in profits, after tax and depreciation, less dividends.
(e) Estimated.

IV: Direct inward investment and the home economy of the United Kingdom

A. Overall importance

10.18 Foreign controlled subsidiaries in the UK accounted for just under 10 per cent of the net output of all manufacturing in 1963.[1] Looked at from the point of view of employment, overseas controlled subsidiaries accounted for about 7 per cent of the labour force in manufacturing industry in the same year. Between 1953 and 1963 employment in foreign controlled manufacturing subsidiaries seems to have doubled.[2] Net output and employment data derived from the Census of Production are only available for 1963 but some idea of the continued growth of foreign investment in the UK economy can be deduced from data on net assets attributable to foreign overseas investors[3] for which more recent figures are published. Including oil[4], overseas interests accounted for about 11 per cent of the net assets of all UK manufacturing companies[5] in 1965 and this percentage had risen to about 14 per cent by 1968. Over these three years the proportion was, therefore, increasing on average at about 1 per cent a year which gives a very approximate indication of the probable orders of magnitude involved.

10.19 So far as all industry—and not just manufacturing—is concerned the figures for the proportions of all UK net assets attributable to overseas investors in 1965 and 1968 were 9 per cent and 11 per cent respectively. The increase is somewhat less than for manufactures but still implies a very rapid rate of growth of overseas investments: total net assets attributable to overseas investors grew by about 12 per cent a year on average over the 1960-68 period.

[1] Net output is roughly equivalent to value added; for a precise definition see the *Census of Production* 1963.

[2] This estimate uses the results of a survey of US firms conducted in 1953; see Dunning *American Investment in British Manufacturing Industry*, 1958.

[3] There are many problems associated with the book values of net assets. In particular they are, of course, likely to be appreciably lower than current market or replacement values. As far as possible, however, the figures are only used for comparative purposes where like is being compared with like.

[4] Estimates for oil are taken from the 'Pink' Book *United Kingdom Balance of Payments.*

[5] Estimates of the net assets of UK companies were derived from *Business Monitor* (*M3 Company Finance*) and *Economic Trends*, February 1965 and November 1967.

10.20 The distinction has to be borne in mind between net assets attributable to overseas investors (which are the figures used in this chapter) and the total net assets of firms subject in some sense to overseas 'control'. The former differs from the latter as follows: excluded are the UK minority interests in overseas controlled subsidiaries and the UK interests in those associate companies where the overseas interest, although less than 50 per cent, effectively controls the company; included is the overseas minority interest in those associates not controlled abroad. The UK minority interest in overseas controlled subsidiaries is not, however, large: it amounted to only about 9 per cent of the total net assets of subsidiaries in both 1965 and 1968. Unfortunately it is not possible from published data to distinguish associates which are effectively controlled by overseas companies from associates where the foreign interest is more of the nature of a portfolio investment. Control is a subtle concept not easily identified. It seems more likely, however, that the above estimates of foreign penetration of the UK economy would be marginally increased rather than diminished if control in its wider sense was used as the criteria.

10.21 Other indications of the relative importance of inward investment are the 1963 Census data relating to the sales and capital expenditure of foreign controlled subsidiaries and branches in manufacturing. Sales of foreign subsidiaries were 9 per cent of total UK sales and the capital expenditure of foreign subsidiaries was 13 per cent of the total for the UK.

B. Organisation[1]

10.22 In the preceding paragraphs one of the difficulties in comparing data drawn from different sources was that the financial statistics on net assets include the overseas share in associate companies but excludes the UK minority interest in subsidiaries while the Census data on net output and employment relates to totals in subsidiaries. For this reason alone it is of interest to give some attention to the structure and organisation of inward investment.

10.23 Table 10.IX below shows the importance of the subsidiary as a form of organisation (90 per cent of all net assets attributable to overseas investors) and the relative unimportance of both branches (2 per cent) and associates (8 per cent).[2]

Table 10.IX

Values of direct investments* by form of organisation and date of establishment (large investments)

Book values of net assets attributable to overseas investors at end 1965 *in £m*

	Before 1946	1946–55	1956–65	*Total values*
Branches	20.1	6.5	10.1	36.7
Subsidiaries	1,246.8	211.1	295.3	1,753.2
Associates	28.6	28.2	92.2	149.0
TOTAL VALUES	1,295.5	245.8	397.6	1,938.9

Source: Board of Trade Journal, 26 January 1968.

* Exclude oil, insurance and banking.

[1] This section excludes oil companies and companies with fixed and current assets less than £¼ million. The latter, although numerically substantial, account for only a very small proportion (2 per cent) of the net assets of overseas investors.

[2] Figures relate to 1965; percentages for 1968 are virtually the same.

About two thirds of the net assets in 1965 were in companies established here before 1946. Although by value of assets pre-1946 firms are the most important, by numbers it is the opposite: 44 per cent of the number of large investments were established in the 1956-65 period. In other words, the initial foreign stake tends to be small and grows over time (see paragraph 10.26).

10.24 An interesting point brought out by Table 10.IX is that 62 per cent of the investments in associated companies occurred in the ten years before 1965, while 71 per cent of the investments in subsidiaries are in companies established before the war. This would imply either that associates are becoming a more popular form of organisation or that many foreign take-overs, while they may initially consist of a minority shareholding, later became converted to a majority shareholding.

10.25 Table 10.X shows there is a strong association between age and degree of ownership.

Table 10.X

Values of direct investments* by degree of ownership and date of establishment (large investors)

Book values of net assets attributable to overseas investors at end 1965 *in £m*

	Before 1946	1946–55	1955–65	*Total values*
Under 50%	31.2	29.0	94.6	154.8
50–74%	112.6	8.3	36.0	156.9
75–99%	152.0	6.4	40.3	198.7
100%	999.7	202.1	226.7	1,428.5
TOTAL VALUES	1,295.5	245.8	397.6	1,938.9

Source: Board of Trade Journal, 26 January, 1968.
* Excludes oil, insurance and banking.

Not only are subsidiaries a preferred form of organisation but there is also a strong preference for complete ownership with about 75 per cent of inward investment in wholly owned subsidiaries and branches.

10.26 The association between age and size is also marked (Table 10.XI) as indicated in paragraph 10.23.

Table 10.XI

Values of direct investments* by size and date of establishment (large investments)

Book values of net assets attributable to overseas investors at end 1965 *in £m*

	Before 1946	1946–55	1956–65	*Total values*
Over £5 m.	926.5	102.0	195.0	1,223.5
£1—£5 m.	285.9	105.3	113.2	504.4
£½—£1 m.	42.6	22.4	42.7	107.7
£¼—£½ m.	28.4	10.9	41.4	80.7
Under £¼ m.	12.1	5.2	5.3	22.6
TOTAL VALUES	1,295.5	245.8	397.6	1,938.9

Source: Board of Trade Journal, 26 January 1968.
* Excludes oil, insurance and banking.

C. Country of ownership

10.27 Overseas investment in the UK is very much United States investment. Table 10.XII shows clearly the completely dominant position of the United States (67 per cent of the net assets) with most of the rest being spread fairly evenly between Switzerland, Canada and the EEC (mostly Dutch) in 1968.[1] (The associated flows of inward investment are given in Table 10.XIII).

10.28 Table 10.XIV shows employment, sales and capital expenditure of foreign controlled manufacturing subsidiaries in 1963 also by country of ownership. The order of importance is much the same as that shown by the net assets of companies. According to the employment data the United States is still easily the most important country of ownership with Switzerland, the Netherlands and Canada the next most important. This group of countries together accounted for 90 per cent of the total employment in foreign owned subsidiaries.

D. Industrial distribution

10.29 The book values of net assets attributable to overseas investors by broad industry groups is shown in table 10.XV. Of the total in 1968, manufactures accounted for nearly 85 per cent. Oil investments accounted for nearly one-third of the total. Some interesting changes have taken place since 1965 in the direction of new inward investment (the flow items are shown in table 10.XVI). The food, drink and tobacco sector has been growing in relative importance and there has also been strong growth in the chemical and engineering sectors. Vehicles and other manufacturing industries have been growing slowly in comparison.

10.30 According to the 1963 employment data mechanical and electrical engineering each accounted for around one-fifth of the total employment in foreign controlled subsidiaries (Table XVII). However, if the employment in foreign controlled subsidiaries in a particular sector is compared with overall employment in that industry the special position of the vehicles sector becomes apparent. A convenient statistic for measuring the degree of concentration of a foreign investment in a particular sector is the concentration quotient defined as the percentage of total employment in foreign subsidiaries in each industry divided by the percentage of total UK employment in the same industry. On the basis of the employment figures in Table 10.XVII foreign companies were most heavily concentrated in vehicles in 1963. There was also above average concentrations in electrical engineering and chemicals while the concentration of employment in mechanical engineering was the same for both foreign controlled subsidiaries and all UK firms.

10.31 To assess the overall degree of concentration of foreign subsidiaries a coefficient of concentration was calculated, defined as the sum (divided by 100) of the plus (or minus) deviations of the percentage of employment in foreign subsidiaries in each industry from the corresponding percentage of employment in all United Kingdom firms.[2] Complete coincidence industry by industry would give a coefficient of zero while complete differentiation gives a

[1] Some of the Canadian and Swiss based companies may themselves have a parent company in the US.

[2] See P Sargent Florence, *Investment, Location and Size of Plant*, Cambridge University Press, 1948.

figure approaching 1. The coefficient calculated from Table 10.XVII was 0.28 indicating that the concentration of foreign controlled subsidiaries, at this level of aggregation, was not markedly different from that for UK industry generally.

10.32 However, this classification is a broad one and Table 10.XVII gives a more detailed analysis for employment only. The first and second columns show the percentage distribution of employment in foreign controlled subsidiaries and in all UK firms respectively. About 13 per cent of the employment in foreign subsidiaries was in the manufacture of mechanical machinery which ranked next in importance after vehicles in 1963. The food sector and the manufacture of radio and electronic apparatus (which includes computers) each accounted for about 7 per cent of the total employment.

10.33 The concentration quotients shown in the last column are, as explained above, the ratios of columns one and two. These figures bring out some rather interesting points. At this more detailed level the pharmaceutical industry had easily the largest concentration of employment relative to the distribution of all UK employment. Other sectors with high quotients were insulated wires and telephones apparatus and rubber. Next came scientific instruments, radio and electronic apparatus, and domestic appliances and only then vehicles. There were also above average concentrations in mineral oil refining, non-ferrous metals and mechanical machinery. The industries with very low concentration quotients were shipbuilding, drink and tobacco, and textiles. Clearly foreign investment has flowed into the newer expanding industries and for this reason alone its importance in the economy is likely to continue to grow.

10.34 The finer the industrial breakdown, the more sensitive is the overall coefficient of concentration. Using the detail of Table 10.XVIII the coefficient rises to 0.38 indicating a moderate degree of concentration. Ten years previously in 1953, Professor Dunning (1958) carried out a survey of US financed firms in the UK (which accounts for the bulk of foreign owned firms—see previous section) and on the basis of an all industry classification came up with a concentration coefficient of 0.35. Over this ten-year period there does not therefore appear to have been any marked increase in the concentration of foreign investment. As indicated in the opening paragraph of this section there has been a continuing strong inflow of foreign investment into the chemical and engineering industries since 1963 but without detailed data for some later year it is impossible to say whether there has been an increase in concentration in these sectors.

E. Regional distribution

10.35 The only data available on foreign investment by regions comes from the 1963 Census and is shown in Table 10.XIX. In terms of absolute numbers, the South-east region is easily the most significant; the North-west comes second, followed by the West Midlands and Scotland. These four regions together contain over 80 per cent of the total employment in foreign subsidiaries with the remaining quarter divided between the other seven regions.

10.36 A location quotient for foreign controlled subsidiaries may be derived in a similar fashion to the concentration quotient described earlier. The two regions with the highest location quotients are the South-east and East Anglia; Wales and Scotland have quotients a little above average. The regions with the next highest quotients are the North-west, Northern Ireland and the West Midlands. The remaining regions have fairly low quotients of employment in foreign controlled subsidiaries.

10.37 The overall coefficient of location was 0.26 which suggests that the location pattern of foreign controlled subsidiaries does not differ substantially from that of British industry as a whole. This conclusion was also reached by Professor Dunning (1958) in respect of the location patterns of US firms ten years previously. But this does not mean that foreign controlled firms do not have a dominent influence in areas smaller than the region.

Table 10.XII

Value of stock of direct inward investments by area and main country*

Book values of net assets attributable to overseas investors at year ends in £m

	1960	*1961*	*1962*	*1963*	*1964*	*1965*	*1966*	*1967*	*1968*
North America	755.1	971.9	1,085.7	1,228.6	1,367.1	1,543.7	1,714.0	1,813.9	2,045.9
USA	613.1	813.5	916.5	1,037.8	1,165.6	1,316.9	1,488.8	1,604.8	1,822.8
Canada	142.0	158.4	169.2	190.8	201.5	226.8	225.2	209.1	223.0
EEC	112.5	131.0	133.7	144.6	163.6	178.4	192.3	248.5	278.2
Belgium	8.6	9.4	8.9	9.7	12.0	12.9	13.2	13.9	14.7
France	19.4	32.0	31.5	34.4	38.3	40.2	43.8	45.9	51.0
Italy	14.0	13.8	13.8	15.2	15.9	17.3	18.0	18.4	17.7
Netherlands	66.7	71.3	73.8	77.0	86.4	95.2	102.3	151.0	168.2
Western Germany	3.8	4.5	5.7	8.3	11.0	12.8	15.0	19.3	26.6
EFTA	123.0	137.2	158.6	184.2	196.0	208.8	234.6	271.6	308.6
of which Switzerland	90.9	101.7	122.5	145.7	154.5	167.0	183.9	206.8	225.6
Other Areas	49.4	49.9	52.0	52.6	66.3	64.0	73.8	90.7	85.4
TOTAL	1,040	1,290	1,430	1,610	1,793	1,995	2,215	2,425	2,718

Source: Department of Trade and Industry, *Business Monitor* (*M4 Overseas Transactions*).

* Excludes oil, insurance and banking.

Table 10.XIII

Net direct inward investment flows by area and main country†: averages 1960-1963, 1964-1967, 1968-1969

£ million

	1960–63	1964–67	1968–69
North America	133	136	214
USA	117	129	206
Canada	16	7	7
EEC	8	22	30
Belgium	1	1	1
France	3	3	5
Italy	—	2	4
Netherlands	3	14	12
Western Germany	1	2	9
EFTA	16	14	21
of which Switzerland	15	12	11
Other Areas	7	9	32
TOTAL	165	181	297

Source: Department of Trade and Industry, *Business Monitor* (*M4 Overseas Transactions*).

† Excludes oil and insurance.

Table 10.XIV

Employment, sales and net capital expenditure in foreign-controlled manufacturing subsidiaries by area and main country, 1963*

	Employment ('000)	*Sales* (£*m*)	*Net capital expenditure* (£*m*)
North America	442.4	2,174.4	110.9
USA	407.9	1,944.4	105.6
Canada	34.5	230.0	5.3
EEC	54.3	171.2	10.0
Belgium	1.6	5.6	0.1
France	15.6	48.1	2.2
Italy	8.5	33.4	2.4
Netherlands	27.6	79.4	5.1
West Germany	1.0	4.7	0.2
Switzerland	23.6	112.3	6.4
Sweden	11.8	34.1	0.9
Others	8.2	33.7	1.1
TOTAL	540.3	2,525.7	129.3

Source: Census of Production, 1963.

* Firms employing 25 persons or more.

Table 10.XV

Values of stock of direct inward investment†

Book values of net assets attributable to overseas investors at year ends

£ million

	1962	1963	1964	1965	1966	1967	1968
Food, drink and tobacco				187	205	218	303
Chemicals and allied industries				227	273	289	330
Metal manufactures				154	159	153	174
Mechanical engineering	n.a.	n.a.	n.a.	337	388	425	471
Electrical engineering				185	219	289	324
Vehicles				304	318	331	352
Other manufactures				249	268	289	309
Total manufactures				1,643	1,830	1,994	2,263
Distribution	n.a	n.a	n.a	244	260	286	286
Other activities				108	125	145	169
TOTAL	1,430	1,610	1,793	1,995	2,215	2,425	2,718
Oil	700	725	750	800	850	1,000	1,150
TOTAL	2,130	2,335	2,543	2,795	3,065	3,425	3,868

Source: Department of Trade and Industry and CSO, *United Kingdom Balance of Payments Yearbooks* and estimates.

† Excludes banking and insurance.

n.a.—not available.

Table 10.XVI

Net direct inward investment flows by industry§: averages 1960-1963, 1964-1967, 1968-1969

£ million

	1960–63	1964–67	1968–69
Food, drink and tobacco	26‡	18	62
Chemicals and allied industries	22‡	23	37
Metal manufactures	4‡	1	9
Mechanical engineering	} 22	33	52
Electrical engineering		26	17
Vehicles	33‡	18	13
Other manufactures	24‡	18	37
Total manufactures	133	136	226
Distribution	18	24	27
Banking	4	10	26
Other activities	12	12	19
TOTAL	165	181	297

Source: Department of Trade and Industry.

‡ 1963 figures only: figures for 1960-62 are not available.

§ Excludes oil and insurance.

Table 10.XVII

Employment, sales and net capital expenditure in manufacturing industries by industry

	Employment ('000)		*Sales* (£*m*)		*Net capital Expenditure* (£*m*)	
Industry group	*Foreign**	*UK*	*Foreign**	*UK*	*Foreign**	*UK*
Food, drink and tobacco	40.9	756.1	278.9	5,174.1	11.2	136.6
Chemicals and allied industries	48.3	396.0	287.2	2,185.1	18.6	119.8
Metal manufactures	27.0	573.0	162.0	2,589.1	6.0	144.0
Mechanical engineering	116.1	1,713.7	361.7	4,127.6	15.4	137.0
Electrical engineering	100.9	767.4	270.7	1,860.3	13.8	66.4
Vehicles	110.7	433.0	647.1	2,081.0	42.8	88.3
Other manufactures	96.4	3,320.4	518.1	9,680.9	21.5	333.1
TOTAL MANUFACTURES	540.3	7,959.6	2,525.7	27,698.1	129.3	1,025.2

Source: Census of Production, 1963.
* Firms employing 25 persons or more.

Table 10.XVIII

Employment in manufacturing industries by industry, 1963

SIC MLH	*Heading*	*Foreign†* *% of total*	*UK %* *of total*	*Concentration quotient*
211–229	Food	7.2	7.2	1.00
231–240	Drink and tobacco	0.4	2.3	0.17
261–263	Coke, ovens, mineral oil refining, greases, etc.	1.1	0.6	1.83
271	Dyestuffs, fertilisers and other chemicals	2.1	2.3	0.91
272	Pharmaceutical and toilet preparations	5.0	0.9	5.56
273–277	Explosives, soap, polishes, etc.	1.9	1.8	1.06
311–313	Iron and steel	2.1	5.5	0.38
320	Non-ferrous metals	2.8	1.7	1.65
331–339	Mechanical machinery	12.7	8.2	1.55
341–349	Industrial plant and other mechanical engineering	3.8	4.6	0.83
351–352	Scientific instruments and watches	4.6	1.7	2.71
361	Electrical machinery	0.7	2.6	0.27
362–363	Insulated wires and telephone apparatus	6.3	1.8	3.50
364	Radio and other electronic apparatus	7.1	3.0	2.37
365–369	Domestic appliances and other electrical goods	4.6	2.2	2.09
370	Shipbuilding and marine engineering	0.2	2.5	0.08
381–389	Vehicles	20.6	10.0	2.06
391–399	Metal goods n.e.s.	4.0	6.4	0.63
411–450	Textiles and clothing	2.9	16.4	0.18
461–479	Bricks, pottery and furniture	1.5	7.2	0.21
481–489	Paper, printing	2.0	7.3	0.27
491	Rubber	5.1	1.5	3.40
492–499	Other manufacturing industries	1.3	2.3	0.57
	ALL MANUFACTURING INDUSTRIES	100.0	100.0	

Source: Census of Production, 1963.
† Firms employing 25 persons or more.

Table 10.XIX

Employment, sales and net capital expenditure in manufacturing industries by region

	Employment ('000)		*Sales* (£*m*)		*Net capital Expenditure* (£*m*)	
	*Foreign**	*UK*	*Foreign**	*UK*	*Foreign**	*UK*
Northern	8.5	397.4	52.3	1,418.0	1.8	59.6
Yorks & Humberside	20.6	823.4	81.6	2,666.7	4.1	121.6
East Midlands	18.3	550.1	83.6	1,724.9	2.1	57.6
East Anglia	17.3	154.4	61.9	528.7	2.9	20.5
South-East	277.9	2,218.4	1,312.6	7,956.4	68.1	269.1
South-West	4.1	347.2	13.9	1,285.9	0.7	41.0
Wales	24.0	282.0	180.4	1,298.2	6.4	58.0
West Midlands	46.1	1,114.5	207.4	3,626.4	10.0	132.1
North Western	70.5	1,265.5	348.0	4,354.5	18.3	149.4
Scotland	45.7	638.4	156.3	2,218.6	8.5	92.5
Northern Ireland	7.3	168.4	27.7	620.8	6.4	23.8
TOTAL	540.3	7,959.7	2,525.7	27,699.1	129.3	1,025.2

Source: Census of Production, 1963.
* Firms employing 25 persons or more.

V: Comparative rates of return[1]

10.38 Some assessment of the efficiency of foreign controlled firms is clearly of interest but 'efficiency is . . . a difficult word to define and is capable of various interpretations' (Dunning: 1958). Many measures of efficiency have been suggested but one that is easier to handle from the point of view of data requirements is the rate of return on capital. In a dynamic world in which technical change is occurring continuously and relative prices are shifting through time, profits under competitive conditions can be considered a return to successful innovation and risk taking. Firms in the forefront of product process innovation, quick to adapt to changing circumstances while still taking proper account of relative factor prices, could be expected to show greater profits than their less adventurous competitors. However, this indicator has both theoretical and practical drawbacks: market imperfections may introduce bias into profits as an index of efficiency and in the case of foreign owned subsidiaries; inter-firm pricing may not reflect market conditions; and the usual measure of profits is less than perfect and data on capital employed are only given at book values.

10.39 The only satisfactory way of coming to firm conclusions on the efficiency of foreign controlled firms is by in-depth studies of a selected number of foreign owned and comparable UK owned firms[2]. All that has been attempted here is some general impressions of comparative average rates of return which can be calculated from published statistics. By only using the rates of return comparatively some of the defects of using book values are reduced.

10.40 The table below compares the rates of return after tax (earnings figures are only available after tax) on foreign investment from the US, EEC and all areas. The United states figures are appreciably greater than those for other countries. Since, on *a priori* grounds, one would expect all foreign owned firms to gravitate towards the more profitable sectors of industry, differential rates of return could be taken as an indication of differing efficiency. However,

[1] We had much helpful advice on this section from Mr Buckingham of DTI's Economic and Statistics Division.
[2] See Chapter 7, Part III.

the EEC countries have a much higher proportion of their investments in distribution although it is doubtful whether this in itself is sufficient to account for the size of the difference between the United States sector and the rest. There is a presumption, therefore, that the rates of return on United States subsidiaries are reflecting the supposed superior technical know-how, managerial techniques, etc of the United States economy.

Table 10.XX

Average rates of return* on direct inward investment†

Per cent

	1965	1966	1967	1968
USA	12.5	11.0	9.2	10.5
EEC	9.9	6.9	5.6	6.3
TOTAL	10.6	9.5	8.1	9.3

Source: Department of Trade and Industry.

* After UK Tax.

† Excludes oil, insurance and banking.

10.41 An attempt was also made to compare the average rate of return on all foreign investment with that on UK companies generally. Only UK quoted companies were used in the comparison since non-quoted companies contain a large proportion of foreign owned companies. The rates of return on the UK quoted companies were calculated after tax[1] and related to the shareholders' interests in the assets and income of the companies. These adjustments were made in order to make the comparison with the rates of return on foreign investment as close as possible. The results for all manufacturing industry are shown in Table 10.XXI. While small differences in these figures cannot be taken as significant there does seem to be evidence that foreign controlled companies do have higher rates of return than UK quoted companies.[2] One reason for expecting a higher overall rate of return on foreign controlled firms is because inward investment has a different industrial distribution to that of UK companies and the higher rates of return might be entirely due to the greater concentration of foreign controlled firms in high profit industries.

Table 10.XXI

Average rates of return in manufacturing industry

Per cent

	1960	1961	1962	1963	1964	1965	1966	1967	1968
Inward investment	11.7	8.8	8.3	10.1	11.1	11.7	8.6	8.3	11.4
UK quoted companies	9.9	8.2	7.4	8.1	8.6	9.6	6.1	5.5	6.3

Source: Department of Trade and Industry, *Business Monitors*

10.42 In order to see if there appeared to be any differences between foreign controlled and UK firms in the same sectors, rates of return were calculated by broad industry groups (Table 10.XXII) for the two years 1965 and 1966.

[1] Including for 1967 and 1968 the tax on distributed profits.

[2] If allowance is made for the fact that UK companies paid tax on their distributed profits at standard rate while foreign owned companies paid, in general, lower withholding taxes, the rates of return on UK quoted companies would be a little over 1 per cent higher in 1967 and 1968.

Table 10.XXII

Average rates of return by industry

Per cent	*Food, drink and tobacco*	*Chemicals and allied industries*	*Metal manufacture*	*Mechanical engineering*	*Electrical engineering*	*Vehicles*	*Other manufactures*
1965							
Inward investment	12.3	17.2	6.5	13.1	10.3	10.9	9.6
UK quoted companies	10.8	9.2	8.6	7.2	9.8	11.8	10.0
1966							
Inward investment	9.8	13.2	4.4	10.1	9.6	4.4	7.8
UK quoted companies	7.1	5.7	3.4	5.2	7.3	6.4	6.4

Source: Department of Trade and Industry, *Business Monitors* and *Statistics on Incomes, Prices, Employment and Production*

The differences in both years for chemicals and mechanical engineering is striking although in the case of the latter the inclusion of shipbuilding in which there is negligible foreign investment pulls down the rate of return on UK quoted companies.

Annex

Statistics from United States sources relating to direct investment in the United Kingdom

A. Introduction

Statistics relating to United States overseas investment have been published for many years by the Department of Commerce, and this provides longer time series for some series than are available from United Kingdom sources. However, a different set of definitions are employed by the American authorities from those used in the United Kingdom. Broadly, the Department of Commerce classifies direct investment by:

(a) branches;

(b) subsidiaries, with 25 per cent or more of the voting shares being owned by a single interest or affiliated groups resident in the United States;

(c) associates with from 10 per cent to 25 per cent of the voting shares being owned in the United States.

These definitions may be compared with those given in paragraph 10.3 of this chapter.

Since the United States sector accounts for such a large proportion of all foreign investment in the United Kingdom, any inferences which can be drawn concerning the United States sector will, to a considerable extent, be true of all foreign investment, and this is the basic justification for using those data.

The tables are discussed very briefly in the following paragraphs: two tables are included for reference on the value of United States direct investment in the world and in Europe.

B. Balance of payments flows

The net capital outflow from the United States (Table 10.XXIII) excludes undistributed profits of subsidiaries. If, however, undistributed profits (Table 10.XXV) are added in, the result will approximate the change in the value of direct investment and this is in fact how the census data on the value of investment is carried forward.

The item which appears in the United States balance of payments accounts as 'income from direct investment' is shown in Table 10.XXIV. This item includes the profits of branches, but excludes the undistributed profits of subsidiaries as well as the taxes paid on distributed profits to the United Kingdom authorities. It includes small amounts of interest and preferred dividend payments.

A comparison of the royalties and fees (Table 10.XXVI) with the income from direct investment shows that a substantial proportion of the return flow to the United States takes the form of royalties and fees.

C. Values of assets, earnings and rates of return

The censuses carried out in 1950 and 1957 provide the bench-marks for the data on the value of direct investments (Table 10.XXVII). A later census has been carried out but results have not yet been published. Briefly, the census data were derived by taking the United States share in the equity, accumulated surplus, long-term debt and other liabilities of each United States direct investment subsidiary and branch defined in the introduction. The intervening years were interpolated from flow data. As the fixed assets were valued at cost, the resulting figures under estimate the market value of the enterprise.

The earnings on direct investment are shown in Table 10.XXVIII, the total having been related to the value of assets at the beginning of the year. The rate of return in the sixties has been about a half of that obtained in the fifties.

Table 10.XXIII

United States direct investment net capital outflows into the United Kingdom

£ million

Industry	1950	1951	1952	1953	1954	1955	1956	1957	1958	1959	1960	1961	1962	1963	1964	1965	1966p	1967p	1968p	1969p
Petroleum	8	6	—9	—1	1	3	79	32	*	19	46	43	16	15	11	50	38	104	64	17
Manufacturing	9	1	3	—3	3	8	21	27	15	46	154	23	44	18	41	41	94	13	63	44
Other	2	*	—1	3	1	1	1	3	8	3	10	4	2	11	21	25	6	7	29	57
TOTAL	18	8	—7	—1	5	11	101	61	23	68	210	70	61	44	74	116	137	124	156	118

Source: US Department of Commerce, *Balance of Payments Statistical Supplement*, revised edition, and *Surveys of Current Business.*

p Preliminary.
* Less than £½ m.

Table 10.XXIV

Income from United States direct investment in the United Kingdom

£ million

Industry	1950	1951	1952	1953	1954	1955	1956	1957	1958	1959	1960	1961	1962	1963	1964	1965p	1966p	1967p	1968p	1969p
Petroleum	*	2	8	8	8	18	26	16	21	41	16	19	8	4	10	—1	—5	—6	—5	1
Manufacturing	19	18	12	16	24	25	36	34	37	46	49	62	54	54	71	73	74	75	87	97
Other	7	7	9	9	9	13	13	13	11	13	13	11	14	14	17	22	21	30	35	38
TOTAL	26	26	28	32	41	55	75	62	69	100	78	92	75	71	99	91	90	99	117	136

Source: US Department of Commerce, *Balance of Payments Statistical Supplement*, revised edition, and *Surveys of Current Business.*

p Preliminary.
* Less than £½ m.
NB Income is the sum of dividends and interest, net after foreign (i.e. UK) withholding taxes, and branch profits.

Table 10.XXV

Undistributed subsidiary earnings of United States direct investment in the United Kingdom

£ million

Industry	1950	1951	1952	1953	1954	1955	1956	1957	1958	1959	1960	1961	1962	1963	1964	1965p	1966p	1967p	1968p	1969p
Petroleum	4	3	8	9	4	9	8	18	3	—1	5	4	—5	13	—7	*	—3	—11	—9	—17
Manufacturing	18	25	24	25	31	33	29	32	29	43	41	30	29	57	59	79	57	40	88	70
Other	3	5	3	1	5	4	7	8	8	8	10	10	9	9	8	8	14	—	7	10
TOTAL	25	32	35	35	40	45	43	57	39	50	57	44	33	78	60	86	68	29	87	63

Source: US Department of Commerce, *Balance of Payments Statistical Supplement*, revised edition, and *Surveys of Current Business*.

p Preliminary.

* Less than £½ m.

NB Undistributed subsidiary earnings are computed as the difference between the United States share of net earnings of subsidiaries and the United States share of gross dividends (dividends before deduction of withholding taxes).

Table 10.XXVI

Royalties and fees from direct investments in the United Kingdom

£ million

	1960	1961	1962	1963	1964	1965	1966	1967	1968	1969
Manufacturing	14	18	21	27	31	40	44	49	58	64
TOTAL	18	24	28	35	39	50	54	60	70	79

Source: Surveys of Current Business and unpublished Department of Commerce data.

Table 10.XXVII

Value of United States direct investments in the United Kingdom at year end

£ million

Industry	1950	1951	1952	1953	1954	1955	1956	1957	1957(a)	1958	1959	1960	1961	1962	1963	1964	1965	1966p	1967p	1968p	1969p
Petroleum	44	55	55	61	66	78	99	150	155	158	176	227	275	288	316	322	390	418	519	651	651
Manufacturing	194	220	247	270	304	346	396	455	442	486	575	774	825	900	978	1,075	1,181	1,326	1,406	1,768	1,898
Other	65	69	71	75	82	87	94	103	108	122	133	154	165	177	196	226	259	276	291	370	434
TOTAL	303	344	372	406	451	510	589	707	705	767	885	1,155	1,265	1,366	1,490	1,624	1,830	2,020	2,217	2,789	2,983

Source: US Department of Commerce, *Balance of Payments Statistical Supplement*, revised edition, and *Surveys of Current Business*.

(a) Census data.
p Preliminary.

Table 10.XXVIII

Earnings of United States direct investment in the United Kingdom and the rate of return

£ million

Industry	1950	1951	1952	1953	1954	1955	1956	1957	1958	1959	1960	1961	1962	1963	1964	1965p	1966p	1967p	1968p	1969p
Petroleum	4	5	16	16	12	27	34	34	23	22	21	14	3	4	16	—2	—9	—19	—19	—25
Manufacturing	37	42	35	41	55	58	64	65	65	89	90	91	81	108	129	150	128	123	184	178
Other	10	12	11	10	14	15	20	19	19	21	22	24	22	22	25	30	33	33	46	50
TOTAL	50	58	62	67	80	99	118	119	107	132	134	128	106	134	169	178	153	137	211	203
Rate of return		19.1	18.0	18.0	19.7	22.0	23.1	20.2	15.2	17.2	15.1	11.1	8.4	9.8	11.3	11.0	7.6	6.2	7.5	

Source: US Department of Commerce, *Balance of Payments Statistical Supplement*, revised edition, and *Surveys of Current Business*.

p Preliminary.
NB Earnings is the sum of the US share in net earnings of subsidiaries and branch profits.

Table 10.XXIX

Value of United States direct investment in world at year end

£ million

Industry	1950	1951	1952	1953	1954	1955	1956	1957	1957(a)	1958	1959	1960	1961	1962	1963	1964	1965	1966	1967	1968	1969p
Mining & smelting	403	461	579	686	738	785	864	923	843	914	1,017	1,053	1,087	1,141	1,203	1,275	1,352	1,541	1,768	2,265	2,348
Petroleum	1,211	1,317	1,526	1,753	1,892	2,107	2,627	3,252	3,234	3,508	3,687	3,861	4,354	4,545	4,876	5,119	5,464	5,788	6,310	7,870	8,327
Manufacturing	1,368	1,553	1,774	1,907	2,107	2,365	2,700	3,005	2,860	3,098	3,467	3,947	4,285	4,732	5,335	6,047	6,907	7,878	8,763	11,006	12,271
Other	1,228	1,304	1,379	1,456	1,560	1,670	1,846	2,204	2,132	2,270	2,481	2,503	2,656	2,878	3,117	3,411	3,895	4,333	4,728	5,935	6,539
TOTAL	4,210	4,635	5,258	5,805	6,297	6,927	8,038	9,385	9,069	9,789	10,653	11,363	12,381	13,295	14,531	15,851	17,617	19,540	21,569	27,076	29,485

Source: US Department of Commerce, *Balance of Payments Statistical Supplement*, revised edition, and *Surveys of Current Business.*

(a) Census data.

p Preliminary.

Table 10.XXX

Value of United States direct investments in Europe at year end

£ million

Industry	1950	1951	1952	1953	1954	1955	1956	1957	1957(a)	1958	1959	1960	1961	1962	1963	1964	1965	1966p	1967p	1968p	1969p
Mining & smelting	11	11	12	13	14	16	18	19	20	19	18	18	17	18	20	20	19	20	22	25	30
Petroleum	152	183	190	218	239	272	354	435	448	471	519	630	769	852	991	1,108	1,224	1,422	1,604	1,932	2,002
Manufacturing	333	384	426	468	528	602	697	800	784	884	1,053	1,359	1,520	1,744	2,012	2,353	2,716	3,170	3,553	4,498	5,094
Other	122	133	140	150	162	181	203	229	232	259	312	384	460	576	671	844	1,035	1,177	1,321	1,631	1,855
TOTAL	619	710	769	848	944	1,072	1,272	1,482	1,483	1,633	1,901	2,390	2,765	3,189	3,693	4,325	4,995	5,789	6,500	8,086	8,981
of which UK	303	344	372	406	451	510	589	707	705	767	885	1,155	1,265	1,366	1,490	1,624	1,830	2,020	2,217	2,789	2,983

Source: US Department of Commerce, *Balance of Payments Statistical Supplement*, revised edition, and *Surveys of Current Business.*

(a) Census data.

p Preliminary.

Bibliography

AITKEN T Jr
A Foreign Policy for American Business
Harper and Bros, 1962

ARCHIBALD G C
'Regional multiplier effects in the UK'
Oxford Economic Papers, 19, 1967

ARROW K J and HURWICZ L
'Decentralisation and computation in resource allocation'
in Phouts, R W *ed*, *Essays in Economics and Econometrics in Honor of Harold Hotelling*
University of North Carolina Press, 1960

BAIN J S
International differences in industrial structure
(Comparative studies in Economics No 6)
Yale, 1966

BALASSA B
'Tariff protection in industrial countries, an evaluation'
Journal of Political Economy
Vol LXXIII, 1965, pp 573-94

BALL G W
'The Promise of the Multinational Corporation'
Fortune Magazine
June 1967, p 60

BALOGH T and STREETEN P P
'Domestic versus Foreign Investment'
Bulletin of the Oxford Institute of Statistics
August 1960

BARDERA V N
Foreign Capital as an Instrument of National Economic Policy
Martinus Nijhoff, 1964

BARKIN S *et al*, *eds*
International labor
Harper & Row, 1967

BARLOW E R
Management of Foreign Manufacturing Subsidiaries
Harvard University Press, 1953

BASI R S
Determinants of US Private Direct Investment in Foreign Countries
Kent State University, 1963

BEHRMAN J N
National Interests and the Multinational Enterprise
Prentice Hall, 1970

BELL P W
'Private Capital Movements and the US Balance of Payments position'
in Factors Affecting the United States Balance of Payments
Joint Economic Committee
87 Cong, 2 sess, 1962. pt 6, pp 395-482

BERLE A A Jr
Power without Property
Harcourt, Brace, 1959

BHAGWATI J N *ed*
Economics and World Order
World Law Fund, 1970

BLAU M and SCOTT W R
Formal Organisations
Chandler Publishing Co, 1962

BRASH D T
American Investment in Australian Industry
Canberra, Australian National University Press, 1966

BRECHER I and REISMAN S S
Canadian/US Economic Relations
Ottawa, Queen's Printer, 1957

BRECHLING F
'Trends and cycles in British regional unemployment'
Oxford Economic Papers, 19, 1967

BRETON A
'The Economics of Nationalism'
Journal of Political Economy, August 1964

BRONFENBRENNER M
'The Appeal of Confiscation in Underdeveloped Countries'
in Argawala, A N and Singh, S P
The Economics of Underdevelopment
Oxford, 1958

BROOKE M Z and REMMERS H L
The Strategy of Multinational enterprise
Longman, 1970

BURNHAM J
The Managerial Revolution
John Day Co, 1941

BUTLER W J
'Public Relations for Industry in Underdeveloped Countries'
Harvard Business Review
September-October 1952

BYE M
Self Financed Multiterritorial Units and their Time Horizon
(International Economic Papers No 8) MacMillan, 1958

CAMPBELL J
'The Role of Big Business in the New Nations'
Optima, September 1963

CAVES R E
Britain's Economic Prospects
(A Brooking's Institution Study)
Allen & Unwin, 1968

COMMISSION ON INDUSTRIAL RELATIONS, Reports:

No 1 *The Associated Octel Company Ltd.* Cmnd 4246
No 3 *W Stevenson & Sons Suttons, Cornwall Ltd.* Cmnd 4248
No 5 *BSR Ltd.* Cmnd 4274
No 6 *Elliotts of Newbury Ltd.* Cmnd 4311
No 7 *Brock's Fireworks Ltd.* Cmnd 4325
No 10 *The International Harvester Company of Great Britain Ltd.* Cmnd 4469
No 11 *Hoover Ltd.* Cmnd 4537
No 14 *Standard Telephones and Cables Ltd.* Cmnd 4598
No 18 *Electrolux Ltd.* Cmnd 4697
No 26 *Engelhard Industries Ltd.* HMSO, Dec 1971

COMMITTEE ON MANPOWER RESOURCES FOR SCIENCE AND TECHNOLOGY
Report on the 1965 triennial Manpower Survey of Engineers, Technologists, Scientists and Technical Supporting Staff
Cmnd 3103. HMSO, 1966

COMMITTEE ON MANPOWER RESOURCES FOR SCIENCE AND TECHNOLOGY
Report of the working group on Migration
(Chairman: Dr F E Jones) Cmnd 3417. HMSO, 1967

DOMHOFF G W
Who Rules America
Prentice Hall, 1967

DUNNING J H
American Investment in British Manufacturing Industry
Allen & Unwin, 1968

DUNNING J H and STEUER M D
'The effects of United States direct investment in Britain on British technology'
Moorgate & Wall Street, Autumn 1969, pp 22-25

DUNNING J H
The Role of American Investment in the British Economy
(with two case studies by W G Jensen)
PEP Broadsheet 507, February 1969

FLANDERS A
The Fawley Productivity Agreements
Faber & Faber, 1964

FLANDERS A
'Great Britain *in* Sturmthal A, *ed, Contemporary collective bargaining in seven countries*
Cornell University, 1957

FLANDERS A
Industrial relations: what is wrong with the system
Faber & Faber, 1965

FLORENCE P S
Investment, location and size of plant
(NIESR, Economic and Social Studies, No 7)
CUP, 1948

FLORENCE P S
Foreign Ownership and the Structure of Canadian Industry, Report of the Task Force on the structure of Canadian Industry (The 'Watkins' Report)
Ottawa, Privy Council Office, 1968

FLORENCE P S
The Fortune Directory
Times Inc, 15 June, 1968; 15 September 1968

FRIEDMAN W
'Some Impacts of Social Organisations on International Law'
American Journal of International Law
Vol 50, 1956, p 1503

GENNARD J
British Labour and Multinational Corporations: a review of responses and attitudes
British North American Research Committee, 1972

GEUTZKOW H
Multiple loyalties: theoretical approach to a problem in international organisation
Publication No 4
Centre for Research on World Political Institutions, Princeton University, 1955

GLASGOW, UNIVERSITY DEPT SOCIAL & ECONOMIC RESEARCH
Greenock Area Local Employment Survey Final Report
(draft), June 1966 (Mimeo)

GOODMAN S
'The political economy of private international investment'
Economic Development and Cultural Change
April 1957

GREENOCK CORPORATION
First Review of the Development Plan
(draft) 1966/?

GROSSMAN G *ed*
Value and Plan: Economic Calculation and Organisation in Eastern Europe
Berkeley, University of California Press, 1960

HAIGHT J T
'United States Controls over Strategic Transactions'
University of Illinois Legal Forum, 1965

HALL E T
'The silent language in overseas business'
Harvard Business Review
Vol 28, No 2, March-April 1960

HARBERGER A C
'Monopoly and Resource Allocation'
American Economic Review
(Proceedings) May 1954, pp 77-87

HARTLAND P
'Private enterprise and international capital'
Canadian Journal of Economics and Political Science
Vol 19, No 1, February 1963

HOTELLING H
Essays in Economics and Econometrics: in Honor of Harold Hotelling
University of North Carolina Press, 1960

HUFBAUER G C and ADLER F M
Overseas Manufacturing Investment and the Balance of Payments
Tax Policy Research Study No 1
Washington, US Treasury 1968

HUNTER A *ed*
Monopoly and Competition
Penguin Modern Economics, 1969

HURWICZ L
'Conditions for Economic Efficiency of Centralised and Decentralised Structures'
in Grossman G *ed*
Value and plan: Economic calculation and organisation in Eastern Europe
University of California Press, 1960

HYMER S
'Direct Foreign Investment and the National Economic Interest'
in Russel P *ed: Nationalism in Canada*
(Economic Growth Centre Paper No 108)
McGraw-Hill, 1966

HYMER S and ROWTHORN R
'Multinational corporations and international oligopoly: the non-American challenge'
in Kindleberger, C P, *ed*
The International Corporation
MIT Press, 1970

In place of strife: a policy for industrial relations
Cmnd 3888, HMSO, 1969

JASEY A E
'The Social Choice between Home and Foreign Investment'
Economic Journal, March 1960

JOHNSON H G
Comparative Cost and Commercial Policy Theory for a Developing World Economy
Wicksell Lectures 1968
Stockholm, Almquist & Wiksell, 1968

JOHNSON H G
'The efficiency and welfare implications of the international corporation'
in Kindleberger C P, *ed*
The International Corporation
MIT Press, 1970

JONES R M
'The direction of industrial movement and its impact on recipient regions'
Manchester School, June 1968, p 151

JONES R W
'International Capital Movements and the Theory of Tariffs and Trade'
Quarterly Journal of Economics, February 1967, pp 1-38

KARSTEN C F
'Should Europe restrict US investments'
Harvard Business Review, 43, 5, September-October 1965, pp 53-61

KAYSEN C
'The Social Significance of the Modern Corporation'
American Economic Review, XLVII
No 2, May 1957

KEMP M C
'Foreign Investment and the National Advantage'
The Economic Record, March 1962

KERR C and SEGAL A
'The Interindustry Propensity to Strike—an International Comparison'
in Kornhauser A, Dubin R and Ross A *eds*
Industrial Conflict
McGraw-Hill, 1954

KEYNES J M
'Foreign Investment and National Advantage'
The Nation and the Athenaeum, August 1924

KINDLEBERGER C P
American Business Abroad, six lectures on direct investment
New Haven, Yale University Press, 1969

KINDLEBERGER C P *ed*
The International Corporation
MIT Press, 1970

KINDLEBERGER C P
'Public Policy and the International Corporation'
in International Aspects of Anti-Trust
US Senate: Hearings before the Sub-Committee on Anti-Trust and Monopoly of the Committee on the Judiciary, 1966, Pt 1, pp 162-173

KNOWLES K G J C
Strikes, a Study in Industrial Conflict
Oxford, Institute of Statistics Monograph No 3
Blackwell, 1952

KORNHAUSER A, DUBIN R and ROSS A *eds*
Industrial Conflict
McGraw-Hill, 1954

LAYARD P R G *et al*
Qualified Manpower and Economic Performance: an Interplant Study in the Electrical Engineering Industry. (LSE Unit for Economic and Statistical Studies on Higher Education, Studies on Education)
Allen Lane. The Penguin Press, 1971

LESTER R A
Hiring Practices and Labour Competition
Princeton, 1954

LILIENTHAL D E
The Multinational Corporation
NY Development and Resources Corporation, 1960

LITVAK I A and MAULE C J
Foreign Investment: The Experience of Host Countries
Prager, 1970

McKERSIE R B
'Changing Wage Payments System'
in Royal Commission on Trade Unions Employers' Associations. Research Paper II, two studies in Industrial Relations
HMSO, 1968

MACMILLAN J and HARRIS B
The American Take-Over of Britain
Leslie Frewen, 1968

MAGDOFF H
'Economic Aspects of US Imperialism'
Monthly Review, November 1964

MARSHALL J J
'Foreign Policy Aspects of American Trade Regulation, Effects on Canada'
Faculty of Law Review, University of Toronto
Vol 24, 1966

MASON E S *ed*
The Corporation in Modern Society
Harvard U P, 1959

MAURER H
Great enterprises: growth and behaviour of the big corporation
MacMillan, 1953

METZGER S D
'Prohibition of trade with Iron Curtain countries'
Law and contemporary problems, 1964

MILLER A S
'Foreign trade and the "Security State" study in conflicting national policies'
Journal of Public Law, vol 7, 1958, pp 46-47

MILLS C W
White Collar
OUP, 1951

MODEL L
'The politics of private foreign investment'
Foreign Affairs, June 1967

MOFFAT G C
'The foreign ownership and balance of payments effects of direct investment abroad'
Australian Economic Papers, June 1967, pp 1-24

NATARAJAN L
American Shadow over India
Bombay, People's Publishing House, 1956

NBPI
Report 123, *Productivity agreements.* Cmnd 4136. HMSO, 1969

'Overseas Investment'
Board of Trade Journal, 30 June 1967, p x

PAUNCH A
'A businessman's philosophy for foreign affairs'
Harvard Business Review, March-April 1957

PEARCE I F and ROWAN D C
'A framework for Research into the Real Effects of International Capital Movements'
in Essays in Honour of Marco Fanno, edited by T Bagiotti
Padua, 1966

PENNER R G
'The Benefits of Foreign Investment in Canada, 1950 to 1956'
The Canadian Journal of Economics and Political Science,
Vol XXXII, No 2, May 1966, pp 172-183

PENROSE E T
'Foreign investment and the growth of the firm'
Economic Journal, vol 66, June 1956, pp 220-235

PERLMUTTER H V
'The tortuous evolution of the multinational corporation'
Columbia Journal of World Business, 1969

PERLO V
American imperialism
NY, International Pub. 1957

PERLO V
The empire of high finance
NY, International Pub. 1957

PHOUTS R W *ed*
Essays in Economics and Econometrics in Honour of Harold Hotelling,
University of North Carolina Press, 1960

REDDAWAY W B *et al*
Effects of United Kingdom Direct Overseas Investment: Final Report
Cambridge University Press, 1968

ROBERTS B C
Evening Standard, 25 March 1971

ROBERTS B C, LOVERIDGE R J and GENNARD J
The reluctant militants: a study of industrial technicians
Heinemann, 1972

ROBERTS B C & GENNARD J
'Trends in plant and company bargaining'
Scottish Journal of Political Economy
June 1970

ROBINSON R D
'Conflicting interests in international business investment'
Boston University Business Review, Vol 7, No 1, Spring 1960

ROYAL COMMISSION ON TRADE UNIONS AND EMPLOYERS' ASSOCIATIONS
Written evidence of the Ministry of Labour
HMSO, 1965

ROYAL COMMISSION ON TRADE UNIONS AND EMPLOYERS' ASSOCIATIONS
Minutes of Evidence, 28, *Philips Industries*, HMSO, 1966
Minutes of Evidence 53, *Association of Supervisory Staffs, Executives and Technicians*, HMSO, 1968

RUSSEL P *ed*
Nationalism in Canada (Economic Growth Centre Paper No 108)
McGraw-Hill, 1966

SAFARIAN A E
Foreign ownership of Canadian Industry
Toronto, McGraw-Hill, 1966

SCHWARZMAN D
'The burden of monopoly'
Journal of Political Economy, December 1960, pp 627-630 *and*
'The effect of monopoly: a correction' *Journal of Political Economy*,
October 1961, p 494

SERVAN-SCHREIBER J J
Le Défi Americain
Plon, 1967 published in England as *The American Challenge*
Hamish Hamilton, 1968

SIMON M and NOVAK D E
Management of international corporations
McGraw-Hill, 1960

SIMON M and NOVAK D E
The Multinational Corporate Family and the Nation State: Some Hypotheses for Test
Harvard Business School (mimeo) [19?]

SIMON M and NOVAK D E
'Some Dimensions of the American Commercial Invasion of Europe, 1871-1914'
Journal of Economic History, December 1964

SOBAJIMA S
'Conflicting views on the economic effects of international private investment'
Osaka Economic Papers, January 1963

SOMMERFIELD S
'Treasury regulations affecting trade with the Sino-Soviet bloc and Cuba'
Business Law, 1966

STEINMETZ L L
The staffing of foreign divisions and branches: a descriptive study of methods and techniques employed by companies in the United States to manage foreign operations (Unpublished PhD dissertation) Michigan, 1964

STEUER M D
American Capital and Free Trade, Effects of Integration
Atlantic Trade Study, October 1969

The Times 500, Leading companies in Britain and Overseas, 1968-69
Times Newspapers Ltd, October 1968

TOBIN J
'Liquidity preference as behaviour towards risk'
Review of Economic Studies, February 1958, pp 65-86

TOWNSEND L A
'The Multinational Corporation: a new force for economic development'
Vital Speeches, May 1 1965

Trades Union Congress Annual Reports, 1965, 1967 and 1968

TUC
Economic Review 1970
TUC, 1970

TURNER L
Politics and the Multi-National Company
(Fabian Research Series 279) December 1969

'The 200 largest industrials outside the US'
Fortune, 15 September 1968
pp 130-136

ULMAN L
'Collective bargaining and industrial efficiency' *in* Caves R E *ed*
Britain's Economic Prospects
(A Brooking's Institution Study) Allen & Unwin, 1968

US STATE DEPARTMENT
Expanding private investment for free world economic growth (Straus Report)
Washington DC, April 1959

VERNON R
'Antitrust and international business'
Harvard Business Review, September-October 1968, p 82

VERNON R
'International Investment and International Trade in the Product Cycle'
Quarterly Journal of Economics, May 1966, pp 190-207

VERNON R
'Multinational enterprise and national sovereignty'
Harvard Business Review, March-April 1967, pp 156-172

VERNON R
'Saints and Sinners in Foreign Investment'
Harvard Business Review, May-June 1963

VERNON R *ed*
The technology factor in international trade
(Universities—National Bureau Conference Series, No 22)
New York, 1970

WANE E E
Business and politics in the Far East
Yale UP, 1932

WELLS L T Jr
'Test of a product cycle model of international trade: US exports of consumer durables'
Quarterly Journal of Economics, Vol LXXIII, February 1969, pp 152-162

Who Owns Whom (UK edition)
A directory of parent, associate and subsidiary companies
O W Roskill & Co, 1968

WILLIAMS F
The American Invasion
Blond, 1962

WILLIAMS S
'Negotiating investment in emerging countries'
Harvard Business Review, Vol 43, 1, January-February 1965

WILLIAMSON O W
The economcs of discretionary behaviour: managerial objectives in a theory of the firm
Prentice-Hall, 1964

WINDMULLER J P
Labor relations in the Netherlands
Cornell UP, 1969

WINSLOW E M
'Who are the economic imperialists now?'
Harvard Business Review, March-April 1960

Printed in England for Her Majesty's Stationery Office by James Townsend and Sons, Ltd., Exeter.
Dd. 506431 K16 6/73